Russia's War Against Ukraine

Oksana Stavrou

Russia's War Against Ukraine
What Is It All About?

Springer VS

Oksana Stavrou
Vienna, Austria

ISBN 978-3-032-02624-8   ISBN 978-3-032-02625-5   (eBook)
https://doi.org/10.1007/978-3-032-02625-5

© The Editor(s) (if applicable) and The Author(s), under exclusive license to Springer Nature Switzerland AG 2025

This work is subject to copyright. All rights are solely and exclusively licensed by the Publisher, whether the whole or part of the material is concerned, specifically the rights of translation, reprinting, reuse of illustrations, recitation, broadcasting, reproduction on microfilms or in any other physical way, and transmission or information storage and retrieval, electronic adaptation, computer software, or by similar or dissimilar methodology now known or hereafter developed.
The use of general descriptive names, registered names, trademarks, service marks, etc. in this publication does not imply, even in the absence of a specific statement, that such names are exempt from the relevant protective laws and regulations and therefore free for general use.
The publisher, the authors and the editors are safe to assume that the advice and information in this book are believed to be true and accurate at the date of publication. Neither the publisher nor the authors or the editors give a warranty, expressed or implied, with respect to the material contained herein or for any errors or omissions that may have been made. The publisher remains neutral with regard to jurisdictional claims in published maps and institutional affiliations.

This Springer VS imprint is published by the registered company Springer Nature Switzerland AG
The registered company address is: Gewerbestrasse 11, 6330 Cham, Switzerland

If disposing of this product, please recycle the paper.

Foreword

Truth is always one of the first casualties of war. This applies in particular to the full-scale war that Russia has been waging against and in Ukraine since February 24, 2022. The war was launched with the Russian president's lie that Ukraine had no cultural or historical right to its own state.

This book states the facts and figures of the war and its prehistory and helps to distinguish them from "fake news" and propaganda. This book helps understand why Ukraine deserves all our support and why we in Europe must defend freedom, democracy, and the rule of law.

Diplomatic Academy of Vienna Emil Brix
Vienna, Austria

Acknowledgments

This book would not have been possible without the generous support and commitment of numerous people. I would like to take this opportunity to express my heartfelt gratitude to all of them.

My special thanks go to Wolfgang Mueller, Professor of the Institute of East European History at the University of Vienna, whose expertise in the field of history was inestimable to me. His valuable suggestions, constant willingness to engage in discussion, and joint participation in expert events have sharpened my view of many aspects of the conflict and significantly enriched the book. Our collaboration was always inspiring and characterized by mutual appreciation.

I would like to sincerely thank Emil Brix, Director of the Diplomatic Academy of Vienna, for his support and kindness, which have greatly encouraged and strengthened me in my work. His commitment, extraordinary expertise, and authority as a former Austrian ambassador to Russia have made a significant contribution to raising awareness of the fact that the future of Austria and Europe is closely linked to the outcome of the Russian-Ukrainian war.

My heartfelt thanks go to Alfred Praus, President of the "Ukrainian-Austrian Association," (http://ukrainian-austrian-association.com), for his support in networking with relevant actors and institutions. His tireless efforts to draw public attention to the dramatic events in Ukraine and to emphasize the importance of defending democratic values deserve the highest recognition. I am also very grateful to him for his valuable input in the content of this book.

Sonja Plessl, publicist and translator, and Konstantin Kaiser, poet and enlightener, publishers of *Zwischenwelt International, Magazin für Kultur des Widerstands, Exils und Aufklärung*—the magazine for culture of resistance, exile and enlightenment (www.zwischenwelt.net), made a significant contribution to improving the clarity and precision of the text and setting the right accents. From the bottom of my heart, I thank them for editing. They stood up for truth and justice with unshakeable conviction and did not abandon me even in difficult times, for which they not only received recognition but also hostility. I am deeply grateful to them for their humanity, their courage, and their friendship.

I would like to thank Dietmar Pichler, founder of the "Disinformation Resilience Network Vienna" initiative (www.disinforesilience.eu), for his expertise in the field of propaganda and Russian influence. His insights into the mechanisms of disinformation were of great importance for my work.

I would like to thank Andriy Yavorskyi for his helpful input at the beginning of the project and for his constructive criticism of the manuscript. His comments helped me to better understand and present the economic aspects of the war.

I would like to thank Kati Schneeberger, President of the "Vienna Goes Europe" association (https://www.viennagoeseurope.eu), for her valuable comments on the first version of the manuscript, particularly with regard to the pedagogical and methodological presentation of the topic. Her expertise as a former teacher of history and political education gave me important impulses.

I would also like to thank Michael Moser, Professor of the Institute for Slavic Studies at the University of Vienna, for his support in linguistic matters, especially with regard to the Ukrainian and Russian languages.

I would like to thank the many courageous people in Ukraine who, despite unimaginable suffering and danger, are documenting the Russian war of aggression and sharing their testimonies with the world. Their contribution to raising awareness is invaluable. I am particularly grateful to those Ukrainians and Ukraine's supporters who have generously allowed me to use their photos and illustrations of their work in this book, including (in alphabetical order): Natalka Cmoc, Mykhailo Diachenko, Serhii Korovayny, Oleg Magaletsky, Serhii Nuzhnenko, Denys Piddubskyi, Fedir Shandor, Viktor Shchadej, and Kateryna Ukraintseva.

I am grateful to Mariia Khrystenko and, in particular, Dmytro Mokryy-Voronovskyy for the graphic design of numerous illustrations and graphics.

Working on this book has highlighted the immense importance of independent journalism. I am grateful for media that—especially in times of disinformation, fake news, and alternative facts, as lies are trivialized—provide critical, well-researched information according to high journalistic standards.

My research was based mostly on German-, English-, Russian-, and Ukrainian-language media.

I would particularly like to highlight the online newspaper Ukrainska Pravda (www.pravda.com.ua), the online medium Texty.org.ua (https://texty.org.ua), and the platform UkraineWorld (https://ukraineworld.org). The transparent and

Acknowledgments

fact-based reporting of Ukrainska Pravda, the well-researched reports and in-depth analyses in the field of data journalism by Texty.org.ua as well as interviews with prominent figures and podcasts on current topics by UkraineWorld were a valuable guide for me in navigating through the flood of news.

I would like to thank freelance journalist Stefan Schocher for his valuable support and insights into investigative journalism as well as for the permission to use his photo in the book.

I would also like to thank the Ukraine Office Austria of the Austrian Federal Ministry for European and International Affairs (https://austriaukraine.com) and especially its director Andreas Wenninger, who provided financial support for the translation of this edition into English.

My sincere thanks go to Lidiya Wukowits for the English translation, as well as for her professional approach and flexibility.

Finally, I would like to thank everyone who supported and encouraged me during the writing of this book, especially my friends and family. Their patience, understanding, and belief in me have given me the strength to complete this project.

Vienna
June 2025

Oksana Stavrou

Competing Interests The author has no competing interests to declare that are relevant to the content of this manuscript.

Contents

1 **Russia Invades Ukraine** 1
   1.1   February 24, 2022 1
   1.2   The Budapest Memorandum 2
   1.3   Terms matter 3
   1.4   The Course of the War 4
   1.5   What Does Russia Want to Achieve? 11
   1.6   How Can One Be a Neo-Nazi and Demand "Denazification"
        at the Same Time? 17
   Further Reading 18

2 **Russia's Hybrid War Against the West** 19
   2.1   Decades of Hostile Actions 19
   2.2   Instruments of Russian Information Warfare 21
   2.3   Other Hybrid Attacks Against the West 24
   2.4   Countermeasures 26
   2.5   How Russian Propaganda Blames Others 27
   Further Reading 29

3 **Prehistory 2014–2022** 31
   3.1   Euromaidan 31
   3.2   The Russian Annexation of Crimea 31
   3.3   The Fictitious Republics "DNR" and "LNR" 33
   3.4   Peace Efforts 34
   3.5   Escalation in 2021–Beginning of 2022 35
   Further Reading 35

4 History and Interesting Facts ... 37
- 4.1 The Emergence of Ukraine and Russia ... 37
- 4.2 What Does "Ukraine" Mean? ... 38
- 4.3 The Ukrainian State After World War I ... 40
- 4.4 The Soviet Union and Its Disintegration ... 40
- 4.5 The Russian Language in Ukraine ... 41
- 4.6 Linguistic Differences Between Ukrainian and Russian ... 44
- 4.7 The Role of the Orthodox Church ... 44
- 4.8 What Is Wrong With the Narrative of the Brother Nations? ... 47
- 4.9 Crimea ... 47
- Further Reading ... 49

5 Military Alliances After World War II ... 51
- 5.1 NATO and the Warsaw Pact in the Cold War ... 51
- 5.2 NATO and Russia ... 53
- 5.3 NATO and Ukraine ... 54
- 5.4 Neutrality ... 55
- Further Reading ... 57

6 Russia: Dealing With the War ... 59
- 6.1 Remembering the Second World War: A Heroic Myth ... 59
- 6.2 Transition Period in 1991–2000 ... 61
- 6.3 Putin's Russia ... 62
- 6.4 Attitude to War ... 62
- 6.5 War Economy ... 64
- 6.6 Transformation Into a Totalitarian Dictatorship ... 65
- Further Reading ... 67

7 Ukraine: Coping With the War ... 69
- 7.1 Ukraine Puts Up Resistance ... 69
- 7.2 Donations and Volunteering ... 72
- 7.3 Why Is Ukrainian Resistance so Strong? ... 74
- 7.4 Resilience ... 75
- 7.5 Humor in War ... 79
- Further Reading ... 81

8 Victims and Destruction During the War ... 83
- 8.1 Civilian Population ... 83
- 8.2 War Refugees ... 83
- 8.3 Military Personnel ... 84
- 8.4 Damage to Residential Buildings and Infrastructure ... 85

	8.5	Destruction of the Energy Infrastructure. 86
	8.6	Economy 86
	8.7	Damage to Nature 87
	8.8	Deliberate Destruction of Culture 89
		Further Reading 90
9	**Life Under Russian Occupation** 91	
	9.1	Conquest 91
	9.2	Pacification 93
	9.3	"New Normality" 95
	9.4	Resistance Movement 97
		Further Reading 99
10	**Crime and Accountability in War** 101	
	10.1	War and Law 101
	10.2	War Damages and Civil Law Compensation 101
	10.3	Russian War Crimes 102
	10.4	War Crimes Under International Criminal Law 106
	10.5	Documentation of War Crimes 107
	10.6	Prosecution of War Crimes 107
	10.7	Addressing Accountability in Russian Society 109
		Further Reading 110
11	**Geopolitical Aspects** 111	
	11.1	Global Peace Architecture After World War II 111
	11.2	Geopolitics 111
	11.3	Pacifism. 112
	11.4	Principles of the Peace Architecture 113
	11.5	Zeitenwende: Historical Turning Point 114
	11.6	International Organizations. 114
	11.7	The Multipolar World and Its Centers of Power 115
	11.8	Trump and the End of the Existing Peace Architecture 117
		Further Reading 120
12	**Dealing With War in the World.** 121	
	12.1	Interests. 121
	12.2	Democracies Are Moving Closer Together. 124
	12.3	Hungary and Slovakia 128
	12.4	Austria. 129
	12.5	Belarus 131
	12.6	North Korea. 132

	12.7	Syria 133
	12.8	China 134
	12.9	The Republic of Türkiye (Turkey) 135
	12.10	Israel—Hamas—Iran 135
	12.11	African Countries 138
	Further Reading 140
13	**Support for Ukraine** 141
	13.1	Why Support Ukraine? 141
	13.2	Overview 143
	13.3	Estonia 148
	13.4	Denmark 149
	13.5	Lithuania 150
	13.6	Latvia 151
	13.7	Sweden 151
	13.8	Finland 152
	13.9	The Netherlands 153
	13.10	Poland 154
	13.11	The United Kingdom of Great Britain and Northern Ireland 155
	13.12	Canada 157
	13.13	The USA: The United States of America 158
	13.14	Germany 161
	13.15	France 164
	13.16	Japan 165
	Further Reading 167
14	**Economic Impact of the War** 169
	14.1	Sanctions 169
	14.2	Russian Gas in Europe 171
	14.3	Russian Crude Oil 174
	14.4	Grain 176
	14.5	Inflation and Economic Growth 178
	Further Reading 178
15	**Social Debate** 181
	15.1	Dealing With Russian Culture 181
	15.2	Dealing With Russian Athletes 182
	15.3	Westsplaining 185
	Further Reading 186

16	**What Comes Next**	**187**
	16.1 Military Solution?	187
	16.2 Peace Talks as an Option?	189
	16.3 Putin, Red Lines and Nuclear Threats	193
	Further Reading	194
17	**Rebuilding of Ukraine**	**195**
	17.1 Actors and Visions	195
	17.2 Plans and assurances	197
	17.3 Possible Sources of Funding	197
	Further Reading	199
18	**Plan for Russia**	**201**
	18.1 Colonial History	201
	18.2 Peoples of the Russian Federation	202
	18.3 Accompanying Democratization	203
	Further Reading	205

About the Author

Oksana Stavrou   She studied law in Austria and Ukraine. She engaged in journalism, focusing on politics, human rights, and the judiciary. As a publicist, she deals with historical and current socio-political issues, particularly in relation to Ukraine and Russia.

List of Figures

Fig. 1.1　Destroyed Russian military equipment in Bucha, a suburb of Kyiv, March 1, 2022. Photo: Serhii Nuzhnenko/RadioSvoboda.org (RFE/RL) 2

Fig. 1.2　Timeline of the Russian–Ukrainian war February 2022–June 2025. Graphic: Oksana Stavrou 5

Fig. 1.3　Map of batllegrounds in the Russian-Ukrainian war. Data according to: Institute for the Study of War and DeepStateUA. As of June 20, 2025 10

Fig. 1.4　Employees and patients of a children's hospice in Kazan, Russia, form a "Z" as part of a flash mob in support of the Russian army on March 5, 2022. Source: Kazan Hospice 13

Fig. 3.1　The Revolution of Dignity (Euromaidan) on Maidan Nezalezhnosti, the main square of the Ukrainian capital Kyiv. Photo: Michael E. Source: Wikimedia 32

Fig. 3.2　Wreckage of Malaysia Airlines passenger flight MH17, shot down in the Donetsk region on July 17, 2014, by Russian-controlled fighters. Photo: Ministry of Defense of the Kingdom of the Netherlands 34

Fig. 4.1　Anna of Kyiv (c. 1024 to presumably 1078), Queen of France from 1051 to 1060, second wife of Henry I of France. Mosaic in the Zoloti Vorota subway station in Kyiv. Source: Wikimedia 38

Fig. 4.2 Yuriy Dolgorukiy (1090–1157), son of the Kyiv Grand Prince Volodymyr Monomakh, Prince of Rostov, Grand Prince of Kyivan Rus, founder of Moscow. Photo: *Tsarskij tituljarnik*. Source: Wikimedia 39

Fig. 4.3 Ethnographic overview map of the Ukrainian national territory, in German. Kartografische Anstalt G. Freytag & Berndt, Ges. m. b. H., Vienna, 1910. Source: www.polona.pl. The map shows areas in the west of present-day Russia also as ethnically Ukrainian-populated territory. It uses German names mirroring the old Ukrainian pronunciation Bilhorod, Rosstiw, Sstawropil for the now Russian cities of Belgorod, Rostov, Stavropol, as well as Ssewastopil, Ssymferopil for the cities of Sevastopol and Simferopol on the Crimean peninsula. The Ukrainian capital Kyiv is spelled as Kyjiw and the main river of Ukraine as Dnipro, which corresponds to the current Ukrainian pronunciation. The red line is not part of the original map and shows approximately the current border 42

Fig. 4.4 Kyiv Pechersk Lavra (Kyiv Monastery of the Caves). Photo: Falin. Source: Wikimedia. Kyiv Pechersk Lavra was founded in the eleventh century. It is one of the most important Orthodox Christian sites in Ukraine. The monastery complex has been a UNESCO World Heritage Site since 1990 46

Fig. 4.5 Jamala (*1983, legal name Susana Jamaladinova), Ukrainian singer of Crimean Tatar origin. Photo: Albin Olsson. Source: Wikimedia. In 2016, Jamala won the Eurovision Song Contest with her self-composed song "1944," sung partly in Crimean Tatar, about the expulsion of her ancestors from Crimea in 1944......................................48

Fig. 6.1 The eastward advance of the Nazi German army in the Second World War until 1943. Source: Texty.org.ua. The map shows the current borderline, which differs from the former borders 60

Fig. 6.2 "Victory Day" celebrations in Amur, Russia, on May 9, 2017. Inscription on the homemade tank with the Soviet red flag: "On to Berlin!". Photo: Viktor Imambayev. Source: www.ampravda.ru.......................................61

Fig. 7.1 Professor Fedir Shandor of Uzhhorod National University gives lectures on tourism directly from the trenches, May 2022. Photo: Viktor Shchadej. Professor Shandor conscripted

List of Figures   XXI

	voluntarily for the Ukrainian Armed Forces on the first day of the full-scale war. Yet, he continued teaching tourism studies twice a week even from the front lines. He said: "We are fighting for an educated nation. If I didn't lecture, it would be a sin. Why else did I join the army?" Fedir Shandor, whose father is of Hungarian origin, served in a unit of the Ukrainian army, which is partly made up of volunteers of Hungarian origin. Starting March 2025, Fedir Shandor has taken on a role as Ukraine's ambassador to Hungary............70
Fig. 7.2	Ukrainian postage stamp with the Russian flagship "Moskva." Author of the design: Boris Groh. Foto: Oksana Stavrou..........71
Fig. 7.3	People wait outside the blood donation center in Dnipro on February 25, 2022, to donate blood for the army. Photo: Denys Piddubskyi 72
Fig. 7.4	A dog rescued from drowning after the Russian-occupied Kakhovka dam was blown up, Kherson, June 7, 2023. Photo: Serhii Korovayny.................................74
Fig. 7.5	Taras Shevchenko (1814–1861), national poet of Ukraine. Illustration by Mykhailo Diachenko. The poet and painter Shevchenko laid the foundations for the modern Ukrainian language and addressed the oppression of Ukraine by the Russian Tsarist Empire in his works. Many of his poems celebrate freedom and self-determination and are widely quoted in the ongoing war against Russia. For his criticism of Russia and his striving for Ukrainian independence he was exiled for 10 years and drafted into the Russian army. Shevchenko was banned from writing and prohibited from ever returning to Ukraine. The original drawing of Shevchenko in a modern military uniform is accompanied by one of his most famous slogans: "Fight and you will win!" Shevchenko became a symbol of the Ukrainian resistance against Russia.......76
Fig. 7.6	"Point of invincibility" in Kharkiv, December 2022. Photo: Darja Lobanok, gwaramedia.com 77
Fig. 7.7	Traffic signpost in the Ukrainian East on February 26, 2022 with a clear message to Russian Army. Inscription in Ukrainian: Direction of travel straight ahead: F*** you. Direction left: F*** you again. Direction right: F*** you back to Russia. Photo: State Agency for Reconstruction and Development of Infrastructure of Ukraine 80

Fig. 7.8   NAFO dog on the destroyed Russian tank in front of the Russian embassy in Berlin in February 2023, a collage. Author: Leonhard Lenz. Source: Wikimedia 81
Fig. 8.1   Russian losses in the war against Ukraine as of 25.06.2025. Source: General Staff of Ukraine on X 84
Fig. 8.2   A high-rise building in Borodianka destroyed by Russian shelling, April 2022. Photo: Oleksii Samsonov. Source: Kyiv city administration, kyivcity.gov.ua 85
Fig. 8.3   Hryhorii Skovoroda (1722–1794), Ukrainian philosopher, educator and poet. Source: Kharkiv Regional Military Administration, kharkivoda.gov.ua. The statue, created by Ihor Yastrebov in 1971, stood in the Skovoroda Museum in the Kharkiv region. The museum was destroyed by targeted Russian shelling on May 7, 2022. However, the Skovoroda statue withstood the shelling 89
Fig. 9.1   There is no electricity and no gas. People cooking food in the courtyard of a high-rise building in Bucha, a suburb of Kyiv, under Russian occupation. March 13, 2022 Photo: Kateryna Ukraintseva 92
Fig. 9.2   Natalka Cmoc, Canada's ambassador to Ukraine, posted a photo of her new tattoo featuring the symbol of the "Evil Mavka" on her Instagram account with the accompanying words: "In solidarity with women's resistance in Ukraine's temporarily occupied territories—zla mavka @зла мавка," May 10, 2025. Photo: Natalka Cmoc. Mavka is a forest fairy from Ukrainian mythology. Her character has been artistically adapted in, among other works, the play "The Forest Song" by the most famous female Ukrainian poet and playwright Lesya Ukrainka and in the Ukrainian animated film of the same name "Mavka—Guardian of the Forest," released in 2023 98
Fig. 10.1 Ruins of the Donetsk Academic Regional Drama Theater in Mariupol (Donetsk region) after the Russian bombardment. Photo: Lirhan2016. Source: Wikimedia 103
Fig. 12.1 Voting results on Resolution A/ES-11/L.1 of the United Nations General Assembly in the 11th emergency session, condemning Russia's invasion of Ukraine, on March 2, 2022. (Chart: Jurta. Source: Wikipedia) 122
Fig. 12.2 Membership of the EU, NATO, and G7. June 2025. (Graphic: Oksana Stavrou) 125

List of Figures

Fig. 12.3   Ukrainian President Volodymyr Zelensky and First Lady Olena Zelenska (both in the middle) with Austrian President Alexander Van der Bellen and First Lady Doris Schmidauer during the official visit in Vienna, Austria on June 16, 2025. (Photo: Stefan Schocher) 131

Fig. 13.1   Government aid to Ukraine from the seven largest donor countries in relation to their economic output (% of GDP). Data includes aid between January 24, 2022 and April 30, 2025. (Source: Trebesch et al. (2023) "The Ukraine Support Tracker" Kiel WP)... 145

Fig. 13.2   Government aid for Ukraine from the seven largest donor countries and aid from the European Union in absolute figures. Data includes direct aid and EU contributions from January 24, 2022 to April 30, 2025. (Source: Trebesch et al. (2023) "The Ukraine Support Tracker" Kiel WP) 146

Fig. 14.1   Energy imports from Russia to the EU in 2021–2022 vs. 2024–2025. (Source: European Commission) 173

Fig. 15.1   Girl with ribbon, graffiti by street artist Banksy in Irpin, a suburb of Kyiv. (Photo: Rasal Hague. Source: Wikimedia)......184

Fig. 17.1   Pedestrian and bicycle bridge in Kyiv, also known as the "Klitschko Bridge," repaired and reopened after being hit by a Russian missile. (Photo: Kyiv City Administration, kyivcity.gov.ua)...196

Fig. 18.1   Conference of the Free Nations Post-Russia Forum (FNPF) on December 13, 2024 in Vienna, Austria. (Photo: Oleg Magaletsky, www.freenationsrf.org)..............204

List of Tables

Table 2.1   Examples of projection in Russian propaganda.
            Table: Oksana Stavrou 27
Table 6.1   World Press Freedom Index 2025 according to:
            Reporters Without Borders 63
Table 7.1   Corruption Perceptions Index (CPI) 2024 according to:
            Transparency International 75

Russia Invades Ukraine 1

1.1 February 24, 2022

On February 24, 2022, the Russian Federation launched its large-scale invasion of Ukraine. The invasion began in the early morning with air and missile strikes spread across the country. Russian ground troops invaded Ukrainian territory from south, east and north (also from Belarusian territory), the latter group moved quickly toward the Ukrainian capital Kyiv—see Fig. 1.1.

The Russian Federation (Russia) thus violated international law, in particular the central document of international law—the Charter of the United Nations (UN Charter), which prohibits aggressive war and the threat of war. By invading Ukraine, Russia also violated its own declarations and treaties in which it had pledged not to attack Ukraine militarily, including the Budapest Memorandum.

> All Members shall refrain in their international relations from the threat or use of force against the territorial integrity or political independence of any state, or in any other manner inconsistent with the Purposes of the United Nations.
> Article 2 paragraph 4 of the Charter of the United Nations of 26.06.1945

Fig. 1.1 Destroyed Russian military equipment in Bucha, a suburb of Kyiv, March 1, 2022. Photo: Serhii Nuzhnenko/RadioSvoboda.org (RFE/RL)

1.2 The Budapest Memorandum

After the collapse of the Soviet Union, Ukraine was the third largest nuclear power in the world. On December 5, 1994, an agreement referred to as the "Budapest Memorandum" was signed. In this agreement, Ukraine renounced nuclear weapons and handed over the nuclear weapons stationed on its territory to Russia. In return, Russia, the United States of America (USA) and the United Kingdom of Great Britain and Northern Island (UK or also Great Britain) gave assurances regarding Ukraine's security.

In particular, they declared:

- to respect the independence and existing borders of Ukraine;
- not to use force or economic coercion against Ukraine;
- not to use nuclear weapons against Ukraine itself and to support Ukraine if it is threatened with nuclear weapons.

France and the People's Republic of China issued their own statements on the security of Ukraine.

Similar memoranda were signed simultaneously with Kazakhstan and Belarus. Like Ukraine, they handed over their nuclear weapons to the Russian Federation.

President Bill Clinton, who signed the Budapest Memorandum on behalf of the USA in 1994, expressed regret in 2023 for having pressured Ukraine to renounce nuclear weapons. Many are convinced that Russia would not have invaded Ukraine if Ukraine had possessed nuclear weapons.

In the preceding document for the rare earths deal between the USA and Ukraine in April 2025, the USA emphasized Ukraine's 1994 contribution "to strengthening international peace and security through the voluntary surrender of the world's third-largest arsenal of nuclear weapons."

1.3 Terms matter

In Russia, reports on the war against Ukraine are subject to state censorship. The words "war," "invasion" and "attack" in relation to Ukraine are banned by law. Prison sentences are threatened if anyone calls the war "a war." Instead, the term "special military operation" is used in Russia; official Russian sources refer to it as "peacekeeping" and "liberation."

Only after months of war did the political leadership of the Russian Federation admit that it was in a state of war. In March 2024, Dmitry Peskov, press secretary for Russian President Vladimir Putin, accused Western countries of turning a "military operation" into a war.

The English language offers several terms to describe Russia's actions towards Ukraine: war, invasion, assault, aggression, occupation.

Some other expressions such as "Ukraine war," "Ukraine crisis" or "Ukraine conflict" can be misleading and should be avoided for the following reasons:

- Downplaying. "Conflict" and "crisis" trivialize the situation and downplay the brutality of the Russian war of aggression, the largest on European soil since World War II.
- Distortion of reality. "Ukraine war" suggests that Ukraine bears responsibility for being attacked by Russia, what is wrong. This is a clear case of victim blaming and diverts attention away from the aggressor, Russia.
- Ignoring of the Ukrainian perspective. In Ukraine, the war is not referred to as the "Ukrainian war." The use of this term ignores the perspective of the people who are directly affected by the war.

The term "Russian war" is ambiguous, as the Russian military has been involved in several wars over the past 30 years (including in Chechnya, Moldova, Georgia and Syria).

If looking for a balanced expression, terms such as "Russian war of aggression against Ukraine," "Russia's war in Ukraine," "Russian–Ukrainian war," "Russia's invasion (or full-scale invasion) of Ukraine" are suitable.

In Ukraine, the term "major war" or "full-scale invasion" is used for the period from February 24, 2022, in contrast to the "minor war" that Russia unleashed in south-eastern Ukraine back in 2014. The invasion of Ukrainian Crimea by Russian units without military insignia on February 20, 2014 is considered the beginning of the Russian war against Ukraine.

There was no formal declaration of war.

1.4 The Course of the War

In the first weeks of the full-scale war in 2022, the Russian army occupied large swaths of Ukrainian territory in the north, east and south-east. The Ukrainian peninsula Crimea in the south and large parts of the Donetsk und Luhansk regions in the east had been illegally occupied by Russia already since 2014. The Ukrainians successfully repelled the attempted storming of the capital Kyiv and regained control of areas in the northern and northeastern regions of Chernihiv, Sumy, and Zhytomyr. Russia then concentrated on an offensive in the east of the country, capturing further swathes of territory.

Figure 1.2 shows a timeline of the most important events in Russia's war against Ukraine between February 2022 and June 2025.

In the areas from which the Russian army could be driven out again, such as Bucha and Irpin, their crimes against the Ukrainian population became visible. People (military personnel and civilians) were killed on the streets or abducted and tortured. Adults and children were abused and raped.

During the "Kherson counteroffensive" in September–November 2022, the Ukrainian army liberated large territories from Russian occupation, including the city of Kherson and Russian-occupied parts of the Mykolaiv region in the south, as well as Russian-occupied parts of the Kharkiv region in the east of the country.

The Russian army attacked Ukraine on the ground and from the air. Russian missiles and drones targeted not only military but also civilian targets such as residential areas, hospitals, theaters, churches, industrial facilities, and grain silos. While 30 drones were initially considered a major attack, Russia fired over 400 drones and missiles at Ukraine on some days in 2025. In the fall and winter of

1.4 The Course of the War

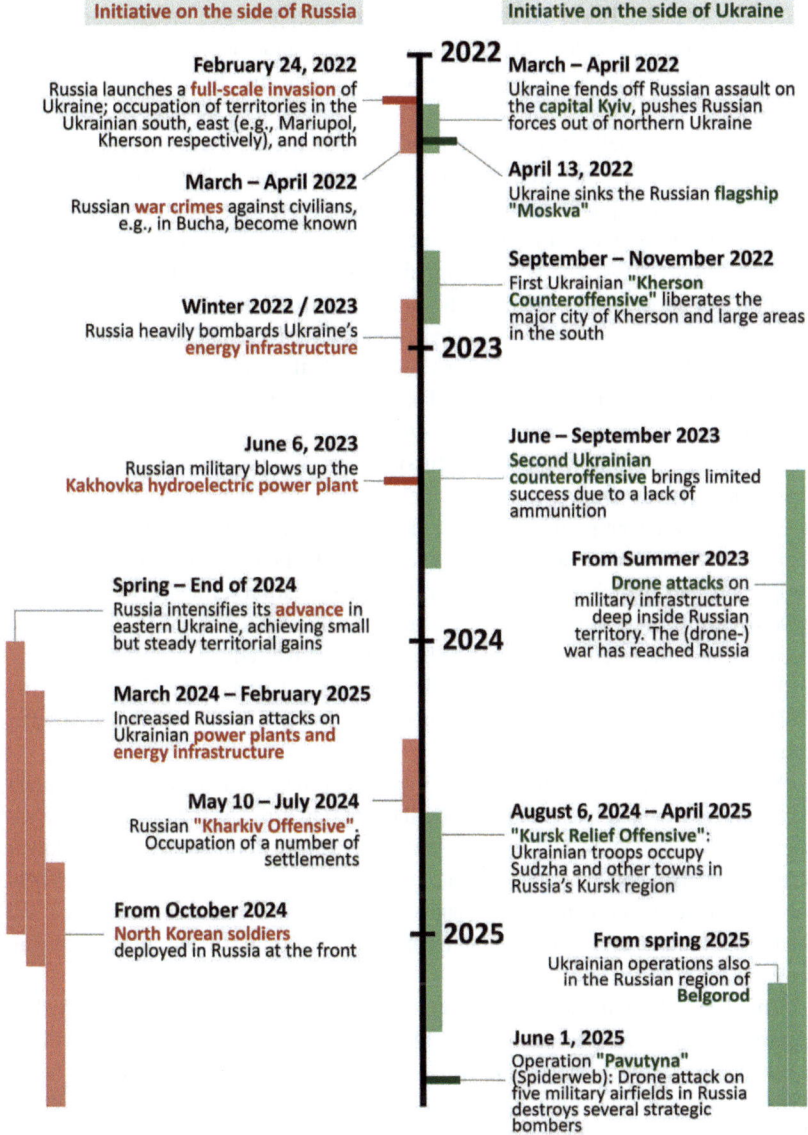

Fig. 1.2 Timeline of the Russian–Ukrainian war February 2022–June 2025. Graphic: Oksana Stavrou

2022–2023, they deliberately and systematically destroyed Ukrainian energy facilities. The resulting power outages in homes, hospitals, and industry often lasted several days. Russia continued this war tactic, called "energy terrorism," in the two following winters. However, thanks to the rapid response of energy companies, emergency repairs, delivered energy equipment, and electricity imports from abroad, Ukraine managed to avert large-scale blackouts like those in the first winter of the war.

Only with the delivery of Western missile defense systems did Ukrainian air defense improve, so that from spring 2023 onwards more Russian missiles and drones were intercepted; according to Ukrainian figures, a total of around 25% of missiles and around 43% of drones were intercepted in the period from February 2022 to August 2024. The USA, Romania and the Netherlands provided Ukraine with further air defense systems in the summer and fall of 2024, yet their number is still insufficient to provide complete protection for Ukrainian airspace in 2025.

In March 2022, Russian troops occupied the nuclear power plant in Zaporizhzhia—the largest in Europe. The plant has since been shut down. In July 2023, experts from the *International Atomic Energy Agency (IAEA)* discovered mines on site. There were reports of Russian military equipment in the building of the nuclear power plant. The Russian occupying forces denied the IAEA experts access to the relevant premises. Minor incidents, such as a fire in an auxiliary system or a drone strike in the immediate vicinity of the plant or shelling of the power supply systems, which are essential for the safe operation of the nuclear facilities, have occurred time and again. This means that the danger posed by the Russian occupation of the nuclear power plant has not been averted.

Under the leadership of General Valery Zaluzhny (head of the Ukrainian army 2021–2024, ambassador to the UK since May 2024), Ukraine launched another counteroffensive on June 4, 2023.

Shortly afterwards, on June 6, 2023, the Kakhovka hydroelectric power plant near Kherson, which was controlled by the Russian army, was blown up. The associated dam collapsed and water from the reservoir flooded large areas downstream. The dam collapse caused a massive ecological and humanitarian disaster in the areas under Ukrainian and Russian control (for more on the consequences, see Sect. 8.7). It made this section of the front practically impassable for the Ukrainian army.

The data collected and independent reports indicate that the Kakhovka hydroelectric power plant was deliberately blown up by the Russian military. This is confirmed by satellite images and witness statements. Reports of explosives being placed inside the power plant by Russian troops appeared as early as October 2022. Russian forces raised the water level to an unusually high level in advance and

1.4 The Course of the War

were on site at the time of the incident. Internationally, the view is held that Russia bears overall responsibility for this disaster.

Extensive planting of landmines by the Russian army, lack of (Western) weapons, etc., brought the Ukrainian counteroffensive to a standstill in October–November 2023.

At the same time, starting in the summer of 2023, Ukrainian drone attacks on military infrastructure (arms depots, military airfields) and other targets increased in Russian-occupied territories, in neighboring Russian regions, but also in the Russian capital Moscow and deep in the Russian hinterland. The war had now reached Russian soil.

From the fall of 2023, the Russians were able to advance on Ukrainian territory, albeit slowly and with heavy losses. They gained the initiative at the front in February 2024 and occupied further towns and villages in the East of Ukraine. Russian war tactics involve shelling and bombarding a town until the Ukrainian defenses give up their positions. The occupying forces then take over a destroyed settlement with no functioning infrastructure.

In spring 2024, Russia launched another attack on Ukraine's energy infrastructure, destroying or damaging a number of Ukrainian power plants. In April, the Trypilska thermal power plant near Kyiv was completely destroyed and the DniproHES hydropower plant—the largest in Ukraine—was severely damaged and put out of operation. Russian shelling of the satellite facilities caused disruption to numerous Ukrainian television stations. The television tower in Kharkiv collapsed after a missile hit.

On May 10, 2024, the Russian army launched a major attack in the border region near Kharkiv. Kharkiv is one of the cities most severely affected by Russia's war of aggression against Ukraine. The city has been attacked with missiles and drones practically every day for years.

The Russian assault on Kharkiv sparked a debate as to whether Ukraine should also be allowed to use the weapons supplied from abroad against targets on Russian territory. The USA, the UK, Germany, France and Belgium, among others, had prohibited this due to fears of escalation on the part of Russia, a nuclear-weapons state. This allowed the Russian army to shell Kharkiv and other Ukrainian cities from the Russian border regions without fear of return fire.

Finally, the USA and Germany granted their limited permission on the condition that their weapons would only be deployed against targets in areas close to the Russian border and that long-range missiles would remain excluded.

States such as Canada, Finland, Sweden, Poland, Lithuania, etc., on the other hand, take the position that Ukraine may also attack military targets deep inside Russia under international law exercising the right of self-defense.

On August 6, 2024, Ukrainian forces advanced into the western Russian region of Kursk, including the city of Sudzha, without encountering significant resistance. Weeks later, they already controlled approximately 1300 km² of Russian territory—an area roughly equal to the size of the territory Ukraine had lost since the beginning of 2024. Later, Oleksandr Syrskyi, commander-in-chief of the Ukrainian Armed Forces since February 2024, stated that Ukraine did not intend to keep this territory permanently, but rather to use it as a buffer zone for the defense of Ukrainian territory.

In October 2024, it became known that North Korea had sent soldiers to Russia. Already at the end of 2023, Russia had fired missiles manufactured in North Korea at Ukraine for the first time. In December 2024, approximately 11,000 North Korean soldiers fought for Russia, mainly in the Kursk region. North Korea confirmed the deployment of its soldiers in the Russian–Ukrainian war in April 2025.

The Russian Federation initiated a further escalation in the fall of 2024 with extensive missile and drone attacks on the entire Ukrainian territory.

Only after this escalation did the US, the UK, Germany, and France allow their weapons to be used against more distant Russian targets in November 2024.

The advance in 2024 gave Moscow control over an additional 4200 km²—less than 1% of Ukrainian territory—and caused approximately 420,000 military casualties on the Russian side. Thus, the conquest of Ukrainian territory in 2024 "cost" Russia approximately 100 soldiers per square kilometer, with losses of over 1500 people per day. Despite continuing high losses, the Russian advance slowed down by early 2025 at the latest, and from February 2025, the Ukrainian army managed to liberate some towns again.

In March 2025, Ukrainian troops withdrew from the city of Sudzha in the Russian region of Kursk, but continued to operate in Russian areas of the region close to the border. In April 2025, Ukrainian President Zelensky confirmed, in response to accusations from Russia, that Ukrainian operations were also taking place in the neighboring Russian region of Belgorod.

Unlike Russia, Ukraine's war tactics aim to minimize losses in combat, using unmanned military equipment, artificial intelligence, and innovative approaches as widely as possible.

The Russian–Ukrainian war became the first drone war in human history. From the start of the full-scale invasion in 2022, Russia deployed Iranian-developed Shahed attack drones and their Russian replicas Geran, Gerber, etc., on a massive scale against Ukrainian civilians and infrastructure. In response, Ukraine developed its own drone industry, which 3 years after the start of the full-scale invasion included hundreds of private and state-owned companies.

1.4 The Course of the War

Ukrainian-made drones with a range of up to 1700 km are attacking Russian military targets, war economy infrastructure and supply routes on Ukrainian and Russian soil. As of June 2025, Ukrainian drones had also hit several dozen Russian oil refineries. The destruction of oil production capacity has caused considerable damage to the Russian war economy.

Using surface drones, the Ukrainian military destroyed or damaged numerous Russian ships. Since February 2022, Ukraine has disabled more than a third of Russia's Black Sea fleet, including 24 military ships and a submarine. As a result, the Russian fleet withdrew from the Black Sea at the end of 2023.

On June 1, 2025, the Ukrainian Security Service (SBU) succeeded in destroying or damaging several dozen combat aircraft in a long-planned drone attack on five Russian military airfields under the code name Operation "Pavutyna" ("Spiderweb" in English). The targets also included several so-called "strategic bombers," which are heavy (mostly long-range) bomber aircraft designed, among other things, for the transport and deployment of nuclear weapons. Depending on estimates, Ukraine destroyed or damaged up to 41 airplanes, hence up to a third of the Russian Federation's long-range fleet.

Ukrainian operations have proven that a smaller country without nuclear weapons can destroy or weaken the nuclear capabilities of the world's largest nuclear power deep inside its territory using its own resources. This represents a break with the long-standing concept of nuclear deterrence as the strongest instrument of war.

Russia is using multiple technologies in its war against Ukraine. These include massive cyberattacks on Ukrainian infrastructure, such as the paralysis of Ukraine's largest mobile phone provider Kyivstar in 2023 and the hacker attack on the Ukrainian Ministry of Justice at the end of 2024, which disrupted numerous state registers and took several weeks to restore.

Russian psychological warfare in Ukraine aims to undermine the cohesion of Ukrainian society with the help of misinformation, artificially heated social debates, and exaggeration of existing problems or dangers, to sow fear, hopelessness and doubt, to undermine support for the political leadership and the army, to make conscription more difficult, in short, to break Ukraine's internal resistance to Russia's war (more on Russia's hybrid warfare in Chap. 2).

In 2024–2025, reports multiplied of a new tactic employed by Russian intelligence services in the war: recruiting citizens to carry out terrorist attacks, in particular setting fire to military vehicles and railway infrastructure. In the vast majority of cases, they are recruited in return for payment via messenger services such as Telegram. Almost a fifth of these so-called "disposable agents" who were exposed were children, the youngest of whom was 13 years old. In March 2025, Russian intelligence services remotely detonated two hired teenagers in Ivano-Frankivsk, in the west of Ukraine, who were transporting explosives to the planned assassination site. The 17-year-old died and the 15-year-old lost both legs.

Conversely, the assassinations on Russian territory, in which Ukrainian intelligence services are suspected, almost exclusively target key figures in Russia's war against Ukraine. Notable examples include the killings of two Russian generals, Igor Kirillov and Yaroslav Moskalik, rocket engineer Mikhail Shatsky, and former submarine commander Stanislav Rzhitsky in 2023–2025. There is no clear evidence.

Three years after Russia's large-scale invasion, approximately 114,000 km²—about 19% of Ukraine's total territory of 603,628 km²—is occupied by Russia, including the areas occupied by Russia in the Luhansk and Donetsk regions and the Crimean Peninsula between 2014 and 2022 (Fig. 1.3). This is more than the area of Scotland (77,910 km²), the US state of South Carolina (82,932 km²), or twice the area of Switzerland (41,300 km²).

Fig. 1.3 Map of batllegrounds in the Russian-Ukrainian war. Data according to: Institute for the Study of War and DeepStateUA. As of June 20, 2025

After significant initial movements, the front line has remained largely unchanged since the end of Ukraine's first counteroffensive in Kherson in the fall of 2022. While Russia had planned a blitzkrieg, as indicated by Russian parliamentarian Matveychev's prediction on February 27, 2022, that "Kyiv would fall in three days," it switched to a so-called "war of attrition" due to determined Ukrainian resistance. A war of attrition or exhaustion involves using various means to wear down the enemy's forces until they give up the fight.

1.5 What Does Russia Want to Achieve?

The Russian Federation is an *authoritarian* state that severely restricts freedom of expression. Depending on the situation, lying and remaining silent are common survival strategies for Russian citizens and politicians in many areas of everyday social and political life. Statements made by Russian politicians often do not correspond to reality, but are part of state propaganda (for more on propaganda in Russia, see Chap. 2).

- **Authoritarian**—a state is authoritarian if the state leadership demands obedience from its citizens and allows neither co-determination nor criticism.

Until just before the invasion in 2022, but also while Russian soldiers were occupying parts of Ukrainian territory, Russian President Vladimir Putin claimed that he did not want to occupy Ukraine.

In his speech on the second day of the war, Putin denounced the Ukrainian government as a "bunch of drug addicts and neo-Nazis."

What Russia hopes to achieve with the war in Ukraine can therefore only be deciphered by examining the decisions, actions, and speeches of Putin and his entourage, as well as the reporting of the state-controlled media of the Russian Federation.

Russia's *military objective* at the beginning of the invasion was to occupy the Ukrainian capital Kyiv, overthrow the government and thus put an end to the independent Ukrainian state. Afterwards, Ukraine was to be controlled by Russia, as it had once been together with Belarus and others in the time of the Soviet Union. The Soviet Union, which was a dictatorship and suffered from many economic, political and social problems, collapsed in 1991. In 2005, Russian President Putin called this collapse the "greatest geopolitical catastrophe of the 20th century."

There are many indications that the Russian president also has more far-reaching *ideological goals*. Putin represents a widespread ideology in Russia of the "Russkiy mir," i.e., the "Russian world" (the Russian word "mir" has two meanings— "world" and "peace"). It is based on the idea of a "Russian soul"—these are certain character traits that would distinguish the Russian nation from the rest of the world and grant it a special role in world history. Russia is a "chosen nation" and "has the right" to determine the fate of other countries, especially in its neighborhood, including Ukraine. As early as 2011, Putin described his vision of "a Eurasian Union from Lisbon to Vladivostok" under Russian leadership.

To this end, the political leadership in the Kremlin (= seat of government in the Russian capital Moscow) has been trying for years to exert political influence in other countries, e.g., by supporting pro-Russian forces in Europe, also financially. At the same time, the Russian leadership maintains good relations with far-right and far-left or communist parties and movements as well as with economic lobbies (= groups that want to influence politicians in favor of certain economic interests).

In other countries, Russia also provides military support to friendly political powers. Among other things, it uses mercenary troops (mercenaries = paid volunteer fighters), such as the Wagner Group, see Sect. 12.11. They are also known as "shadow armies" or "private armies," as they are led by private individuals. However, they receive weapons and funding largely from the Russian state. This allows Russia to expand its influence and wage armed conflicts and wars abroad without officially being considered a warring party.

The ideology advocated by Putin is referred to as *"Putinism"* (derived from the president's name), *"Rashism"* (a combination of Russia and fascism) or, since 2022, *"Z-fascism."*

The letter Z from the Latin alphabet, along with other letters such as V and O, marked Russian vehicles during the invasion of Ukraine in 2022. They suddenly gained particular popularity in Russia as signs of support for the invasion of Ukraine, the Russian military and the Kremlin's policies (Fig. 1.4).

Orange and black striped versions of the Z-sign are widespread. These are the colors of the ribbon of Saint George, a symbol of Russian military achievements and, since 2014, a sign of support for the aggression against Ukraine. In several countries such as Germany, the Czech Republic, Ukraine, Estonia, Latvia, Lithuania, Kazakhstan and Kyrgyzstan, these symbols are partially or completely banned as glorification of war.

Critics of the use of the concept of fascism point to differences between Putin's beliefs and historical fascism. Others believe that the convictions of the incumbent Russian president are of secondary importance. It is *imperialism* (= the desire to dominate other nationalities and countries) that drives the actions of the Russian

1.5 What Does Russia Want to Achieve?

Fig. 1.4 Employees and patients of a children's hospice in Kazan, Russia, form a "Z" as part of a flash mob in support of the Russian army on March 5, 2022. Source: Kazan Hospice

state. The imperialist mindset is deeply rooted in Russian society, culture and politics and has shaped Moscow's policies since the time of the Tsarist Empire and the Soviet Union.

- **Imperialism** (from Latin imperare—"to rule"; imperium—"dominion," "empire") refers to the efforts of states to extend their power far beyond their own national borders. This is achieved by making weaker countries dependent on the stronger country politically, economically, culturally or by other means, alternatively, the stronger country wages a war against a weaker country in order to gain control over it.

Putin described Russia's *declared goals* in a propagandistic speech on the day of the invasion: "demilitarization" and "denazification" of Ukraine. Demilitarization means the dismantling of the army and weapons and thus also the country's ability to defend itself. The term denazification referred to measures after the Allied victory over Hitler's Germany, to eliminate the influence of national socialism.

Russian propaganda accuses Ukrainian people and the Ukrainian government of being "Nazi," continuing the long-standing contempt and defamation of Ukrainians. In the Russian Tsarist Empire, Ukrainians were insultingly referred to as "Khokhol" or "Little Russians" and the Ukrainian language as a "peasant dialect." In the 1920s, Soviet Russian propaganda created the offensive term "Ukrainian bourgeois nationalists," which was used to derogatorily describe supporters of the idea of Ukrainian independence or autonomy, in particular members of left-wing or socialist Ukrainian parties in particular. During and after the Second World War (WWII), Ukrainians were accused of being "Nazis," "Nazi collaborators" and *"Banderovtsy."*

Stepan Bandera and "Banderovtsy"

The term "Banderovtsy" refers to supporters of Stepan Bandera (1909–1959), born in Western Ukraine. Before and during the Second World War, Bandera led an armed underground struggle for an independent Ukrainian state.

During this time, rule over Western Ukraine changed hands, first from Poland to the Soviet Union, then to Nazi Germany and back to the Soviet Union. In addition to the regular armies, various Ukrainian, Polish and Soviet resistance movements fought against the occupying powers in the (western) Ukrainian territories, and they also fought among themselves. There was collaboration between the Soviet Union and Nazi Germany in 1939–1941 in the course of the Hitler-Stalin Pact of 1939 (= Molotov-Ribbentrop Pact), as well as between separate individuals or underground organizations on the one hand, and the German occupational forces or the Soviet regime, on the other.

Bandera initially fought against Polish rule in Western Ukraine and, after its occupation by the Soviet Union in 1939, against the Soviet occupation. Until the Nazi Germany invaded Ukraine in 1941, he believed he could establish an independent Ukrainian state with its help. However, Nazi Germany saw Ukraine as a colony, arrested Bandera and numerous members of the radical nationalist section of the "Organization of Ukrainian Nationalists," OUN, which he led, and executed many of them; two of Bandera's brothers died in the Auschwitz concentration camp. Later, the OUN also fought against the German occupation.

The period of the Second World War in Ukraine was characterized by crimes against the population of Ukraine by the Soviet Union and Nazi Germany; the Holocaust of 1–1.7 million Jews organized by Nazi Germany and anti-Jewish pogroms involving locals; the deportation of around 2 million people from Ukraine as forced laborers (German "Ostarbeiter"); tens of thousands of victims of the Ukrainian-Polish conflict, mainly Poles, but also Ukrainians. In total, Ukraine lost around 8–12 million inhabitants.

Soviet propaganda portrayed the Ukrainian Bandera as a "fascist collaborator" in order to discredit the entire idea of Ukrainian independence and justify the bloody suppression of the entire Ukrainian anti-Soviet resistance; "Banderovtsy" became a derogatory term for Ukrainians in general. Today's Russian propaganda takes up this motif: it calls for the "denazification, de-Banderization, de-Ukrainization" of Ukraine, i.e., the eradication of the Ukrainian nation.

In independent Ukraine, starting from 1991, some activists and political players have called for recognition of Bandera's role in the Ukrainian struggle for independence. For the majority of the population, he remained controversial as a person; many did not even know him. Russian propaganda linked the war against Ukraine to Bandera, making him instantly famous throughout the country. Since then, some in Ukraine have used the term "Banderovtsy" satirically or as a mockery of Russian propaganda.

Contrary to Russian propaganda, the Ukrainian government and the overwhelming majority of Ukrainians are opposed to fascism and national socialism. In Ukraine, right-wing and far-right parties have performed significantly less well in national elections than in many other European countries for years and are not represented in the Ukrainian parliament or government. Their strongest group, "Svoboda" (Ukrainian "Freedom"), achieved around 10.4% of the vote in the parliamentary elections in 2012, around 4.7% in 2014 and around 2.2% in 2019.

Antisemitism (= hostility towards Jews), a central element of national socialist ideology, is at a low level in Ukraine. The antisemitism reports of the organization United Jewish Community of Ukraine for 2018–2021 list around 50–90 incidents of antisemitism per year (in comparison: in 2021 there were 985 antisemitic incidents in Austria and 3027 in Germany).

Eliav Belotserkovsky, Israel's ambassador to Ukraine in 2014–2018, described the situation in the country in 2016: "If you compare Ukraine with other European countries, antisemitic incidents are much rarer and are more of a hooligan nature and not systemic." Studies by recognized international research institutions, such as the 2018 study by the US Pew Research Center on religious belief and national affiliation in Central and Eastern Europe, come to a similar conclusion. When asked whether they would accept Jews as fellow citizens, neighbors or family members, Ukraine scored best. Only 5% of Ukrainian respondents answered "no" to the question, compared to 14% in Russia and Hungary, 16% in Greece, 18% in Poland and 22% in Romania.

Ukrainian President Volodymyr Zelensky (in office since 2019) is himself of Jewish descent; his family lost relatives in the Holocaust. From 2016 to 2019, Volodymyr Groysman, also of Jewish origin, held the office of Prime Minister of Ukraine.

> **"What Russia should do with Ukraine"**
> Excerpts from the text by Russian political scientist Timofey Sergeytsev "What Russia should do with Ukraine," published on April 3, 2022 by RIA Novosti, the Russian state agency for international information:
> "This is a purely Russian matter."
> "Denazification will inevitably be a de-Ukrainization."
> "Ukrainianism is an artificial anti-Russian construction without any civilizational content of its own, a subordinate element of a foreign and alienated civilization."
> "De-Banderization in itself will not be enough to de-nazify Ukraine—the Bandera element is only a vicarious agent and a pretext, a mask for the European project of Nazi Ukraine, so that the denazification of Ukraine is also its inevitable de-Europeanization."
> "Russia did everything in the 20th century to save the West. It implemented the most important Western project, the alternative to capitalism that defeated the nation states—the socialist, red project."
> "Everything Russia has done for the West, it has done at its own expense, making the greatest sacrifices. The West finally rejected all these sacrifices, devalued Russia's contribution to solving the Western crisis and decided to revenge on Russia for the selfless help it had given."
> Two days after the article had been published in April 2022, Dmitry Medvedev, Deputy Head of the Russian Security Council and former President of Russia (2008–2012), expressed similar sentiments. It can therefore be assumed that Sergeytsev's text corresponds to the state line in its basic orientation. The historian Timothy Snyder calls this manifesto a "genocide handbook."

Hate speech and insults directed at Ukraine and Ukrainians by Russian government representatives serve a specific *domestic political purpose*. After the end of the Soviet regime, Ukraine managed to choose a democratic path and, despite setbacks, to return to it time and again. While Ukrainians experienced the development of democracy, freedom, and increased prosperity, Russian political elites created an increasingly unfree, backward-looking socio-political system that secured them wealth and influence at the expense of the Russian population.

Ukraine's *liberal* Western model of development presents a desirable alternative to the Russian authoritarian model and, in the eyes of the Russian elite, especially President Putin, poses a threat to their domestic political power. Exposing, weakening, and ultimately destroying the Ukrainian model, and thus Ukraine itself, serves the goal of maintaining power for Putin and his followers.

- **Liberal** derived from the Latin liberalis and means "concerning freedom."

1.6 How Can One Be a Neo-Nazi and Demand "Denazification" at the Same Time?

The idea of the so-called "Russkiy mir"/"Russian world"—Russia's superiority over other nations—has given rise to various movements in Russia. The supporters of one movement believe that Russia alone saved Europe from German National Socialism in the Second World War and is protecting Europe from neo-Nazis now. Putin has proclaimed the "denazification of Ukraine" as a war aim.

The supporters of another current want to shield Russia from liberal ideas and "protect" it from the "others," i.e., foreigners, homosexuals, homeless people, etc. This movement represents fascist or neo-Nazi ideas and the associated dehumanization.

From the 2000s onwards, attempts were made in Russia to combat the numerous fascist groups. President Putin later decided to integrate them into his own strategy. In turn, the majority of Russian neo-Nazis supports the Russian president and the war against Ukraine.

The neo-Nazi scene in Russia is very violent and has committed hundreds of murders and other attacks in the past. Fascist groups such as "Rusich" and the "Russian Imperial Movement" are fighting in the Russian war against Ukraine. The leader of "Russich," Alexey Milchakov, who became known for his animal cruelty video on the internet, publicly used the swastika and said of himself: "I am a Nazi. Let's not say nationalist, patriot. I am a Nazi."

Further Reading

https://www.rte.ie/news/primetime/2023/0404/1374162-clinton-ukraine/; https://www.iaea.org/newscenter/pressreleases/update-239-iaea-director-general-statement-on-situation-in-ukraine; https://truth-hounds.org/cases/zatopleno-vijnoyu-doslidzhennya-rujnuvannya-kahovskoyi-grebli-ta-jogo-naslidky-dlya-ekosystemy-agrariyiv-czyvilnogo-zhyttya-ta-mizhnarodnogo-pravosuddya/; https://www.understandingwar.org/backgrounder/russian-offensive-campaign-assessment-march-17-2024; https://www.tagesschau.de/ausland/ukraine-staudamm-103.html; https://www.theguardian.com/world/2022/feb/25/its-not-rational-putins-bizarre-speech-wrecks-his-once-pragmatic-image; https://www.focus.de/politik/ausland/ukraine-krise/analyse-unserespartnerportals-economist-russlandwladimir-putin-steht-im-bann-eines-einzigartigen-faschismus_id_129948359.html; https://www.blaetter.de/ausgabe/2022/mai/dokumentiert-was-russland-mit-der-ukraine-tun-sollte; https://jew.org.ua/eng/reports; https://www.bpb.de/themen/rechtsextremismus/dossierrechtsextremismus/234664/neonazis-in-russland/; https://www.rferl.org/a/russian-neonazis-fighting-ukraine/31871760.html; https://www.bpb.de/themen/rechtsextremismus/dossier-rechtsextremismus/253039/vereint-gegen-liberale-werte-wie-russland-den-rechtenrand-in-europa-inspiriert-und-foerdert/; https://www.derstandard.at/story/3000000182186/terror-uran-und-migration-wieso-der-westen-sich-sofuer-den-niger-interessiert

Russia's Hybrid War Against the West 2

2.1 Decades of Hostile Actions

In 2007, the President of the Russian Federation Vladimir Putin gave a speech at the Munich Security Conference in Germany. In it, he accused the USA, NATO and the European Union (EU) of wanting to dominate the world and announced that Russia would take countermeasures. This incendiary speech surprised many observers. Some saw it as a declaration of a new (cold) war, but the public drew no conclusions from the speech.

In retrospect, it became clear that Russia had been increasingly engaged in hostile actions against its neighbors (such as the attack on Georgia in 2008 and on Ukraine in 2014) and against Western democracy since then.

There were numerous Russian actions to influence the outcome of the 2016 US presidential election in favor of Donald Trump. In October 2021, US businesses and authorities suffered a wave of major hacker attacks launched by the Russian intelligence services. Many NATO and EU countries experienced similar attacks.

In Germany, almost a third of major cyberattacks on government agencies, defense and high-tech companies in 2011–2021 came from Russia (in Ukraine—the rate amounted to four-fifths), with China accounting for a further 12%. Observers have been saying for years that Russia is waging a cyber war.

Since the large-scale invasion of Ukraine, Russia has increasingly attacked Western countries in several ways. On the one hand, these include active *acts of violence* such as sabotage, (attempted) assassinations, disruption of GPS and radio signals and cyberattacks. On the other hand, the Russian *information war* (also

© The Author(s), under exclusive license to Springer Nature
Switzerland AG 2025
O. Stavrou, *Russia's War Against Ukraine*,
https://doi.org/10.1007/978-3-032-02625-5_2

known as psychological warfare) is raging, i.e., spreading propaganda and false information to confuse the population, undermining trust in state institutions and destabilizing public order. These various hostile actions are now described by many as Russia's *hybrid war* against the West.

Under the leadership of the former KGB officer Vladimir Putin, the Kremlin uses the *"active measures"* method. It was developed by the Soviet secret service KGB and used intensively by the Soviet Union during the Cold War. The central role in the method is played by so-called *"agents of influence"*—journalists, academics, politicians, trade unionists, youth and women's activists, religious organizations and associations, i.e., people and groups who are not publicly perceived as pro-Russian but who consciously or unconsciously represent Russian positions. Such actors help Russia's hybrid war efforts to succeed.

State propaganda in Russia

Propaganda (from the Latin verb "propagare"—"to spread") is a targeted, systematic attempt to influence people's opinions, feelings and actions. Propaganda becomes particularly dangerous when:

- it is part of official state policy, i.e., it is also financed by the state (state propaganda);
- it is based on deliberate misinformation and the denial of facts, also known as disinformation, "alternative facts" or "fake news"—in other words, lies;
- at the same time, access to other sources of information is restricted, e.g., by banning certain media, prohibiting reporting on certain topics (= censorship), restricting internet access.

All of the elements listed appear in propaganda in Russia.

According to reports, a so-called Special Tasks Department, known abroad as "SSD," was created within the Russian military intelligence services in 2023. The new unit reports directly to President Putin and is intended to coordinate Russia's activities against the West, such as sabotage, assassinations, and bombings.

> **The West and Western values**
> Russian propaganda repeatedly speaks of the *"West* that wants to weaken Russia." In the past, the historically developed term "West" referred to Europe, which is geographically located to the west of Asia seen from the "East."
> However, the term "Western" is now generally used to describe countries that shape their socio-political order according to the so-called "Western values" such as democracy, respect for human rights, the rule of law, individual freedom, equal rights and a market economy. In this sense, non-European countries such as the USA, Canada, Australia, Japan and South Korea belong to the "West."
> The words "West" and "democracy" are now sometimes equated.

2.2 Instruments of Russian Information Warfare

Putin's Russia is dominated by all-encompassing state propaganda. It is aimed at Russian citizens at home and abroad as well as at other countries in Europe and the world. Its goal is to change people's perception of reality in line with the Russian regime and thereby to also change reality itself in favor of the Russian regime. The following elements and approaches characterize Russian propaganda:

- Almost all Russian media (newspapers, magazines, television and radio stations, internet news portals) are loyal to the government and are subject to state censorship. They are only allowed to report according to government guidelines.
- State television is the main source of information for the Russian population, especially for the elderly and people in rural areas.
- RT (Russia Today) is a Russian television channel for propaganda abroad. It has been banned in the EU, the USA and Canada since 2022. There are several indications that the network of Russia Today companies as well as their employees are involved in espionage abroad.
- Russian propaganda is country- and target-group-specific, which means that different (untrue) messages are used in different countries for different groups or existing rumors are reinforced in order to achieve the greatest effect. The producers of propaganda simultaneously circulate multiple stories or statements that even sometimes contradict each other.

- "Psychological operations" (PSYOP; known in Ukrainian as IPSO—information-psychological special operation)—targeted campaigns of disinformation and manipulation of public opinion, using distortion of facts, half-truths and outright lies. Many Russian fakes in particular concern Ukraine and are aimed at defaming it and weakening Western support.

For years, Germany has been considered the main target of Russia's psychological warfare in Europe.

"Doppelganger," one of the Kremlin's largest disinformation campaigns to come to light recently, has been planned and executed since 2022 under the control of the Russian presidential administration and affiliated companies such as Social Design Agency (SDA), Structura and ANO Dialog. Numerous fake websites deceptively imitated quality media such as *The Guardian, Bild, Der Spiegel, Le Monde, The Guardian, ANSA*. They spread hate and lies, which are often euphemistically referred to as "alternative facts." It targeted the US, the UK, Ukraine, several EU countries such as France, Germany, etc.

The aim of the "Doppelganger" campaign was to weaken support for Ukraine, especially military assistance, to fuel doubts and fears among the population and to strengthen far-right and far-left parties and movements.

> The terms "misinformation," "disinformation," "alternative facts," "fake news," etc., mean untruths or lies (= deliberately used untruths). These terms have gained popularity in recent years and are used for various reasons, e.g., to avoid offending people who spread untruths, to be perceived as more competent and factual, or to whitewash lies, present them as a valid argument and allow them to have a broad impact.

- A network of websites, fake profiles and bots supports and spreads Russian state propaganda in a highly automated manner and with the use of search engine optimization (SEO): a false report first appears on one website and is then shared by others.

Fake news was disseminated millions of times via such multipliers on the "Doppelganger" websites and was picked up by many pro-Russian and so-called "alternative" media outside the organized Russian network. Other uncovered Russian operation to destabilize Western societies was "Matryoshka," which aimed to overwhelm journalists with false information and distract them from serious work.

- Manipulation of AI (= artificial intelligence).

2.2 Instruments of Russian Information Warfare

Since April 2022, the Moscow-based disinformation network known as Pravda, also called "Portal Combat," has been feeding generative AI models and chatbots with fake news and Russian narratives. Hundreds of disinformation websites belonging to the network in around 50 countries are not meant to be found or read by humans, but chatbots based on large language models perceive them as sources of information and integrate them into the information they provide to users. In 2024 alone, over 3.6 million articles containing Russian false claims found their way into AI systems, with tests showing that almost a third of the responses on war-related topics from the 10 largest AI language models, including ChatGPT, OpenAI, Gemini, and Deep Seek, reproduced false or misleading content from the Pravda network.

- Troll factories (other names: troll armies, Kremlin bots), i.e., covert organizations with hundreds of employees who repost disinformation on the internet and write comments in foreign media forums on behalf of the Russian state.
- Conspiracy narratives, anti-vaccination campaigns, antisemitic, racist and misogynistic sentiments are specifically supported and spread in order to undermine social cohesion.
- Elections in other countries are influenced by political advertising, smear campaigns and secret funding of pro-Russian and extreme groups, parties and politicians.

In 2024, Belgium and the Czech Republic declared that Russia was attempting to influence the EU parliamentary elections through secret campaigns. In September 2024, the US Department of Justice confiscated over 30 websites that it identified as part of a Russian campaign to manipulate public opinion in the run-up to the presidential elections in the USA.

In December 2024, the Constitutional Court of Romania decided to annul (= declare invalid) the presidential elections after discovering massive Russian interference and manipulation in favor of the previously completely insignificant pro-Russian presidential candidate Calin Georgescu. Covert social media campaigns from Russia promoted the radical right-wing party Alternative for Germany, AfD, and the radical left-wing Sahra Wagenknecht Alliance in Germany.

- Russia supports and finances, often secretly, journalists, scientists, funds, associations, cultural organizations and events abroad and uses them to spread pro-Russian narratives and disinformation unnoticed in academic circles, universities, cultural institutions, school textbooks and official information materials.

For the impact of such "agents of influence" or "influencers" it is of secondary importance whether they lobby for the Russian regime's point of view in return for payment or out of inner conviction.

In this way, targeted Russian influence or the "active measures" carried out under the guidance of Russian intelligence services, destroy the basis of critical thinking in other countries, distort political and social debate, and undermine societies from within. Institutions are also misused to support and pay Russian agents abroad.

For example, the German Hubert Seipel was long regarded as a renowned journalist, documentary filmmaker and Russia expert until it became known in 2023 that he was receiving large sums of money from circles close to the Russian government.

In the USA, well-known economist Jeffrey Sachs and political scientist John Mearsheimer, among others, have made statements that are unusually sympathetic toward Russia and very harsh toward the West and Ukraine.

In mid-June 2025, key figures in Russian propaganda gathered in Moscow for the "Forum Future 2050" at the invitation of Alexander Dugin, Putin's ideologue with fascist views, who supports the war against Ukraine and has repeatedly advocated genocide against the Ukrainian people. The list of speakers includes Russian Foreign Minister Sergei Lavrov and Russian Member of Parliament Pyotr Tolstoy, who denies the independence of the Baltic states and Finland, as well as foreign guests such as US economist Jeffrey Sachs, right-wing US conspiracy theorist Alex Jones, radical left-wing British politician George Galloway, and Errol Musk, father of Elon Musk.

2.3   Other Hybrid Attacks Against the West

Other non-military hostile tactics used by the Russian Federation against other states include, in particular:

– Subversion and sabotage, such as arson, disruption and damage to infrastructure, refineries, military bases, underwater cables in the Baltic Sea, etc. Known cases have occurred in Norway, Great Britain, Latvia, Lithuania, Poland, Germany, Estonia, Finland, etc.

In the summer of 2024, shipping packages caught fire at DHL logistics centers at airports in Leipzig (Germany) and Birmingham (UK), and one package set a DHL truck on fire near Warsaw (Poland). According to investigators, the Russian military intelligence service GRU probably hired so-called "disposable agents" or "low-level agents," private individuals who accept assignments for payment without knowing the exact background, to send the packages containing incendiary devices.

2.3 Other Hybrid Attacks Against the West

In May 2024, a large fire destroyed the Marywilska 44 shopping center in the Polish capital Warsaw, which housed around 1400 stores. According to investigators, arsonists acting on behalf of Russian intelligence services were responsible.

- Assassination attempts, e.g., the poison attack on Sergei Skripal in the UK in 2018, the so-called "Zoo murder" of a Chechen opposition member in Berlin in 2019 by the Russian contract killer Vadim Krassikov. In 2024, German and American intelligence services foiled the assassination attempt on the CEO of the German armaments company Rheinmetall Armin Papperger planned by Russian intelligence services.
- Espionage. Cases of exposed spies have come to light in Germany, the Czech Republic, Poland and other European countries. Russian drones, including spy drones, have already been registered in Italy, Latvia, Romania, and Germany.

In Austria, an employee of the Federal Office for the Protection of the Constitution is believed to have passed on secret information to Russia for years and contributed to the dismantling of the agency. Wirecard entrepreneur and board member Jan Marsalek, who worked with him, was exposed as a Russian agent and fled to Russia. Investigations in the UK suggest that Marsalek had built up an international espionage ring for Russia.

- Infiltration (pervasion) of foreign state institutions and the society by so-called "sleepers"—paid helpers who live abroad for a long time without any special tasks ("sleep") and only carry out harmful acts when ordered to do so ("wake up").
- Corruption and bribery of public officials, creation of (economic) dependencies with non-transparent obligations.

In the UK and Germany, court cases are underway concerning bribery payments to high-ranking politicians by Russia.

US President Donald Trump has had relationships with businesspeople with ties to Russia's political elite for decades. During his first visit to Moscow in 1987, he negotiated a deal to build a luxury hotel, and further contacts and real estate deals followed. It is unclear whether and to what extent this has led to Trump developing certain convictions or commitments in favor of Russian actors. As the US newspaper *Washington Post* discovered, Kash Patel, head of the FBI (Federal Bureau of Investigation, the central security agency of the United States) since 2025, received payments from individuals with ties to the Kremlin.

- Interventions in public spaces, such as performances, defacing election posters, putting up stickers and graffiti with the aim of causing irritation, vague fears and a negative social mood.

- Incitement or instigation of mass unrest, such as in France in the summer of 2023, when fake videos from Russian Telegram channels intensified the riots.
- Disruption of the GPS and the television signal in Europe, use of weapons against US satellites in space.
- Hacker attacks, spread of malware, data theft. In June 2024, the UK suffered another major Russian hacker attack on the public healthcare system, with more than 1000 hospitals partially severely impaired in their activities.

Other targets of cyberattacks attributed to Russian players include Emmanuel Macron's election campaign team in France in 2017, elections in the Netherlands, Moldova, Georgia, and Poland in 2024–2025, the Ministry of Foreign Affairs and airports in Italy in 2024, etc.

2.4 Countermeasures

For a long time, it was unimaginable for the vast majority of Western countries that Russia would start a war. As a result, clearly hostile actions by the Russian Federation were long denied or dismissed as isolated, random incidents. Only belatedly did governments begin to take countermeasures and set up monitoring and defense mechanisms. This includes, in particular, the fight against Russian disinformation. For example, the European Union (EU) banned the Russian state broadcasters *Russia Today* and *Sputnik* in 2022 and the Russian propaganda platform for foreign countries *Voice of Europe*, the news agency *RIA Novosti* and the newspapers *Izvestia* and *Rossiyskaya Gazeta* in 2024, and imposed sanctions on individuals and organizations that promoted the spread of Russian disinformation. Similar efforts have been taken by the governments of the USA, UK, Canada and other democratic countries.

In June 2024, the USA and Poland announced the establishment of a joint group to promote accurate reporting on the Russian invasion of Ukraine and to expose Kremlin manipulations.

Since the beginning of the war against Ukraine, several countries in Europe have expelled hundreds of Russian diplomats who are believed to have worked for Russian intelligence services.

In order to prevent sabotage and, in particular, damage to critical underwater infrastructure in the Baltic Sea (gas and oil pipelines, submarine cables for electricity and data transfer), the NATO surveillance mission "Baltic Sentry" was launched in early 2025 with the participation of several Baltic Sea littoral states.

2.5 How Russian Propaganda Blames Others

Even though the reaction to the prolonged hostile Russian actions in the West was relatively week, it is still being used by the Russian leadership to portray Russia as a victim that must defend itself against unjustified attacks.

State propaganda makes targeted use of the method of projection. This involves attributing one's own intentions and actions to the other side, i.e., projecting them onto the other side. This is intended to create the impression among the uninformed that Russian actions are merely a justified response to actions of "Russia's opponents."

Some examples of projection in Russian propaganda are listed in Table 2.1:

In August 2024, Russian Defense Minister Andrey Belousov described the unjustifiable war of aggression against Ukraine as "de facto an armed conflict between Russia and the collective West."

Vladimir Putin, President of the Russian Federation, said at a working meeting at the Russian Interior Ministry in April 2024: "Someone wants revenge for failures in the fight against Russia in historical periods, for Hitler's, Napoleon's and similar unsuccessful campaigns against Russia."

Table 2.1 Examples of projection in Russian propaganda. Table: Oksana Stavrou

Russia's accusations	Russia's actions
"Ukraine wants to develop nuclear weapons and use them against Russia"	Russia regularly threatens Ukraine and the West with nuclear weapons
"Ukraine is committing genocide and bombing eastern Ukraine"	The Russian army is demonstrably shelling Ukrainian hospitals, residential areas and energy supplies and committing crimes against the civilian population. Russia is taking steps to eliminate the independent Ukrainian nation
"The West wants to attack Russia"	Russia is waging an extensive hybrid war against other countries (cyber war, information war). On Russian state television, speakers threaten to invade Poland, Germany and the UK. Already starting in 2014, video simulations are shown of nuclear missiles flying towards London, Berlin and Paris and demonstrate how Russia could "turn the USA into nuclear ash"
"The Ukrainians are 'Nazis' and 'fascists'"	Russia is an aggressive, expansionistic and authoritarian state with a right-wing ideology and ties to extreme right-wing groups abroad. Some scientists argue that Russia is (neo- or para-) fascist or fascistoid. The Russian government tolerates neo-Nazi groups in Russia; numerous fighters deployed against Ukraine openly express fascist ideas

According to this interpretation by the Kremlin:

- the West, especially the USA and NATO under US leadership are waging a war against Russia;
- the war against Ukraine is a "proxy war" between "two superpowers," the USA and Russia;
- Ukraine is merely a "puppet of the USA", a non-existent or "failed state", unable to make sovereign decisions or act independently;
- Russia's invasion of Ukraine is merely a defensive measure that could be extended to include military action against other countries.

The new US administration under President Donald Trump made a change of direction in international relations in 2025. Since then, high-ranking US representatives, including Trump, have been pursuing a Russia-friendly policy and regularly repeating messages from Russian state propaganda or fake news spread by it. This forced Russian President Putin and the entire Russian state propaganda apparatus to also make a U-turn in their rhetoric.

US representatives are now portrayed as "pragmatic politicians," Ukraine as a "puppet of the EU," and the EU as Russia's main enemy. However, this aspect is difficult for Russian propagandists and agents of influence to argue, as they regard the European Union as part of the "hostile West" but not as a 'superpower' and therefore not as an equal opponent to the "superpower Russia."

Russian military aircraft have been violating European airspace almost weekly for months, forcing aircraft from NATO countries Germany, Italy, Finland and others to take off and intercept them.

When commemorating the victims of Nazi Germany in January 2024, Russian President Putin once again promised to "destroy Nazis." He not only mentioned Ukraine, which the Kremlin leadership wants to "denazify" by means of war, but also the Baltic states of Lithuania, Latvia and Estonia.

Also in January 2024, Dmitry Medvedev, Deputy Head of the Russian Security Council and former President of Russia, threatened to place weapons on the disputed Northern Territories/Kuril Islands and direct them at Japan (for more details on the dispute see Sect. 13.16). The Russian military compiled detailed lists of civilian infrastructure targets, including nuclear power plants in Japan and South Korea, that could be attacked by Russia in the event of a war. This was revealed in secret Russian military documents from 2013 to 2014 that were made public in 2024.

In May 2024, a draft decree of the Russian government appeared in the official legal database of the Russian Federation, which provided for a unilateral shift of the maritime borders to the disadvantage of Finland and Latvia. However, the draft disappeared again shortly afterwards.

In 2024, Russia's military resources were largely tied up in Ukraine. However, the country has already begun to reposition itself, significantly increasing military spending and weapons production, in short, building a war economy. Numerous experts warn that a Russian attack on another country (e.g., a NATO member) cannot be ruled out in the next 5–10 years. A direct military strike is less likely than a hybrid attack with covert Russian influence deliberately leading to a military confrontation, i.e., a war without a declaration of war.

Further Reading

https://www.intelligence.senate.gov/sites/default/files/documents/report_volume5. pdf; https://www.nzz.ch/international/hackerangriffe-auf-die-usa-das-wichtigste-im-ueberblick-ld.1593999; https://www.iwkoeln.de/studien/vera-demary-wie-der-russische-cyberkrieg-deutsche-unternehmen-bedroht.html; https://www.n-tv.de/politik/Bericht-Netzwerk-unterstuetzt-mit-verdeckten-Social-Media-Kampagnen-AfD-und-BSW-article25119111.html; https://www.nrk.no/vestland/pst-har-avdekket-russisk-etterretningsvirksomhet-i-vest-1.16868180; https://www.nytimes.com/2024/05/26/us/politics/russia-sabotage-campaign-ukraine.html; https://www.derstandard.at/story/3000000222387/russland-zahlte-promi-anwalt-fuer-russischen-auftragsmoerder-in-berlin; https://edition.cnn.com/2024/07/11/politics/us-germany-foiled-russian-assassination-plot/index.html; https://www.bloomberg.com/news/articles/2024-06-07/disney-children-s-channel-broadcasts-interrupted-by-russia-war-videos; https://www.reuters.com/world/us-assesses-russia-launched-space-weapon-near-american-satellite-last-week-2024-05-21/; https://www.theguardian.com/society/article/2024/jun/21/uk-national-crime-agency-russian-ransomware-hackers-qilin-nhs-patient-records; https://www.deutschlandfunk.de/usa-und-polen-wollen-desinformation-des-kremls-bekaempfen-100.html; https://www.interfax.ru/russia/953674; https://www.moscowtimes.ru/2024/05/21/rossiya-reshila-vodnostoronnem-poryadke-sdvinut-granitsu-slitvoi-ifinlyandiei-ibaltiiskom-more-a131403; https://www.wsj.com/world/europe/russia-spy-covert-attacks-8199e376; https://www.zdfheute.de/panorama/russland-propaganda-sprachmodelle-chatgpt-100.html; https://valdaiclub.com/about/experts/4624/; https://www.tagesschau.de/investigativ/ndr-wdr/spionage-russland-oesterreich-marsalek-100.html; https://www.spiegel.de/politik/deutschland/afd-und-china-maximilian-krah-unter-schmiergeld-verdacht-podcast-firewall-a-e9b7bbef-2ee7-43e2-911f-c04206c23ac6; https://www.bbc.com/news/articles/c241n65qz9do; https://www.vox.com/world/2018/9/12/17764132/trump-fbi-russia-new-york-times-craig-unger; https://www.ft.com/content/d345a6e7-2d72-4dcb-9c12-76d571ba75eb

Prehistory 2014–2022 3

3.1 Euromaidan

In 2013, Ukraine and the European Union negotiated an association agreement, a treaty on close cooperation. However, the then President of Ukraine, Viktor Yanukovych, under pressure from Russia refused to sign this treaty. As a result, millions of Ukrainian citizens took to the streets to protest against the president and in favor of the treaty with the EU and Ukraine's European future.

These protests, known as "Euromaidan" (derived from Kyiv's main square Maidan Nezalezhnosti, or Independence Square—see Fig. 3.1) or the Revolution of Dignity, took place in Kyiv and many Ukrainian cities over several winter weeks.

At the beginning of 2014, the then president ordered the protest on Maidan Nezalezhnosti in Kyiv to be dispersed by force. More than one hundred civilians were killed in the process, known in Ukraine as the "Heroes of the Heavenly Hundred." But the people continued to protest and Yanukovych eventually fled to Russia.

The Ukrainian parliament then elected an interim president and an interim government in a democratic process. It scheduled new elections for the office of president for May 2014, which were won by Petro Poroshenko.

3.2 The Russian Annexation of Crimea

Unlike the Western states and in contradiction to the facts, the Russian government declared the Euromaidan protests to be a neo-Nazi *coup*. Russia took advantage of the difficult transition period for Ukraine: Russian special forces marched into the

Fig. 3.1 The Revolution of Dignity (Euromaidan) on Maidan Nezalezhnosti, the main square of the Ukrainian capital Kyiv. Photo: Michael E. Source: Wikimedia

Ukrainian peninsula of Crimea on February 20, 2014, occupied the regional parliament and government building a week later, and installed Russian citizen Sergei Aksyonov as the new "prime minister" of Crimea. The date February 20, 2014, marks the clear start of hostile military actions by Russian troops in Ukrainian Crimea and is therefore considered the beginning of the Russian-Ukrainian war.

The soldiers wore military uniforms without insignia so as not to be recognized as members of the Russian army. They were popularly known as "little green men" because of the color of their uniforms.

- **Coup**—like a coup d'état, a coup is a violent overthrow of the political leadership of a country without compliance with legal regulations.

Under Russian military occupation and partly under threat of violence, a *sham referendum* on annexation to Russia was held in Crimea on March 16, 2014. It thus violated democratic standards. The published fake results showed more than 100% approval among respondents in some places. Two days later, Russia officially annexed Crimea when Russian President Vladimir Putin proclaimed it to be a part of the Russian Federation.

The sham referendum and the *annexation* of Crimea are not recognized by the international community. Under international law, the Crimean Peninsula is Ukrainian territory.

- **Annexation**—appropriation of a foreign territory.

3.3 The Fictitious Republics "DNR" and "LNR"

Following the annexation of Crimea, the Russian Federation started the military intervention in the east of Ukraine, where officials loyal to Yanukovych and later Russian intelligence services had co-organized and financed protests against Euromaidan, known as "Antimaidan." By May 2014 at the latest, Russia gained control of large parts of the Donetsk and Luhansk regions in the Ukrainian East by military and non-military means. The Ukrainian administration was violently expelled under the leadership of Russian officers with the participation of Russian special forces, Russian weapons, Russian funding, and the support of local collaborators. Two fictitious republics were proclaimed: "DNR—Donetsk People's Republic" and "LNR—Luhansk People's Republic."

On July 17, 2014, Russian-controlled fighters in the Donetsk region shot down Malaysia Airlines flight MH17, a Boeing 777 flying from Amsterdam to Kuala Lumpur—see Fig. 3.2. A Russian BUK missile brought down the passenger plane. All 298 people on board were killed. Two former Russian army officers and a Ukrainian collaborator were convicted of murder in absentia by a Dutch criminal court in 2022. In May 2025, the International Civil Aviation Organization (ICAO, a specialized agency of the United Nations) ruled that the Russian Federation was responsible for the shooting down of Malaysian aircraft MH17 over Ukraine.

In contrast to Crimea, the "separatists," as the supporters of the Russian-led "DNR"/"LNR" have often been called since 2014, encountered resistance from the local population, volunteers and the Ukrainian armed forces. In April 2014, the Ukrainian interim president Oleksandr Turchynov declared the so-called Anti-Terrorist Operation, ATO. The war and the Russian occupation in these areas have continued ever since. By 2022, about 14,000 people had been killed in the fighting. Around two million people had fled the Russian-occupied areas.

- **Separatists** are parts of the population who want to break off—to separate—from the state in which they live.

The sham republics "DNR" and "LNR" have been controlled by the Russian state with the help of Russian citizens since 2014. The latter are neither "separatists" nor

Fig. 3.2 Wreckage of Malaysia Airlines passenger flight MH17, shot down in the Donetsk region on July 17, 2014, by Russian-controlled fighters. Photo: Ministry of Defense of the Kingdom of the Netherlands

"rebels" in the strict sense of the word. Instead, the correct terms *Russian-controlled militias/fighters* or *occupiers* (for Russian citizens) or "*collaborators*" (for local residents) should be used.

According to opinion polls, the majority of the population wanted the territories to remain part of Ukraine. Nevertheless, in May 2014, the Russian-controlled administration held sham referendums similar to those in Crimea and declared the independence of the "DNR" and "LNR" from Ukraine, not recognized internationally. On February 21, 2022, 3 days before the full-scale invasion of Ukraine, Putin recognized the "independence" of the pseudo-republics. Their formal incorporation into the Russian Federation then followed in October 2024.

3.4 Peace Efforts

From 2014 until the start of the large-scale Russian invasion in 2022, talks on possible peace solutions were held with the participation of Ukraine, Russia and numerous Western politicians. The so-called "Minsk Peace Agreements" were signed in Minsk, the capital of Belarus, but their provisions were never fully implemented.

Russia was unwilling to end its unlawful interference in Ukraine and broke the ceasefire shortly after it had been signed. Ukraine adheres to the borders of 1991, which are valid under international law and to which the Minsk Agreements also refer. Since 2014, the Ukrainian army and Russian-controlled units in the occupied regions of Donetsk and Luhansk have repeatedly fought heavy battles.

3.5 Escalation in 2021–Beginning of 2022

Over the course of 2021, Russia relocated around 150,000 soldiers to the border with Ukraine. Ukrainian and foreign politicians tried to draw the world's attention to the Russian deployment and avert the attack on Ukraine through talks with Russian President Vladimir Putin.

On July 12, 2021, Putin published an essay "On the historical unity of Russians and Ukrainians" in which he questioned the existence of Ukraine as a separate nation. Experts saw this as preparation for an attack. Massive Russian cyberattacks on Ukraine's critical infrastructure from January 2022 confirmed this assumption.

Putin claimed until just before February 24, 2022 that he did not want to invade Ukraine.

> We have no plans to occupy Ukrainian territories. We are not going to impose anything on anyone by force.
> Vladimir Putin, President of the Russian Federation, in his speech in the early morning of February 24, 2022, at the same time announcing the start of the "special military operation," i.e., the invasion of Ukraine.

Further Reading

https://www.courtmh17.com/en/insights/news/2022/transcript-of-the-mh17-judgment-hearing/; https://www.youtube.com/watch?v=wvRkV6DuZ7k; https://www.airliners.de/icao-russland-mh17-abschuss-verantwortlich/80748; http://kremlin.ru/events/president/news/66181

History and Interesting Facts

4.1 The Emergence of Ukraine and Russia

The Ukrainian capital Kyiv was founded in the fifth century. From the ninth to the thirteenth century, the city was the center of a large empire of Kyivan Rus, inhabited by Eastern Slavs, Wikings, Finns, Normans and others, and stretching from the Black Sea in the south to the Baltic Sea in the north. It included large parts of present-day Ukraine, Belarus and western Russia. Its princes adopted Christianity and built up Kyiv in a magnificent way.

Kyiv maintained lively exchanges with other European countries, including a successful marriage policy. For example, Anna Yaroslavna, also known as Anna of Kyiv, daughter of the Grand Prince Yaroslav the Wise of Kyiv and his wife Ingegerd of Sweden, became the second wife of King Henry I of France and thus Queen of France (Fig. 4.1).

In the twelfth century, a son of the prince of Kyiv, Prince Yuriy Dolgorukiy (Fig. 4.2), had a fortification built on the banks of the Moskva River. This new town, which was named Moscow after the river, developed rapidly.

When Kyiv was plundered as a result of the Mongol invasion, Kingdom of Galicia-Volhynia (twelfth to fourteenth century) took over from Kyivan Rus. However, the term "Rus" or "Ruski" was still used for a long time to refer to this region as well as north-eastern areas as far as Moscow.

After the collapse of the Kingdom of Galicia-Volhynia, the territories of present-day Ukraine came under the rule of Poland-Lithuania, the Habsburg Monarchy and the Moscow Tsarist Empire over the next few centuries. In the south, they were controlled by the Crimean Khanate and the Ottoman Empire.

© The Author(s), under exclusive license to Springer Nature Switzerland AG 2025
O. Stavrou, *Russia's War Against Ukraine*,
https://doi.org/10.1007/978-3-032-02625-5_4

Fig. 4.1 Anna of Kyiv (c. 1024 to presumably 1078), Queen of France from 1051 to 1060, second wife of Henry I of France. Mosaic in the Zoloti Vorota subway station in Kyiv. Source: Wikimedia

In the seventeenth century, a Cossack state emerged in central Ukraine. It later fell under the rule of the Moscow Tsarist Empire.

Over the centuries, the Grand Principality of Moscow conquered and controlled large areas from the Baltic Sea to Kamchatka and the Sea of Japan, from Siberia to the Caucasus. It became a huge empire with a tsar as head of state and Moscow or St. Petersburg as its political center.

4.2 What Does "Ukraine" Mean?

The modern name "Russia" was increasingly used for the Tsardom of Moscow from the seventeenth century onwards. In the eighteenth century, Tsar Peter I of Moscow officially renamed it the Russian Empire. The western neighboring regions and their languages were called "White Russian" (today's Belarus) and

4.2 What Does "Ukraine" Mean?

Fig. 4.2 Yuriy Dolgorukiy (1090–1157), son of the Kyiv Grand Prince Volodymyr Monomakh, Prince of Rostov, Grand Prince of Kyivan Rus, founder of Moscow. Photo: *Tsarskij tituljarnik.* Source: Wikimedia

"Little Russian" (today's Ukraine). The local population and intellectual elites found the term "Little Russia" inappropriate or insulting and increasingly adopted the name "Ukraine" or "Ukrainian."

The word Ukraine (Ukrainian "Ukrayina") means "the land" or "country" (Ukrainian "krayina", "kray") and can already be found in writings dating back to the twelfth century.

4.3 The Ukrainian State After World War I

At the beginning of the twentieth century, the western regions of present-day Ukraine (especially Galicia) belonged to the Austro-Hungarian Monarchy and central and eastern regions were part of the Russian Tsarist Empire. Both empires collapsed during or as a consequence of the First World War. Several new states emerged in their place, including Ukraine. After the First World War, the "Ukrainian People's Republic" was proclaimed in the central and eastern part of Ukraine and the "Western Ukrainian People's Republic" in the western. The two republics united in 1919.

After the Russian Revolution in 1917, the Bolsheviks or Communists seized power in Russia under the leadership of Vladimir Ilyich Ulyanov (Lenin). The Russian Bolsheviks then invaded central and eastern regions of Ukraine and annexed it to the Soviet Union in 1922 after several years of war. During the same period, the Polish army invaded western Ukraine and annexed it to Poland.

In 1939, as a consequence of the Hitler-Stalin Pact, the Soviet Red Army occupied Western Ukraine, which had previously been under Polish administration, as well as Estonia, Latvia and Lithuania, and annexed them to the Soviet Union.

4.4 The Soviet Union and Its Disintegration

The Union of Soviet Socialist Republics, USSR or Soviet Union, was founded in 1922. It ultimately consisted of 15 republics, the most populous of which were the Russian Soviet Federative Socialist Republic and the Ukrainian Soviet Socialist Republic.

The USSR was a *dictatorship* of the Russian Communist Party controlled from Moscow. Anyone who disagreed with it was persecuted or eliminated. All important decisions were made in the Russian capital, Moscow. Abroad, the Soviet Union was therefore often simply called "Russia."

- **Dictatorship** means that one person (= dictator) or a group of people in a state have unlimited political power. A dictatorship is the opposite of democracy, in which the people decide on politics. In a dictatorship, there are no free elections, the dictator is not bound by laws or human rights, critics are persecuted, protests and non-conforming opinions are suppressed by force.

At the end of the 1980s, signs of disintegration increased in the Soviet Union. The Baltic Soviet republics of Estonia, Latvia and Lithuania declared their independence in 1990. They were followed by other republics, including Ukraine on August 24, 1991. In December 1991, the heads of republics of Russia, Boris Yeltsin, of Ukraine, Leonid Kravchuk, and of Belarus, Stanislav Shushkevich, signed a treaty on the dissolution of the Soviet Union. The end of the Soviet Union followed on December 25–26, 1991, with the resignation of the then President of the Soviet Union Michail Gorbachev and a parliamentary resolution.

4.5 The Russian Language in Ukraine

In the Russian Empire, tsars banned the Ukrainian language, books, school lessons, church services and theater performances in Ukrainian several times throughout history.

> The Little Russian language did not exist, it does not exist and cannot exist.
> The Valuyev Circular of 1863 on the Ukrainian language. This secret decree by Peter Valuyev, Minister of the Interior of the Russian Empire, forbade the publication of textbooks and religious texts in Ukrainian.

Nevertheless, Ukrainian continued to be used. The eastern Ukrainian regions (Kharkiv, Donetsk, Luhansk) and the neighboring western regions of the present-day Russian Federation (Belgorod, Taganrog, Kuban, Rostov-on-Don) have also long been inhabited by ethnic Ukrainians who traditionally spoke Ukrainian—see Fig. 4.3.

During the Soviet era, the Ukrainian-speaking population in Ukraine dwindled as a result of violence and the targeted policy of *Russification*. The famine organized artificially by the Soviet state in 1932–1933, known as the *"Holodomor"* in Ukrainian, caused the deaths of around four million Ukrainians. Ukraine lost a further 8–12 million inhabitants in the Second World War.

Fig. 4.3 Ethnographic overview map of the Ukrainian national territory, in German. Kartografische Anstalt G. Freytag & Berndt, Ges. m. b. H., Vienna, 1910. Source: www.polona.pl. The map shows areas in the west of present-day Russia also as ethnically Ukrainian-populated territory. It uses German names mirroring the old Ukrainian pronunciation Bilhorod, Rosstiw, Sstawropil for the now Russian cities of Belgorod, Rostov, Stavropol, as well as Ssewastopil, Ssymferopil for the cities of Sevastopol and Simferopol on the Crimean peninsula. The Ukrainian capital Kyiv is spelled as Kyjiw and the main river of Ukraine as Dnipro, which corresponds to the current Ukrainian pronunciation. The red line is not part of the original map and shows approximately the current border

The Holodomor
In the 1920s, under the leadership of dictator Josef Stalin, the Soviet Union launched *forced collectivization,* the restructuring of agriculture into large state farms, the so-called "kolkhozes." Farmers were forced to give up their land and livestock and work on the collective farms. They received no wages, but a share of the harvest. To intimidate them, hundreds of thousands of farmers living in the Soviet Union were expropriated and deported to remote areas.

To punish the Ukrainian farmers for their resistance to collectivization, Moscow obliged the Ukrainian Soviet Republic in 1932 to hand over so much harvest that there was too little food left for the farmers themselves. Soldiers confiscated food and seeds and surrounded villages so that starving people could not flee to the cities.

4.5 The Russian Language in Ukraine

> In central and eastern Ukraine, known as the "breadbasket of Europe" thanks to its fertile black soil and rich harvests, a famine broke out that claimed around four million lives. This famine is called the Holodomor, derived from "killing by hunger." Over 30 countries have officially recognized the Holodomor as genocide against the Ukrainians, including Germany, France, Belgium, Switzerland, the USA, Canada, Brazil, Mexico, etc.
>
> In other areas of the Soviet Union, such as Kuban, which was predominantly populated by ethnic Ukrainians, and the Republic of Kazakhstan millions more died in 1932–1933.

In place of the Ukrainian workforce that was now missing, Russian citizens were systematically settled in Ukraine. They worked in coal mines and heavy industry factories (mechanical engineering, metal processing) in the Ukrainian East, including in the Donbas region (= Donets Basin).

In the Soviet Union, Russian was effectively the official language and was compulsory in schools. All other languages were considered subordinate to Russian. Ukrainian intellectuals, artists and cultural workers were repeatedly persecuted, hundreds of them were executed and thousands were deported to the Soviet Far East, where many of them died in penal and labor camps, the so-called *"Gulags."*

The period in the 1930s, when the Ukrainian cultural elite was particularly persecuted and Ukrainian artists were executed, is known in Ukraine as the *"executed Renaissance."*

The use of the Ukrainian language in public life, film and theater, in books and the press was restricted during the Soviet era. In some places in the Ukrainian East and South, such as Luhansk, Donetsk, Simferopol and Mykolaiv, there was not a single Ukrainian school in the 1980s. Russian was the only language of instruction at the universities there. Many children of Ukrainian-speaking parents were ultimately only able to speak Russian.

This targeted language policy led to an extensive Russification of the ethnic Ukrainian areas.

In Ukraine, which has been independent since 1991, Ukrainian is the state language. In recent years, there have been some efforts to reduce the continuing dominance of Russian in several areas. In 2020, for example, the circulation of Ukrainian-language magazines in Ukraine amounted to 31% of all magazines, while that of Russian-language magazines was 67%. At the same time, 73% of the population defined Ukrainian as their mother tongue and only 26% named Russian as their native language.

The vast majority of the inhabitants of Ukraine speak both languages. Regardless of the language used, most Ukrainians feel that they are citizens of the Ukrainian state. Ukrainian President Zelensky himself grew up in a Russian-speaking family and even used Russian frequently in public appearances until his presidency.

Since the beginning of the Russian aggression against Ukraine, many Ukrainians no longer want to use the Russian language; for them, it has become the language of the aggressors.

4.6 Linguistic Differences Between Ukrainian and Russian

Ukrainian and Russian belong to the Slavic linguistic family. Polish, Czech, Slovakian, Bulgarian, Belarusian, Serbian, Croatian, Slovenian, Bosnian, Macedonian, etc., are in the same language family. Yet, there are many words in the Slavic languages that sound similar but have a different meaning. Hence, it is possible to understand each other on simple topics, but not to communicate freely.

Most Ukrainians also speak Russian, as they had to learn it for a long time. Russians cannot speak Ukrainian without having learned it beforehand. For them, Ukrainian sounds about the same as a Spanish speaker perceives Portuguese.

4.7 The Role of the Orthodox Church

In 988, Prince Volodymyr the Great of Kyiv adopted Christianity of the Byzantine tradition (forerunner of later Orthodoxy) and introduced it as the state religion of Kyivan Rus. This event is known as the "Baptism of Rus." From Kyiv, the Christian faith spread to the neighboring territories, including the Moscow Tsardom. As the Ukrainian territories increasingly came under the rule of the Moscow Tsarist Empire, the Moscow Orthodox Church expanded its overall influence and the control over the Ukrainian Orthodox Church.

Tsar Peter I placed the Russian Orthodox Church under state control in the eighteenth century. The communist regime of the Soviet Union initially fought against all religions, including the Orthodox Church. However, the Soviet dictator Josef Stalin saw the Russian church as an instrument for influencing the population and allowed it to resume under state control. Other religious communities continued to be persecuted. From this re-establishment onwards, clergymen of the Russian Orthodox Church were firmly integrated into state structures, including

4.7 The Role of the Orthodox Church

secret services. Even in today's Russia, the Orthodox Church is closely intertwined with the state.

In Ukraine, there are numerous religions and religious denominations beside Orthodoxy: the Ukrainian Greek Catholic Church (also known as the Uniate Church), the Roman Catholic Church, Islam, Judaism, Protestant churches and some others.

As one's religious affiliation is not officially recorded in Ukraine, corresponding data is based on surveys and estimates. According to these, the Christian Orthodox faith is the largest religious community in Ukraine, accounting for 70% of the population. According to one of the surveys, around four-fifths of Orthodox believers belong to the independent *Orthodox Church of Ukraine (OCU)*. It was recognized as autocephalous (= independent) by the Ecumenical Patriarch of Constantinople (= honorary head of the Orthodox Christians), Bartholomew I, in 2019.

One fifth of Orthodox believers in Ukraine belonged to the *Ukrainian Orthodox Church (UOC)* before 2022. This was and still remains largely under Russian influence, even though it has been administratively separated from the Russian Orthodox Church since 2022. Due to the Russian aggression against Ukraine, the spread of Russian propaganda and the collaboration of numerous clergymen with the Russian occupying forces, believers have been turning away from this church since 2014 and especially since 2022. In surveys in 2024, only 8% of Orthodox believers still professed allegiance to the UOC.

The Russian Orthodox Church openly supports the Russian war against Ukraine, which Patriarch Kirill, the head of the church, calls a "holy war." In the Russian-occupied areas of Ukraine, the independent Orthodox Church of Ukraine and other religious denominations are being persecuted, in some cases expropriated and priests arbitrarily arrested and tortured. Church services in the Ukrainian language are banned.

The Ukrainian state has now begun to abolish the existing privileges for the Russian-friendly UOC, in particular by terminating lease agreements for land used by the UOC (for example, in 2023 for part of the famous Kyiv Pechersk Lavra, see Fig. 4.4).

A Ukrainian law passed in August 2024 prohibits the activities of the Russian Orthodox Church on the territory of Ukraine and provides for the possibility of banning religious organizations with a proven connection to the aggressor state Russia or the Russian Orthodox Church through the courts. The law, which has been partly criticized, does not explicitly mention the UOC. Its parishes and religious sub-organizations are separate legal entities under Ukrainian law. Whether one or more of them fall under the legal ban will have to be decided by a court on a case-by-case basis at the request of the authorities.

Fig. 4.4 Kyiv Pechersk Lavra (Kyiv Monastery of the Caves). Photo: Falin. Source: Wikimedia. Kyiv Pechersk Lavra was founded in the eleventh century. It is one of the most important Orthodox Christian sites in Ukraine. The monastery complex has been a UNESCO World Heritage Site since 1990

Christmas on December 25 or January 7?

The Russian Orthodox Church still follows the old Julian calendar and celebrates Christmas on January 7, similar to Orthodox believers in Belarus and Serbia, for example. Other Orthodox churches, e.g., in Greece and Bulgaria, as well as Catholic and Protestant churches, follow the new Gregorian calendar and celebrate Christmas on December 25.

Until recently, Christians in Ukraine celebrated religious holidays according to the old Julian calendar at the same time as Russia. Already in 2017, December 25 was legally introduced in Ukraine as a non-working holiday for Christmas alongside January 7. A Ukrainian law from July 2023 moved Christmas to December 25, while January 7 is no longer an official holiday. The law was preceded by respective decisions by the Ukrainian Greek Catholic Church and the Orthodox Church of Ukraine.

All Orthodox churches, with the exception of Finnish, continue to follow the Julian calendar for Easter.

4.8 What Is Wrong With the Narrative of the Brother Nations?

Russia sees a historical "kinship" in the fact that the Russian capital Moscow was founded by a Kyivan prince, large parts of present-day Ukraine, Belarus, and Russia were under the sovereignty of Kyiv in the Middle Ages, and they adopted the Orthodox faith from Kyiv.

Russian propaganda calls the three countries Belarus, Russia and Ukraine "brother nations," with the idea that Russia is the "big brother", and claims therefore the right to determine the fate of the "little brothers" Ukraine and Belarus. The Ukrainians reject the propaganda term "brother nations" on the grounds that every nation has the right to decide for itself and does not need any "brothers" to do so.

4.9 Crimea

The Crimean Peninsula has been inhabited by Crimean Tatars for centuries. In the course of the collapse of the Turk-Mongol Golden Horde, the Crimean Khanate emerged in the fifteenth century. It was conquered by the Russian Tsarist Empire in 1783 followed by the Russification of the peninsula. After the collapse of the Tsarist Empire in 1917, Crimean Tatars proclaimed the "People's Republic of Crimea." It was occupied by Russian Bolsheviks and annexed to the USSR. In the meantime, the once 90%-majority of Tatars had been reduced to a 25%-minority.

During WWII, Crimea was occupied by the Wehrmacht, the Nazi German army, from 1941 to 1944. After regaining control of Crimea in 1944, Soviet ruler Stalin ordered all Crimean Tatars to be deported to Central Asia. They were collectively accused of collaborating with Nazi Germany. Mass deportations of Greeks, Bulgarians, Armenians and other nationalities from Crimea followed. Thousands of people died in the process. Their homes were made available to Russian settlers, so that Russians soon became a 70%-majority in Crimea. The expelled Crimean Tatars were not officially allowed to return to Crimea until 1989.

After the Second World War, Crimea lay in ruins. Administratively, the peninsula was part of the Russian Soviet Federative Republic, but had no land connection with it. Crimea did not have enough drinking water and was dependent on the supply of electricity and goods from the Ukrainian mainland. To promote the reconstruction of Crimea and facilitate its administration, Crimea was transferred to the jurisdiction of Ukraine in 1954, although the inhabitants were predominantly Russian.

Administrative border shifts took place several times in Soviet history, regardless of the ethnic composition of the territories. In the 1920s, the Soviet government handed over Kuban and areas around Belgorod and Taganrog in the south and east of Ukraine to the Russian Soviet Republic, although the majority of their population was Ukrainian.

In the all-Ukrainian referendum in December 1991, the majority of Crimea's inhabitants voted for the independence of Ukraine within the existing borders.

As part of the Ukrainian Soviet Socialist Republic, Crimea had the status of an oblast (= region, an administrative unit) alongside 24 other oblasts until 1991. In independent Ukraine, the peninsula enjoyed the special status of an "autonomous republic" with extensive decision-making powers, a regional parliament, and a regional government, in contrast to the 24 oblasts.

Crimea has been illegally occupied by Russia since 2014, and since then the Crimean Tatars have once again been persecuted, as have the parents of the Ukrainian singer Jamala, who is of Crimean Tatar origin (Fig. 4.5) and whose house in Crimea was confiscated by the Russian occupation authorities in 2024.

For more information on the annexation of Crimea in violation of international law and life under Russian occupation, see Sect. 3.2 and Chap. 9.

Fig. 4.5 Jamala (*1983, legal name Susana Jamaladinova), Ukrainian singer of Crimean Tatar origin. Photo: Albin Olsson. Source: Wikimedia. In 2016, Jamala won the Eurovision Song Contest with her self-composed song "1944," sung partly in Crimean Tatar, about the expulsion of her ancestors from Crimea in 1944

Further Reading

https://kiis.com.ua/?lang=ukr&cat=reports&id=1443&page=1; https://www.understandingwar.org/backgrounder/russian-offensive-campaign-assessment-march-29-2024; https://razumkov.org.ua/images/2023/02/13/2022_Religiya_SITE.pdf; https://www.tagesschau.de/ausland/europa/ukraine-priester-spionage-101.html; https://www.consultant.ru/cons/cgi/online.cgi?req=doc;base=ESU;n=16497#DhwzXhTURetAhnP41; https://voxukraine.org/gazety-j-zhurnaly-v-ukrayini; https://ratinggroup.ua/files/ratinggroup/reg_files/rg_ua_1000_independence_082022_xvii_press.pdf

Military Alliances After World War II

5.1 NATO and the Warsaw Pact in the Cold War

After the end of the Second World War in 1945, the victorious Allied powers—the USA, Great Britain, France and the Soviet Union—could not agree on how the world should develop and which ideology should be decisive—communism or Western democracy.

> **Communism**
> Communism as an ideology (= collection of political ideas) emerged in the nineteenth century. According to it, there should be no private property, but all important objects in a state, such as land, houses and companies, should be owned by the state. In theory, state ownership should lead to all people in the country being equal and receiving everything necessary for life.
>
> In practice, every state that proclaimed communist principles has so far turned into a dictatorship or authoritarian regime, where one party controls politics, suppresses other world views and persecutes their representatives. The Soviet Union, China, North Korea, Cuba, Vietnam and Laos are just a few such examples.

The conflict between Soviet communism and Western democracies without a direct military confrontation is known as the "Cold War." The Soviet Union on one side and the United States of America on the other were the main players in the

© The Author(s), under exclusive license to Springer Nature Switzerland AG 2025
O. Stavrou, *Russia's War Against Ukraine*,
https://doi.org/10.1007/978-3-032-02625-5_5

Cold War, also referred to as two opposing "superpowers" or two "poles." This gave rise to the term "bipolar world" (from the Latin "bi-" for "two," "both") for the period after World War II until the end of the 1980s.

To protect themselves from a threat from the Soviet Union, the United Kingdom, France and eight other European countries as well as the USA and Canada founded a defense alliance in 1949—the *North Atlantic Treaty Organization (NATO)*.

NATO

NATO, the "North Atlantic Treaty Organization" is an alliance for the joint self-defense of its members. Its most important principle is embodied in the Article 5 of the NATO founding treaty, the so-called "collective defense clause" stating that an attack on one member is considered as an attack on all, thus, all other members are obliged to support the attacked one.

NATO members also commit to not attacking other members militarily.

Each member has the right to veto NATO decisions (= can prevent the decision).

The USSR also founded a military alliance, the *Warsaw Pact*, in 1955. Other members of the pact were neighboring countries under the influence of the Soviet Union: Poland, the then Czechoslovakia, Hungary, Romania, Bulgaria, Albania and the German Democratic Republic (GDR).

With the collapse of the Soviet Union in 1991, the Warsaw Pact was dissolved. Russia initiated the founding of a new military alliance, the *Collective Security Treaty Organization (CSTO)*. Nine ex-Soviet republics joined the alliance, three of which later withdrew, and Armenia froze its membership in 2024. The CSTO military alliance currently has five active members: Russia, Belarus, Kazakhstan, Kyrgyzstan and Tajikistan. Serbia enjoys observer status in the CSTO.

As the former members of the Warsaw Pact were free to choose after 1991, all of them joined NATO over the years instead of the Russian-led CSTO. The three Baltic ex-Soviet republics Estonia, Latvia and Lithuania did so too.

NATO now has 32 members. Admission to the alliance takes place in a multistage process. Following successful preparatory steps, a country can declare its wish to join in a written application for membership and is invited by NATO to negotiate.

In 1994, the Partnership for Peace (PfP) initiative was launched to strengthen military cooperation and mutual trust between NATO and European and Asian countries that were not members of NATO. At various times, all former Soviet republics, countries of the former Warsaw Pact, countries of the former Yugoslavia, and neutral states (Austria, Switzerland, Ireland, Malta) participated in the PfP program.

After Russia invaded Ukraine, the previously neutral states of Sweden and Finland gave up their neutrality and submitted applications for NATO membership. At the beginning of April 2023, Finland officially became the 31st member, and in March 2024, Sweden became the 32nd member of the Western defense alliance.

5.2   NATO and Russia

After the dissolution of the Soviet Union, the NATO countries expressed their intention to build a trusting strategic relationship with the Russian Federation. Until then, NATO had been regarded as a US led defense mechanism against the threat posed by communist Moscow. Now it was open to all countries that sought peace and security.

In 1994, the Russian Federation became a member of the NATO "Partnership for Peace" program. In 1997, the "NATO-Russia Founding Act" was signed, in which NATO and Russia declared their intention to "build together a lasting and inclusive peace in the Euro-Atlantic area on the principles of democracy and cooperative security."

The North Atlantic Alliance and Russia worked together within the framework of the newly created *NATO-Russia Council*. Russia sent permanent representatives to NATO and NATO opened a permanent representation in Moscow. No other country has been given such a special position by NATO.

The Russian Federation had the option of applying for NATO membership. The country did not do so.

Instead, Russian President Putin and Russian propaganda criticized NATO ever more blatantly and accused the alliance of wanting to encircle Russia. In reality, the Russian Federation shares approx. 4% of its overall border or approx. 11% of its continental border with a NATO country (following Finland's accession to NATO).

Relations between Russia and NATO deteriorated, particularly following Russia's illegal annexation of Crimea and the invasion of the East Ukraine by Russian units in 2014.

At a meeting of the NATO-Russia Council on 12 January 2022, Russia demanded that NATO block the accession of further states and refrain from stationing defense weapons in countries bordering Russia. Jens Stoltenberg, the Secretary General of the Alliance in 2014–2024, rejected this demand with reference to the right of self-determination of the states. This means that every independent state can decide for itself which alliances it wants to join and how it wants to defend itself. This was the last meeting of the NATO-Russia Council to date.

Russian President Putin's position is that NATO is to blame for Russia "having to" invade Ukraine.

5.3 NATO and Ukraine

In 1990, Ukraine declared its intention to strive for permanent *neutrality* in the "Declaration of State Sovereignty of Ukraine." It also declared that it would not belong to any military alliances and would not possess any nuclear weapons. As a non-aligned state, Ukraine became a member of the NATO partnership programs "Partnership for Peace" (PfP) and "Euro-Atlantic Partnership Council" (EAPC) alongside Switzerland, Austria, Russia and other countries.

In the 2000s, Ukrainian politicians began a discussion about the meaningfulness of future NATO membership. Society largely rejected the idea. The Ukrainian law of 2010 defines *non-alignment* (= non-participation in military alliances) as one of the most important principles of Ukraine's foreign policy.

Following the illegal annexation of Crimea by Russia and the start of fighting in the East of Ukraine, the opinion of the Ukrainian population changed significantly: while only around 20% of the population were in favor of joining NATO in 2012, approval rose to around 50% in 2015. In a survey in the summer of 2022, 85% of Ukrainians were in favor of Ukraine joining NATO because they believed it would protect them from Russia.

The annexation of Crimea and the start of Russian hostilities in the Ukrainian East in 2014 showed that the neutral or non-aligned status could not guarantee the country's security. In December 2014, a new law officially ended Ukraine's non-aligned status and defined NATO membership as a goal.

Owing to the Russian war of aggression, the President of Ukraine Volodymyr Zelensky submitted an application for accelerated NATO accession in September 2022.

A general prerequisite for joining NATO is that the candidate country must not be involved in international conflicts and disputes over border demarcations. In February 2024, the then NATO Secretary General Jens Stoltenberg confirmed

Ukraine's future: "Ukraine will join NATO. It's not a question of if, but of when." It is not yet clear when this will happen.

A new body was created in 2023 for closer cooperation on Ukraine's path to NATO membership: the *NATO-Ukraine Council*. The Council serves the purpose of political dialog and exchange in crisis situations. It met for the first time in July 2023.

Two further NATO-Ukraine institutions were created. *NSATU*, NATO Security Assistance and Training for Ukraine in Wiesbaden, Germany, coordinates the delivery of weapons and training of Ukrainian army personnel starting July 2024. 31 NATO members (all except Hungary) participate in it. The training center *JATEC*, Joint Analysis, Training and Education Centre, is housed in Bydgoszcz, Poland, starting January 2025.

5.4 Neutrality

A state can declare itself neutral; this is often done in a written document, e.g., in a law or treaty. By neutrality, a state signals that it does not wish to attack anyone militarily and, in the event of war, will not take part in the war either on the side of the attackers or the attacked. Neutrality also includes non-participation in military alliances (= non-alignment or non-bloc status).

Neutrality gives no guarantee that the neutral country itself will not be attacked militarily.

Which actions are inadmissible due to neutrality greatly depends on the configuration of neutrality.

In Austria, the Neutrality Act of October 26, 1955, expressly contains two prohibitions. Austria "shall not join any military alliances and shall not permit the establishment of military bases of foreign states on its territory." Other actions, e.g., the training of the army personnel of other countries or the demining (= removal of mines) of former war zones, are not mentioned in the law and are therefore at the discretion of politics. After joining the EU in 1995, Austria committed to participating in the EU foreign, security and defense policies.

Austria declared neutrality 10 years after the end of the Second World War, which happened only after the withdrawal of foreign (US, British, French and Soviet) troops from its territory. Neutrality was the price for the Soviet Union's consent to withdraw its troops.

Switzerland has been neutral since 1815 and thus has the longest tradition of military neutrality in Europe. The Swiss Federal Constitution gives the government the mandate and the Federal Assembly the task of taking "measures to safeguard Switzerland's external security, independence and neutrality."

The content of Swiss neutrality is not legally defined. This allows the country to be flexible in its use of the term. Switzerland joined the EU sanctions against Russia due to the invasion of Ukraine in 2022. When other countries wanted to transfer their Swiss-produced weapons to Ukraine, the Swiss government refused to give its consent citing neutrality. In June 2024, however, the National Council's Security Policy Committee voted in favor of supplying Swiss weapons to Ukraine. The final decision is to be made by the Swiss Parliament.

As neutral countries, the three neighbors Austria, Switzerland and Liechtenstein are not themselves members of NATO, but border NATO member states (and each other) on all sides.

> Should there be an attack on Switzerland, [...] then neutrality will fall away.
> Swiss President and Defense Minister Viola Amherd in Vienna in April 2024. Among other things, she addressed the European Sky Shield air defense initiative, to which Switzerland and Austria belong alongside a dozen other countries.

Other neutral or non-aligned states in Europe are: Ireland, Malta, Cyprus, the Vatican, Moldova and Serbia. Cyprus is considering joining NATO, as its president declared at the end of November 2024. Outside Europe, there are about a dozen other neutral states, the largest of which include Mexico, Mongolia, Turkmenistan, Uzbekistan and Japan.

Sweden and Finland gave up their neutrality in the face of the Russian invasion of Ukraine in 2022 and are now members of NATO.

Russia is demanding neutrality from Ukraine, which is to be set out in writing in a treaty. The Ukrainian leadership and society reject this demand. They argue that Ukraine was practically neutral until the Russian aggression in 2014. This did not protect it from Russian aggression. By invading Ukraine, Russia broke numerous treaties. A new treaty with Russia provides no security, as there is no guarantee that Russia will not break this treaty as well (see the Budapest Memorandum in Sect. 1.2).

Some advocates of neutrality propose alternative concepts. They argue that Russia's neutrality would be much more conducive to sustainable peace in the region. Whether and by what means this can ever be achieved is the subject of controversial debate.

Further Reading

https://orf.at/stories/3307007/; https://www.ris.bka.gv.at/GeltendeFassung.wxe?Abfrage=Bundesnormen&Gesetzesnummer=10000267; https://fedlex.data.admin.ch/filestore/fedlex.data.admin.ch/eli/cc/1999/404/20220213/de/pdf-a/fedlex-data-admin-ch-eli-cc-1999-404-20220213-de-pdf-a-4.pdf

Russia: Dealing With the War 6

6.1 Remembering the Second World War: A Heroic Myth

Many in Russia are convinced that the Soviet Union alone defeated Nazi Germany in the Second World War. The role of the other Allies—the USA, France and UK—is downplayed. Russia sees itself as the exclusive heir to the Soviet Union and as the greatest victim of the Nazi regime. Yet other Soviet republics, such as Belarus and Ukraine, contributed significantly to the victory of the Soviet Union and suffered proportionally greater losses than Russia. This fact is often neglected, as is the fact that the Soviet Union collaborated with Germany in the first years of the war.

> **Ukraine's Sacrifices in the Second World War**
> Victory in the Second World War claimed many victims on part of the Soviet Union. The then Soviet Republics Ukraine and Belarus suffered the highest losses in relation to their size. Around 27 million people from the Soviet Union lost their lives in the war. Ukraine lost 8–12 million people (a quarter of the Ukrainian population, around 37% of the USSR's total losses), Belarus around 2.5 million (a third of the population) and Russia around 13.4 million (a tenth of the population).
> Ukraine and Belarus were completely occupied by the Germans—see Fig. 6.1. By contrast, only 3% of Russia's territory was occupied. Ukraine suffered almost half of the Soviet Union's material losses. Almost every second USSR forced laborer (= "Ostarbeiter") came from Ukraine as did every fifth soldier in the Red Army.

Fig. 6.1 The eastward advance of the Nazi German army in the Second World War until 1943. Source: Texty.org.ua. The map shows the current borderline, which differs from the former borders

The Second World War is known in Russia as the "Great Patriotic War," and "Victory Day" on May 9 is an official holiday (see Fig. 6.2). For Russians, the war began in 1941 when Germany attacked the Soviet Union. The rest of the world considers September 1939 to be the start of World War II, when German troops invaded Poland from the west and the Soviet Red Army invaded what is now Western Ukraine, then part of Poland, from the east.

The idea that Russia would continue to protect Europe from the Nazis is widely held in Russian society. This perspective was created by Soviet state propaganda and continues to be promoted by the propaganda of the Russian Federation.

As of September 2023, uniformly updated history textbooks were introduced in Russian schools. They claim, for example, that it is a "firm idea of the West to destabilize the situation inside Russia," discuss the "revival of Nazism" in the Baltic states, and emphasize the necessity of the "special military operation," the euphemistic term used in Russia for the war against Ukraine.

Fig. 6.2 "Victory Day" celebrations in Amur, Russia, on May 9, 2017. Inscription on the homemade tank with the Soviet red flag: "On to Berlin!". Photo: Viktor Imambayev. Source: www.ampravda.ru

6.2 Transition Period in 1991–2000

After the collapse of the Soviet Union in 1991, the newly elected President of the Russian Federation Boris Yeltsin initiated a series of reforms: state-owned companies were privatized, meaning that they passed into private ownership (= privatization), prices were no longer set by the state but were allowed to form freely on the market (= liberalization). The 1993 constitution, which remains in force, defined Russia as a democratic constitutional state and guaranteed basic democratic rights such as freedom of information, freedom of assembly, the right to private property, the right to vote, etc. The constitution granted the president great power.

Yeltsin's reforms were necessary, but they did not only bring positive results. Many people lost their savings due to a poorly implemented currency reform. Several financial crises resulted in massive job losses (= unemployment). Prices skyrocketed (= high inflation). Criminal gangs emerged, which the police failed to control efficiently. Politics was plagued by corruption scandals and power struggles between different factions and oligarchs (= people who had become rich through privatization). The period of democratic reforms in Russia from 1991 to 2000 was generally highly unstable and remains a negative memory for large segments of the Russian population.

6.3 Putin's Russia

When former Prime Minister Vladimir Putin succeeded Boris Yeltsin as President of Russia in 2000, his main promise was stability and economic prosperity. In the early years of Putin's presidency, the situation in the country stabilized, salaries began to rise, people had more money for consumption and criminal gangs were combated. There was now more order and prosperity compared to the turbulent 1990s, even if the standard of living remained far behind that of most European countries.

At the same time, Putin began to establish an authoritarian system around himself. Politicians and activists who criticized the government were arrested. Putin's opponents and dissidents were eliminated; there were political murders. Freedom of the press was gradually restricted (see Table 6.1), forcing many independent newspapers and television channels to shut down. NGOs (= non-governmental organizations) that opposed the state's agenda were either banned or severely limited in their activities. Even permitted demonstrations were sometimes violently dispersed, the protesters arrested and convicted.

Criticizing Putin was practically forbidden. A *personality cult* (= excessive worship of a person) developed around Putin.

Although there were some protests against these developments, the majority of the population accepted them. The restriction of freedom and democracy was tolerated as the price for stability. Putin was re-elected as Russian president even after his first term of office had expired and has remained Russia's most powerful politician since 2000.

6.4 Attitude to War

The mood of the Russian Federation's population regarding the war against Ukraine is displayed in three overlapping, yet sometimes contradictory tendencies: fear of persecution, depoliticization, and hatred (of Ukraine and of the West).

When Russia began its large-scale invasion of Ukraine in 2022, many in the West hoped for a widespread Russian anti-war movement. However, it failed to materialize. Instead, the regime harshly punished individuals who opposed the war, in some cases sentencing them to years in prison. This was intended to intimidate the population and prevent protests.

The well-known Russian opposition leader Aleksei Navalny also criticized the Russian invasion of Ukraine in 2022. In February 2024, he died in a Russian penal colony. In Ukraine itself, Navalny was a controversial figure, as he had made a

6.4 Attitude to War

Table 6.1 World Press Freedom Index 2025 according to: Reporters Without Borders

Position 2025	Country	Index, global score	Press freedom situation
1	Norway	92.31	1–7: Good
2	Estonia	89.46	
3	Netherlands	88.64	
4	Sweden	88.13	
5	Finland	87.18	
6	Denmark	86.93	
11	Germany	83.85	8–42: Satisfactory
20	United Kingdom	78.89	
21	Canada	78.75	
25	France	76.62	
29	Australia	75.15	
57	United States	65.487	43–90: Problematic
62	Ukraine	63.96	
66	Japan	63.14	
124	Mexico	45.55	91–138: Difficult
166	Belarus	25.73	139–180: Very serious
171	Russia	24.57	
176	Iran	16.22	
178	China	14.80	
179	North Korea	12.64	

The World Press Freedom Index is compiled annually by the NGO Reporters Without Borders. It assesses whether and to what extent the state monitors and censors the media in the country, whether journalists have been illegally arrested, physically abused or kidnapped, or have had to flee the country due to intimidation or threats

number of imperialist and anti-Ukrainian statements during his lifetime, even if he later toned them down somewhat.

Over the years, Putin has transformed the Russian state into a dictatorship. Russian citizens, in turn, showed less and less interest in politics. They were largely indifferent to Russia's wars (in Chechnya, Georgia, Syria, Ukraine since 2014, etc.).

This public indifference to politics is called *depoliticization*. People do not want to be informed about the decisions of their own government; they think that politics does not affect them or that they cannot change anything anyway (= fatalism). Such people passively accept Russia's political actions, including the war against Ukraine.

Many Russians even actively support the Kremlin's policy based on propaganda. The main messages of Russian state propaganda are above all hatred of the West and its liberal-democratic system as well as the demonization of NATO, the USA and the EU. Russia's uniqueness, size, and strength are asserted, while Ukraine is denounced as a "Nazi country," "failed state" and a "non-existent nation." These messages are spread by Russian politicians, diplomats and the media, but also by many artists and cultural organizations, kindergartens and schools. All of this contributes to the all-encompassing *indoctrination* of the Russian population.

- **Indoctrination**—a targeted, intensive form of teaching that allows neither discussion nor contradiction, often using one-sided information, psychological techniques or coercion.

Years of indoctrination of the Russian population have an impact, especially in the war against Ukraine. Many people living in Russia actually say that the invasion of Ukraine is justified, that Russia is defending itself against Western threats and that the Russian soldiers are only fighting supporters of Nazism in Ukraine.

These views are shared by many Russians living abroad. Large-scale demonstrations by Russians against the Kremlin's regime and the war are almost unheard of in European countries.

Some Russian opposition activists living in exile (= forced emigration), including Navalny's widow, organized a small demonstration in Berlin, Germany, in November 2024. However, they lack impact and vision for the transformation of Russian society.

Outside the Russian Federation in countries that allow this, Russians openly wear the Z-sign and the black and orange St. George's ribbon (symbols of support for the Russian war) as well as Russian and Soviet flags at certain events, for example, in Serbia, Cyprus, Austria, Turkey, Kyrgyzstan, China, etc., every year on May 9, the Soviet "Victory Day."

However, not everyone wants to personally take part in the fighting on Ukrainian territory. After the mobilization in autumn 2022, many Russians fled the country. To compensate, the Russian government has been trying to recruit volunteers with high financial incentives, offering up to €54,000 per year for signing a military contract. This is several times the average salary in Russia and a comparatively easy way for many Russian families to make money, even if a family member dies in the process.

6.5 War Economy

Following the imposition of Western sanctions in spring 2022, Russia went through a brief economic crisis. In mid-2022, the Russian government began transitioning to a war economy, significantly increasing military spending to boost arms production, and the economy now follows the needs of war. Reliable data on the state of the Russian economy is scarce, as Russia has both classified certain statistics and published falsified numbers.

However, several indicators point to problems in the Russian economy:

- rising inflation which officially reached 9.1% in July 2024 and 10% in February 2025, in reality it is estimated to be much higher;
- temporary export bans on fuel (due to the decline in production following Ukrainian drone attacks) and sugar;
- rising key interest rate; in October 2024, the National Bank of Russia raised the key interest rate to 21%, the highest level since its introduction in 2013;
- increase in the cost of consumer loans with interest rates of up to 44% in 2025;
- ban on capital outflows;
- increase in labor shortage.

Such conditions are reminiscent of the state-controlled planned economy of the Soviet Union.

The power outages and issues with water supply and the internet are particularly frustrating for the population. Due to the increasing centralization of power under Putin, local communities have fewer financial resources at their disposal, urgent municipal tasks remain unfulfilled, infrastructure is deteriorating, and buildings and facilities are collapsing at an increasing rate.

In southern Russia, the supply infrastructure is further strained due to increased consumption as a result of the war and has been thrown off balance by Ukrainian attacks on refineries. This has led to repeated protests, such as in Krasnodar and Anapa in July 2024, where some districts were left without electricity or water for days.

6.6 Transformation Into a Totalitarian Dictatorship

During the war against Ukraine, the Russian state resorted to growingly rigorous measures to maintain control over society. Russia is increasingly showing signs of a totalitarian dictatorship, with state censorship, all state institutions aligned with the president, the destruction and banning of non-governmental organizations, repressive laws, suppression of social resistance, all-encompassing propaganda, distortion of history, and revanchism.

- **Revanchism**—efforts by a state or certain groups to avenge past events that are perceived as political or military defeats (from the French "revanche"—revenge).

In March 2024, presidential elections were held in the Russian Federation, which Vladimir Putin won as expected. The election is internationally regarded as a sham, as it was neither free nor fair, opposition members were not allowed to run and voting was illegally held in the occupied Ukrainian territories. The EU Parliament condemned the elections in a resolution as illegitimate and did not recognize the results.

In June 2024, the regime blocked the population's access to 81 media outlets from the European Union, including *Die Zeit* and *Der Spiegel* from Germany, ORF from Austria, *El Mundo* and *El País* from Spain, *La Stampa*, *La Repubblica* and RAI from Italy as well as *Le Monde*, *Libération*, Radio France and the AFP news agency from France.

In August 2024, the Kremlin banned access to the messaging app Signal in Russia, and in December it blocked Viber in an effort to hinder communication among regime critics. YouTube was throttled so that videos only load slowly and was finally blocked in December. Large social networks owned by US companies, such as X (Twitter) and Facebook, had already been blocked in Russia and can now only be accessed via VPNs.

Young army. How Russia is militarizing children (= preparing for war)
Numerous paramilitary groups (= militarily equipped or armed groups that are not part of the army) have existed in Russia since the 2000s, including many youth organizations. In 2016, a state youth organization, the "Young Army" ("Yunarmiya" in Russian), was founded on the initiative of Defense Minister Sergei Shoigu.

The declared aim of Young Army is to inspire children and teenagers between the ages of 8 and 18 to join the Russian army and "get young people to defend Russia with weapons in their hands." The Young Army is under the control of the Russian Ministry of Defense, is part of a state program for the "patriotic education" of young people and had over one million members in 2023. The children receive basic military training and learn how to handle weapons as part of the program.

Since December 2024, the Young Army has been led by Russian military officer Vladislav Golovin, who was awarded the title "Hero of the Russian Federation" for his participation in the storming of Mariupol, Ukraine, in 2022.

Before that, Olympic and world champion gymnast Nikita Nagorny led the Young Army. Other Russian athletes also support the youth army, such as world champion skier Veronika Stepanova and Olympic bobsledder Dmitri Trunenkov.

The Young Army is also militarizing children in Russian-occupied areas of Ukraine. It recruits Ukrainian youths to be used in Russia's war against their homeland.

The Young Army has been on the sanctions list of the European Union and several countries, including Switzerland, since 2022. In 2023, the US, Canada, and Japan, among others, imposed sanctions on the Young Army, followed by the UK and Australia in 2024.

Further Reading

https://uinp.gov.ua/pres-centr/novyny/informaciyni-materialy-do-vidznachennya-dnya-pamyati-ta-prymyrennya-i-dnya-peremogy-nad-nacyzmom-u-drugiy-svitoviy-viyni; https://texty.org.ua/projects/103857/okupaciya_de/; https://pobedarf.ru/2020/05/09/statistiki-podschitali-poteri-rossii-v-vojne/; https://www.dw.com/de/russland-neues-geschichtsbuchrechtfertigt-krieg-gegen-die-ukraine/a-66494138; https://www.n-tv.de/politik/Moskau-lockt-Kaempfer-mit-Zehntausenden-Euro-an-die-Front-article25109764.html; https://www.theguardian.com/commentisfree/article/2024/jul/24/russia-economic-growth-western-sanctions-vladimir-putin-moscow; https://www.europarl.europa.eu/news/en/press-room/20240419IPR20543/meps-condemn-russian-election-as-farcical-performance; https://www.merkur.de/politik/russland-wladimir-putin-propaganda-ukraine-krieg-jugendarmee-newszr-91940102.html; https://iz.ru/1850543/evgenii-grachev/vstat-ssuda-idet-realnye-stavki-po-potrebkreditam-podnialis-do-37; https://tass.ru/obschestvo/22760737

Ukraine: Coping With the War 7

7.1 Ukraine Puts Up Resistance

From the first hours after Russia's full-scale invasion of Ukraine, the Ukrainian leadership and society put up determined resistance. On February 24, 2022, thousands of people volunteered for the Ukrainian military, including many women.

> Women are not subject to compulsory military service in Ukraine. In 2025, over 70,000 women served in the Ukrainian armed forces, around 10% of whom were directly on the front line. In 2022, women made up around a quarter of the Ukrainian army, one of the highest proportions of women in the military worldwide. Compulsory conscription, which mostly affects men, increased the proportion of men in the army during the war.

Among the volunteers who signed up to go to the front was Fedir Shandor, professor of tourism and, since March 2025, Ukraine's ambassador to Hungary (Fig. 7.1).

Ukrainian President Volodymyr Zelenskyi remained at his official residence in Kyiv despite repeated attacks on him.

> The fight is here. I need ammunition, not a ride.
> Ukrainian President Volodymyr Zelensky responding to a US offer to evacuate him from Ukraine at the beginning of the Russian invasion.

Fig. 7.1 Professor Fedir Shandor of Uzhhorod National University gives lectures on tourism directly from the trenches, May 2022. Photo: Viktor Shchadej. Professor Shandor conscripted voluntarily for the Ukrainian Armed Forces on the first day of the full-scale war. Yet, he continued teaching tourism studies twice a week even from the front lines. He said: "We are fighting for an educated nation. If I didn't lecture, it would be a sin. Why else did I join the army?" Fedir Shandor, whose father is of Hungarian origin, served in a unit of the Ukrainian army, which is partly made up of volunteers of Hungarian origin. Starting March 2025, Fedir Shandor has taken on a role as Ukraine's ambassador to Hungary

The local population met the invaders with courage and defiance: residents stood in front of the Russian tanks, attacked Russian drones, people in the Russian-occupied areas demonstrated for weeks against the invasion, Ukrainian farmers towed Russian tanks away with tractors.

The radio message of one of the 12 border guards on the Ukrainian Snake Island (Zmiinyi Island) became particularly well known. When ordered by the Russian flagship "Moskva" to surrender, he famously replied: "Russian warship, f*** you."

7.1 Ukraine Puts Up Resistance

Fig. 7.2 Ukrainian postage stamp with the Russian flagship "Moskva." Author of the design: Boris Groh. Foto: Oksana Stavrou

The Ukrainian postal service dedicated a stamp to this event, depicting a Ukrainian soldier giving the middle finger to the ship Moskva—see Fig. 7.2. The stamp was issued on April 12, 2022. Two days later, on April 14, 2022, the Moskva, the largest warship in the Black Sea region, sank after being hit by Ukrainian missiles on the previous day.

Ukraine has been under martial law since February 24, 2022. With a few exceptions (e.g., students, parents with 3 or more underage children, single parents, etc.), conscripted men between the ages of 18 and 60 are not allowed to leave the country. Men aged 25 and older can be drafted into the military.

As the war continued, the Ukrainian population became progressively more dissatisfied with the conscription process, which was increasingly criticized as unfair; the number of conscientious objectors has increased. Additionally, delays and shortages in military equipment, ammunition, and weapons have further weakened willingness to serve.

The legal reform of mobilization and the establishment of professional recruitment centers for volunteers in spring 2024 somewhat improved the perception of conscription among the population again.

The increased domestic production of weapons and ammunition partially compensates for delayed and missing deliveries from abroad.

Public sentiment is overwhelmingly negative toward men, especially oligarchs, who attempt to buy their way out of military service. Such cases of corruption in the military are strongly condemned.

7.2 Donations and Volunteering

Ukrainians at home and abroad formed a widespread volunteer movement. Large charitable foundations, small private initiatives and individuals procure equipment such as bulletproof vests, night vision devices, helmets and drones as well as medicines for the front lines and Ukrainian hospitals, evacuate civilians from the embattled areas, supply Ukrainian troops with food, donate blood for the wounded (Fig. 7.3), weave camouflage nets, rescue orphaned pets and take in people displaced by the war.

Numerous volunteer initiatives have taken on key roles for the Ukrainian armed forces. The so-called "printing army," a coordinated network of individuals and organizations that own over 10,000 3D printers at home and abroad, prints medical equipment, replacement parts for assault rifles, walkie-talkies and drones on behalf

Fig. 7.3 People wait outside the blood donation center in Dnipro on February 25, 2022, to donate blood for the army. Photo: Denys Piddubskyi

7.2 Donations and Volunteering

of the military. According to its own figures, the network produced 275 tons of products for the Ukrainian army in 2 years of war.

The Social Drone Initiative, built on a similar principle as a network of volunteers, manufactures drones and supplies them to the army free of charge. People participate in the network in various functions such as assembly (no prior experience required), training, quality control, testing, logistics, etc.

Some of the volunteer work takes place exclusively online. The IT army or cyber army, established by the Ukrainian government, brings together thousands of Ukrainian and foreign volunteers with IT expertise. They expose Russian fake news online, fend off Russian hacker attacks on Ukrainian infrastructure, and coordinate attacks on important Russian websites.

Voluntary (financial) support for the Ukrainian armed forces became the social norm during the war. In 2024, according to a survey, 92% of Ukrainians donated to the army or to war victims. The four largest Ukrainian donation initiatives (launched by the National Bank of Ukraine, the United 24 Foundation of President Zelensky, the Prytula Foundation and the "Come Back Alive" Foundation) have collected over 1 billion euros from domestic and foreign donors since the beginning of the war.

> **"People's satellite"**
> In August 2022, the foundation named after founder Serhiy Prytula launched a crowdfunding campaign for the purchase of Turkish Bayraktar combat drones for the Ukrainian armed forces and subsequently raised 16.2 million euros in donations. As the Bayraktar manufacturer provided the drones free of charge, the Prytula Foundation used the amount raised for over a year of access to the ICEYE satellite for the Ukrainian military. The Finnish ICEYE satellite provides high-resolution images of the territory, even at night and in cloudy conditions.

Ukrainian aid and rescue operations are not only aimed at people, but also at animals. For example, after the flooding caused by the destruction of the Kakhovka dam on June 6, 2023, presumably by the Russian military, Ukrainian aid workers rescued hundreds of animals from the water and evacuated them (see Fig. 7.4).

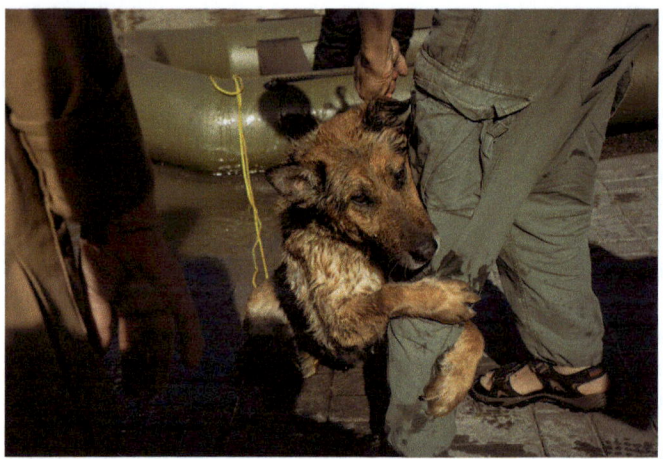

Fig. 7.4 A dog rescued from drowning after the Russian-occupied Kakhovka dam was blown up, Kherson, June 7, 2023. Photo: Serhii Korovayny

7.3 Why Is Ukrainian Resistance so Strong?

Russia's authoritarian regime offers no desirable future for Ukrainian society. The main reasons for Ukrainian resistance to Russian rule are as follows:

- Russia's political leadership openly denies Ukraine's *right to exist*. With its large-scale invasion, Moscow has confirmed its intention to destroy Ukraine as an independent state.
- *Freedom and self-determination* are highly valued in Ukraine. In 2020, Ukraine scored 62/100 points on the Freedom House Index, Russia—20/100. Even before the war, personal freedoms, press freedom, and freedom of speech and assembly were severely restricted in Russia.
- The eastern and southern regions of Ukraine, where Russian is widely spoken, have suffered the most from the Russian invasion. This contradicts *Russia's claim* of "protecting Russian-speaking people."
- *Violence, lawlessness and economic decline* in the Russian-occupied parts of the Donetsk and Luhansk regions and on the Crimean Peninsula since 2014 (see Chap. 9) serve as a warning. The brutality towards the population in the territories occupied after 2022 reinforces this impression.

Table 7.1 Corruption Perceptions Index (CPI) 2024 according to: Transparency International

Rank 2024	Country	Corruption Perceptions Index score
1	Denmark	90
2	Finland	88
8	Sweden	80
9	Netherlands	78
10	Australia	77
15	Canada	75
15	Germany	75
20	Japan	71
20	United Kingdom	71
25	France	67
28	United States	65
76	China	43
96	India	38
105	Serbia	35
105	Ukraine	35
107	Brazil	34
107	Turkey	34
140	Mexico	26
151	Iran	23
154	Russia	22
170	North Korea	15

The Corruption Perceptions Index (CPI) assesses 180 countries and territories worldwide according to the perceived level of corruption in the public sector. The results are presented on a scale from 0 (highly corrupt) to 100 (very clean)

- Although Russia's economy is larger than Ukraine's, corruption (Table 7.1) and privileges for people close to Putin mean that the Russian population outside the metropolitan areas of Moscow and St. Petersburg live in *great poverty*. In 2021, 11% of the population in Russia lived below the poverty line—twice percentage in Ukraine (5.5%).

7.4 Resilience

Ukrainian society is showing great resilience in the war.

Corresponding experiences and structures had already emerged during the Russian hostilities since 2014. Ukrainian civil society is an active socio-political force that pushes state institutions to take actions, initiating change and often taking on tasks where the state struggles.

Immediately after the beginning of the large-scale invasion in 2022, a well-functioning network of authorities, institutions, companies, associations, private initiatives and individual activists quickly emerged. This network supported the Ukrainian armed forces in stopping the Russian advance and reduced the feeling of powerlessness among the population by enabling them to help. Self-help groups formed rapidly, and acts of solidarity towards strangers increased significantly.

Works by outstanding figures in Ukrainian history, such as the national poet and painter Taras Shevchenko (see Fig. 7.5) and the most famous Ukrainian female

Fig. 7.5 Taras Shevchenko (1814–1861), national poet of Ukraine. Illustration by Mykhailo Diachenko. The poet and painter Shevchenko laid the foundations for the modern Ukrainian language and addressed the oppression of Ukraine by the Russian Tsarist Empire in his works. Many of his poems celebrate freedom and self-determination and are widely quoted in the ongoing war against Russia. For his criticism of Russia and his striving for Ukrainian independence he was exiled for 10 years and drafted into the Russian army. Shevchenko was banned from writing and prohibited from ever returning to Ukraine. The original drawing of Shevchenko in a modern military uniform is accompanied by one of his most famous slogans: "Fight and you will win!" Shevchenko became a symbol of the Ukrainian resistance against Russia

poet, playwright, and feminist Lesya Ukrainka (1871–1913), gained importance as a source of spiritual support.

The external threat from Russia initially strengthened societal unity and increased confidence in Ukraine's political leadership. In order to demoralize the population and break their resistance, the Kremlin leadership relied from the outset on terrorizing civilians with drone and missile strikes. Ongoing Russian attacks destroy hospitals, universities, stores and other civilian facilities and kill peaceful citizens across the country every day.

In response to Russia's destruction of Ukraine's energy infrastructure in the winter of 2022–2023, Ukrainian authorities set up several thousand "points of invincibility" (Fig. 7.6)—places of refuge for residents equipped with heating and power generators where people could warm up during winter power outages, charge their electronic devices, and receive urgent assistance.

Still, regular blackouts and air raids, during which people are forced to seek shelter, make everyday life quite difficult. They interrupt work processes and school lessons and cause great psychological stress due to the constant threat of death across the country.

This clouded the mood in society. Particularly in May 2024, when Russia repeatedly shelled large areas of Ukraine's energy infrastructure and launched an

Fig. 7.6 "Point of invincibility" in Kharkiv, December 2022. Photo: Darja Lobanok, gwaramedia.com

offensive on Kharkiv while Western defensive weapons were delayed, many people adopted a pessimistic view of the future. Despite this, surveys in the country showed no willingness to give up the fight against the aggressor or to cede territory to Russia. This determination is fueled by the awareness of Russian atrocities, decline of life in the Russian-occupied territories as well as declared intention of Moscow to eradicate Ukraine as a nation.

The political leadership of Ukraine, above all President Zelensky, has mirrored the resilience of the Ukrainian people in both rhetoric and actions.

In 2019, Volodymyr Zelensky ran for president on the promise of ending the war in the east of Ukraine that Russia unleashed in 2014. He was elected with 73% of the vote. However, as has been the case with all presidents of independent Ukraine since 1991, his popularity ratings began to decline shortly after the elections, reaching a low of 37% before the Russian invasion in 2022.

His decisive leadership at the beginning of the full-scale war brought Zelensky the highest approval rating of 93% of the population in May 2022. Since then, trust in the president has fallen again among Ukrainians, but according to surveys it was still 52% in December 2024—significantly higher than before the war.

Zelensky gained the backing and increased trust of Ukrainians after the scandal in the Oval Office of the White House at the end of February 2025. At that official meeting at the US seat of government, the newly elected US President Donald Trump and his Vice President JD Vance accused the Ukrainian president in a rude manner of ingratitude and unwillingness to end the war. Zelensky remained composed and objective.

In 2024, both Zelensky's 5-year presidential term and the Ukrainian parliament's legislative period officially expired. However, no new elections were held, as they are not permitted under martial law and are also rejected by the vast majority of Ukrainian citizens.

Despite the war, Ukraine is implementing further reforms, especially after the start of accession talks with the European Union in 2023.

Additionally, Ukraine has seen innovations and new solutions emerge in response to wartime challenges.

In May 2024, classes began in the first underground school in Kharkiv. Other underground schools followed in the Zaporizhzhia and Mykolaiv regions. By the end of 2024, 139 underground schools and dozens of other educational facilities were under construction.

After initially fleeing abroad, at least three million people have returned to Ukraine despite the ongoing war.

The Ukrainian economy grew by approximately 5% in 2023—following a slump of one third in 2022—and slowed to approximately 3% in 2024. Numerous companies relocated from the east of Ukraine to the west of the country after the start of the full-scale invasion.

Loans and non-repayable grants from abroad secured Ukraine's economic survival and covered all non-military socio-economic expenditures in 2024. All of Ukraine's tax revenues in 2024 went entirely toward its military expenditures, which amounted to 34% of the gross domestic product (GDP), according to a report by the Stockholm International Peace Research Institute (SIPRI). This meant that Ukraine bore the highest military burden in the world relative to its economic output, ahead of Israel (8.8% of GDP), Algeria (8%), Saudi Arabia (7.3%), and Russia (7.1%). In absolute terms, however, Russia spent more than twice as much on the war in 2024 as Ukraine did on its defense.

7.5 Humor in War

Humor is firmly anchored in Ukrainian culture and plays multiple roles in the defense against Russia. It helps to mentally process traumatic war experiences, to cope with war-related difficulties, but also to counter Russian propaganda.

Numerous newly created social media channels produce and distribute hundreds of memes every day on current topics relating to war, politics and society. Many of them are witty spontaneous reactions by ordinary citizens to war events. These include a woman in a high-rise building in Kyiv who downed a Russian drone with a jar of home-pickled tomatoes, but also the remark of a resident of occupied Henichesk telling a Russian soldier to carry fresh sunflower seeds so that sunflowers would grow where he would die in Ukraine. Other memes focus on Russian disinformation.

When it became apparent at the start of the Russian invasion 2022 that the invaders were using outdated maps from the 1980s, the State Restoration Agency of Ukraine called for the removal of place-name signs in the affected regions on the third day of the invasion. Instead, in many towns, signs were put up with a clear message to the enemy army—see Fig. 7.7. One of these signs was auctioned off in June 2022 for the equivalent of 20,000 euros, with the money going to the Ukrainian armed forces as a donation.

Fig. 7.7 Traffic signpost in the Ukrainian East on February 26, 2022 with a clear message to Russian Army. Inscription in Ukrainian: Direction of travel straight ahead: F*** you. Direction left: F*** you again. Direction right: F*** you back to Russia. Photo: State Agency for Reconstruction and Development of Infrastructure of Ukraine

In October 2022, the Russian defense minister accused Ukraine of working on a "dirty bomb" with radioactive materials. The response from the Ukrainian internet community was: "It is a lie that Ukraine has a dirty bomb. A Ukrainian bomb can only be well-cleaned, ironed and neatly folded."

Internationally, NAFO, the North Atlantic Fella Organization (a play on the North Atlantic Treaty Organization—NATO), has dedicated itself to providing humorous yet serious support to Ukraine (Fig. 7.8). NAFO is an internet phenomenon that originated from an initiative by Kamil Dyszewski from Poland. Several thousand members worldwide comment on current events related to the Russian war on the internet, combat Russian propaganda with the help of reworked, sometimes funny and absurd images of Shiba Inus—a Japanese dog breed—("Fellas"), and collect donations for the Ukrainian military.

Fig. 7.8 NAFO dog on the destroyed Russian tank in front of the Russian embassy in Berlin in February 2023, a collage. Author: Leonhard Lenz. Source: Wikimedia

Further Reading

https://www.merkur.de/politik/russland-ukraine-kriegit-digitalisierung-internet-hacker-ukraine-kampf-starlink-91897333.html; https://freedomhouse.org/sites/default/files/2021-08/FIW2020_book_JUMBO_PDF.pdf; https://www.kommersant.ru/doc/5251853?from=lenta; https://epravda.com.ua/publications/2024/10/31/721234/; https://www.socialdrone.com.ua/en; https://www2.deloitte.com/ua/en/pages/press-room/press-release/2024/consumer-behavior.html; https://www.pravda.com.ua/news/2024/07/23/7466999/; https://www.pravda.com.ua/news/2024/06/13/7460542/; https://kiis.com.ua/?lang=ukr&cat=reports&id=1441&page=1; https://orf.at/stories/3360984/; https://www.sipri.org/sites/default/files/2025-04/2504_fs_milex_2024.pdf

Victims and Destruction During the War

8.1 Civilian Population

The criminal Russian war of aggression cost the lives of at least 13,000 Ukrainian civilians, including over 600 children, in Ukrainian-controlled areas between February 2022 and May 2025. The actual number of victims is likely much higher. The NGO Human Rights Watch estimated that, in addition to confirmed figures, around 8000 people died as a result of acts of war alone in Russian-occupied Mariupol in 2022.

Approximately 16,000 Ukrainian civilians were in Russian captivity as of December 2024. In addition, around 20,000 Ukrainian children were forcibly taken (= deported) to Russia. Both the detention of civilians and abduction of children for the purpose of re-education are war crimes, the latter is also classified as genocide.

8.2 War Refugees

The Russian invasion in 2022 forced the Ukrainian population to flee. A year later, more than 13 million people—a third of Ukraine's population—had been displaced. In mid-2025, approximately 6.3 million Ukrainian war refugees (over 80% of whom were women and children) were still living in Europe and approximately 3.7 million in Ukraine (internally displaced persons).

Increased Russian attacks throughout Ukraine and, in particular, the Russian shelling of energy infrastructure and thus fear of winter without heating and water once again drove Ukrainians to flee abroad in the fall of 2024.

© The Author(s), under exclusive license to Springer Nature Switzerland AG 2025
O. Stavrou, *Russia's War Against Ukraine*,
https://doi.org/10.1007/978-3-032-02625-5_8

8.3 Military Personnel

As a result of the Russian invasion, 46,000 Ukrainian soldiers have been killed since 2022—this death toll was announced by Ukrainian President Volodymyr Zelensky in February 2025. Prior to that, in December 2024, Zelensky estimated Russian losses at 198,000 dead.

In June 2024, Russian President Putin casually said that around 5000 Russian soldiers were probably killed every month.

Estimates of the number of wounded on both sides are less accurate. In December 2024, Zelensky spoke of around 370,000 injured on the Ukrainian side, half of whom had returned to the front after treatment. For Ukraine, there was an estimate in 2024 that the number of war-related amputations alone was over 50,000. For the Russian side, the Ukrainian president named 550,000 wounded.

The General Staff of Ukraine publishes daily estimates of Russian losses, including those killed and wounded—see Fig. 8.1.

Representatives of NATO, the USA and the UK have repeatedly announced their estimates of Russian and Ukrainian war losses, which are roughly in line with the figures given. However, it is not yet possible to definitively verify the data.

Among the 11,000 North Korean soldiers who have been fighting for Russia at the front in Kursk region since October 2024, British intelligence reports indicate that by June 2025, approximately 6000 had already been killed or wounded.

Fig. 8.1 Russian losses in the war against Ukraine as of 25.06.2025. Source: General Staff of Ukraine on X

8.4 Damage to Residential Buildings and Infrastructure

The Russian attacks have reduced many Ukrainian villages and towns to rubble. The shelling of residential areas with missiles and drones has also destroyed homes deep inside the country. By January 2024, a total of around 250,000 apartments and houses are estimated to have been damaged or destroyed, most of them in the regions of Donetsk, Kyiv (see, for example, Borodianka, a suburb of Kyiv in Fig. 8.2), Luhansk, Kharkiv, Chernihiv, and Kherson. Numerous administrative buildings, factories, airports, roads, hospitals and other civilian facilities suffered damage as a result of the war, including one in seven schools in the country.

Medical facilities and emergency responders have been frequent targets of Russian attacks. In July 2024, a Russian missile struck Ukraine's largest children's hospital, Okhmatdyt, in Kyiv, shortly after which a Kyiv maternity clinic was also hit, killing dozens. In three years from February 2022 and February 2025, the World Health Organization (WHO) has recorded 2254 attacks on Ukrainian health infrastructure—the highest number ever recorded in a conflict.

Fig. 8.2 A high-rise building in Borodianka destroyed by Russian shelling, April 2022. Photo: Oleksii Samsonov. Source: Kyiv city administration, kyivcity.gov.ua

Russia is using the "double tap" tactic (= double strike; considered a war crime), as it did during the Russian military operation in Syria: a target is hit twice in succession. After the initial strike, they wait until first responders, police, firefighters, emergency services and journalists are on the scene before launching a second strike to hit as many emergency workers and civilians as possible.

8.5 Destruction of the Energy Infrastructure

In the winter of 2022–2023, Russia fired several hundred missiles and drones at energy facilities in Ukraine. The targeted bombing of substations, power grids and other objects led to widespread power outages and forced power cuts throughout the country, as well as the failure of heating and water supplies in the middle of winter. It was part of the strategy to wear Ukraine down and force it into surrender. Despite severe power supply issues, Russia failed to cause a total blackout.

At the end of March 2024, the Russian Federation resumed its systematic attacks against Ukraine's energy infrastructure, primarily targeting power plants. Russia used its most expensive missiles—aeroballistic Kinzhal and ballistic Iskander—which Ukraine is barely able to fend off due to the lack of air defense systems. By the fall of 2024, Russian attacks had destroyed or damaged all of Ukraine's thermal power plants and a significant part of its hydropower plants.

Increased Russian reconnaissance drone activity near Ukrainian nuclear power plants and the fact that satellite images of these facilities were taken by China suggested that Russia was planning attacks on Ukraine's three operational nuclear power plants. In August 2024, German Foreign Minister Annalena Baerbock described these threats as a "waging war by freezing" with the aim of "letting people freeze to death in winter if necessary."

Occupied by Russian troops since March 2022, the Zaporizhzhia nuclear power plant—the largest in Europe—had to be shut down. Repeated incidents such as the fire in a cooling system in the summer of 2024 and regular Russian shelling of nearby objects highlight the acute danger of a nuclear disaster.

8.6 Economy

In 2022, Ukraine's *gross domestic product* and therefore the country's economic output shrank by almost 30%. The full extent of the damage caused by Russia's war can only be accurately assessed once the conflict ends. The World Bank, in coordination with the EU and the Ukrainian government, estimates the reconstruction costs at over $524 billion, the equivalent of around €506 billion (as of December 2024, published in February 2025). This exceeds by comparison Norway's annual economic output (GDP 2024—$504 billion) as well as a seventh of the UK's annual economic output (GDP 2024—$3840 billion).

- **Gross domestic product**, or GDP for short, is the value of all goods and services produced in the country. If GDP is rising, the economy is considered to be growing; if GDP is falling, the economy is shrinking.

Trade, industry, agriculture and the construction, transportation and energy sectors have been particularly severely impacted by the war. Ukraine has lost a significant portion of its agricultural production capacity as a result of the war, partly due to Russia occupying 20% of Ukraine's farmland, and partly due to extensive landmines, soil contamination, destruction of storage and processing facilities, and disrupted transport routes.

Before the full-scale invasion, Ukraine exported electricity, primarily to Europe. Following the massive destruction of its energy production facilities by Russia, the country has to buy electricity from abroad in order to meet domestic demand.

The largest mining and metal processing companies are located in the east of Ukraine. Some fell under Russian control as early as 2014, while others got occupied in 2022. Numerous large factories in the Russian-occupied territory were dismantled and moved to Russia. Many mines are no longer operational. Due to the destruction of facilities, and disruption of supply chains and transportation options, many factories had to shut down, causing Ukraine economic losses in the billions.

Despite these challenges, Ukraine's economy grew by 3–5% in both 2023 and 2024. However, it remains far from pre-war levels.

8.7 Damage to Nature

Ukraine has the greatest biodiversity on the European subcontinent, it is home to 35% of all European plant and animal species and is therefore very important for the European ecosystem. Almost a third of Ukraine's territory consists of natural and semi-natural ecosystems and nature reserves, 16% of which are forests.

The biggest ecological and humanitarian disaster of the war was caused by the Russian blowing up of the Kakhovka dam north of Kherson on June 6, 2023. The resulting flood wave from the reservoir covered an area of over 600 square kilometers, including 80 villages on both banks of the Dnipro River. In the city of Nova Kakhovka, water levels rose by 12 m. Around 40,000 people were affected, with 20,000 evacuated, and dozens who lost their lives.

The flood carried landmines, pesticides, machine oil, waste and chemicals into the Black Sea. The disappearance of the reservoir left people and agriculture in the Dnipro, Kherson, Zaporizhzhia and Crimea regions without a water supply. Dozens of cultural sites and museums were ruined or damaged. Countless animals, including in three national parks, died.

The destruction of the hydroelectric power plant resulted in the loss of enormous power generation capacity. The interruption to shipping on the Dnipro meant that Ukrainian exports, including grain, were blocked.

The destruction of the Kakhovka dam by Russia has been labeled as *ecocide*.

- **Ecocide**—criminal act that can cause massive or long-term damage to the environment.

Observers suspect that the Kremlin is using the destruction of Ukrainian natural environment as a deliberate war tactic. In March 2022, the Russian president authorized the military leadership on site to log Ukrainian forests without restrictions, for personal use and for sale. The occupiers indiscriminately cut down large areas of forest, including in nature reserves, as well as protective forests meant to prevent soil erosion and sandstorms.

In August 2024, the Russians contaminated the two rivers Seim and Desna in the Russian-Ukrainian border region with chemical waste from a sugar factory. North of the Ukrainian capital Kyiv, the Desna flows into the Dnipro, the largest river in Ukraine and one of the largest in Europe. The natural ecosystem of both the Seim and the Desna on the Ukrainian side collapsed and more than 30 tons of dead fish had to be disposed of. Only emergency measures prevented the poisoning of Kyiv's drinking water.

Other serious environmental damage caused by war includes forest fires, the destruction of nature reserves and unique animal and plant species, such as the death of thousands of dolphins in the Black Sea due to the noise of explosions at sea and the sonar technology of Russian warships.

The combat zone is home to many heavy industry facilities. Chemical leaks frequently occur, allowing heavy metals and toxic chemicals to seep into the groundwater, contaminating drinking water sources and rendering agricultural land unusable.

Ukraine is currently one of the most heavily mined regions in the world. Explosions and gunfire release toxic substances. According to a study by Dutch climate researcher Lennard de Klerk and others, 3 years of Russia's full-scale war caused 230 million tons of CO_2 equivalent—as much as 120 million cars with combustion engines emit in a year.

8.8 Deliberate Destruction of Culture

United Nations experts accuse Russia of deliberately destroying Ukrainian culture. Russian military attacks in Ukraine have destroyed or damaged numerous sites of cultural, historical and religious significance, including monuments, museums (see Skovoroda Museum in Fig. 8.3), theaters, churches, libraries, schools and universities.

In museums and archives, Russian occupiers consistently follow the same looting tactics during their advance. Unique exhibits are either discarded, irreversibly destroyed or stolen and transported to Russia.

As of September 2024, the Russian war destroyed or damaged around one thousand libraries and with them millions of Ukrainian books. The shelling of the Faktor-Druck printing plant in Kharkiv in May 2024 alone destroyed over 50,000 books.

The targeted destruction of Ukrainian cultural assets as a tactic of war is aimed at eradicating the Ukrainian people's cultural identity.

Fig. 8.3 Hryhorii Skovoroda (1722–1794), Ukrainian philosopher, educator and poet. Source: Kharkiv Regional Military Administration, kharkivoda.gov.ua. The statue, created by Ihor Yastrebov in 1971, stood in the Skovoroda Museum in the Kharkiv region. The museum was destroyed by targeted Russian shelling on May 7, 2022. However, the Skovoroda statue withstood the shelling

In the Russian-occupied territories, Ukrainian teaching materials were removed from schools and replaced by Russian materials with a distorted Russian presentation of history. Teachers were "retrained" or transferred from Russia to the occupied territories. More than 3000 schools in Ukraine were damaged or destroyed.

Further Reading

https://www.worldbank.org/en/news/press-release/2025/02/25/updated-ukraine-recovery-and-reconstruction-needs-assessment-released; https://www.zeit.de/2023/26/urkaine-krieg-kachowka-staudamm-sprengung-schaeden; https://www.sueddeutsche.de/politik/kachowka-staudamm-ukraine-1.5904713; https://www.hrw.org/feature/russia-ukraine-war-mariupol/report; https://reliefweb.int/report/ukraine/ukraine-complex-emergency-factsheet-10-fiscal-year-fy-2024; https://www.uno-fluechtlingshilfe.de/hilfe-weltweit/ukraine; https://data.unhcr.org/en/situations/ukraine#_ga=2.171723040.1002354476.1678196051-1692816759.1678196044; https://de.statista.com/statistik/daten/studie/1297855/umfrage/anzahl-der-zivilen-opfer-durch-ukraine-krieg/; https://www.who.int/europe/news/item/24-02-2025-three-years-of-war-rising-demand-for-mental-health-support-trauma-care-and-rehabilitation; https://www.fr.de/politik/verluste-russland-ukraine-krieg-zahlen-daten-aktuell-opfer-militaer-news-zr-93249292.html; https://www.n-tv.de/mediathek/bilderserien/panorama/Kriegsversehrte-Ukrainer-suchen-den-Weg-zurueck-ins-Leben-article24877218.html; https://kse.ua/ua/about-the-school/news/zagalna-suma-zbitkiv-zavdana-infrastrukturi-ukrayini-zrosla-do-mayzhe-155-mlrd-otsinka-kse-institute-stanom-na-sichen-2024-roku/; https://life.pravda.com.ua/society/v-ukrajini-cherez-viynu-poshkodzheni-ponad-3-5-tisyachi-zakladiv-osviti-300221/; https://www.who.int/ukraine/news/item/19-08-2024-grim-milestone-on-world-humanitarian-day%2D%2Dwho-records-1940-attacks-on-health-care-in-ukraine-since-start-of-full-scale-war; https://ec.europa.eu/commission/presscorner/detail/en/ip_24_801; https://www.bpb.de/themen/europa/ukraine-analysen/nr-288/541010/analyse-die-oekologischen-folgen-des-russischen-angriffskrieges-in-der-ukraine/; https://ngl.media/2024/04/08/zrubati-vse/; https://en.ecoaction.org.ua/wp-content/uploads/2025/02/20250224_ClimateDamageWarUkraine36monthsENprelim-1.pdf

Life Under Russian Occupation 9

9.1 Conquest

In the first weeks of the large-scale Russian invasion of Ukraine on February 24, 2022, the Russian army occupied large areas in the North, East and South of Ukraine, in the oblasts (regions) of Kyiv, Zhytomyr, Chernihiv, Sumy, Kharkiv, Mykolaiv, Kherson, Zaporizhzhia, Luhansk, and Donetsk. Large parts of the Luhansk and Donetsk regions, including their regional capitals—the cities of Luhansk and Donetsk—had already been occupied by Russians in 2014, along with the Crimean peninsula. Thanks to determined defense in February-April and the Kherson counteroffensive in September-November 2022, the Ukrainian army was able to push the invaders back from many areas.

By the end of 2022, under Russian control were parts of the Luhansk, Donetsk, Kherson, and Zaporizhzhia regions and the Crimean Peninsula completely.

Russia's large-scale war of aggression caused a mass exodus of the Ukrainian population, especially from the newly occupied territories. However, many people remained in place.

Initially, there was hardly any access from outside to the Ukrainian territories newly occupied by Russia; it was either life-threatening or prohibited by the Russian occupation administration. Insightful reports about life in the first months of Russian occupation in 2022 came from refugees and residents of Ukrainian towns that have since been liberated. For example, Kateryna Ukraintseva, a member of the Bucha City Council, reported on social media about her experiences during the Russian occupation of the city (Fig. 9.1).

From the first days of the invasion, the invaders persecuted Ukrainian activists, journalists, priests, former soldiers, police officers and elected representatives.

Fig. 9.1 There is no electricity and no gas. People cooking food in the courtyard of a high-rise building in Bucha, a suburb of Kyiv, under Russian occupation. March 13, 2022 Photo: Kateryna Ukraintseva

Many were arrested, tortured and killed or disappeared. Russian soldiers ransacked houses in search of food and valuables.

Parents hid their children for fear of their deportation. According to official Ukrainian figures, around 20,000 Ukrainian children were separated from their families or abducted from care facilities and deported to Russia in the first months of the occupation.

Adults were also forced to leave their homes in the occupied territories. Estimates of Ukrainian citizens deported to Russia range from several hundred thousand to three million people. Russian authorities call them "evacuees" or "refugees."

Heavily bombed towns such as Mariupol, Bakhmut, and Avdiivka (all in the Donetsk region) were almost completely destroyed. The remaining residents lived for weeks without electricity or heating and with limited access to drinking water. It was often impossible to give those who had been killed or died a proper burial. Some were buried in mass graves, others individually in parks or in the yards of private homes.

There was a shortage of medicines, and long queues formed outside medical facilities. Basic medical care for Ukrainian civilians was hardly available, as medical supplies were stolen by the Russians and used for their own soldiers, and there was a shortage of medical personnel.

Instead of the Ukrainian currency, the hryvnia, the Russian ruble was introduced as the means of payment in the occupied territories. ATMs were out of service. Food became scarce and prices rose. Numerous shops and factories closed.

Russia pressured Ukrainians in the occupied territories to accept Russian citizenship. A Russian passport became a requirement for receiving humanitarian aid, medical treatment, employment, school certificates, or pension payments, registering property or accessing electricity and water services, traveling to neighboring towns, or even moving within the local area.

Ukrainian internet, mobile phone networks, television, and radio were shut down. Residents were now cut off from information from Ukraine and the world and received news only through Russian propaganda television and radio channels.

Russian checkpoints and surveillance cameras were installed throughout public spaces. The occupiers conducted regular ID and smartphone checks. If photos of Russian soldiers or Ukrainian-language texts were found, arrest was imminent.

9.2 Pacification

After taking control, Russian occupation forces renovated some streets, houses, and infrastructure. Russian propaganda uses these reports as evidence of the supposed improvement in quality of life under Russian administration.

The introduction of the Russian currency and financial incentives initially brought some benefits for residents of the occupied territories: pensions and salaries up to 2.5 times higher than in Russia, subsidies for school enrollment, and exemption from utility costs. The occupying authorities hoped that this would buy the loyalty of the local population and encourage migrants from the Russian Federation to settle in the region.

In 2024, Russia discontinued this practice, pensions and salaries fell by half or more, and demands for back payments for utility costs and mass layoffs followed.

In Russian-occupied areas of Ukraine, owners must register their apartments and houses in the Russian land registry, otherwise they are considered "ownerless." This requires physical presence and a Russian passport—two conditions that many Ukrainians cannot or do not want to fulfill. Corresponding regulations have been in force in all occupied territories since spring 2024. As a result, tens of thousands of properties belonging to Ukrainian citizens are being expropriated.

If locals refuse to accept Russian citizenship, they are considered foreigners and must go through the corresponding approval procedures or abandon their homeland.

They are being replaced by Russian citizens from distant regions of the Russian Federation. A similar resettlement policy was pursued on a large scale in the Soviet Union, serving to Russify non-Russian populations and non-Russian territories.

In Mariupol, the Russian occupation administration has reportedly demolished several hundred high-rise buildings in the three years since the city was captured in 2022, renamed streets, and thus rendered the property documents of former Ukrainian residents obsolete.

Damaged apartments and houses abandoned by Ukrainian residents are referred to as "razruschka" ("little ruins" in Russian) by pro-Russian real estate agents on site. Such properties are repaired as needed and used by Russian immigrants who receive support for their resettlement into the occupied territories.

There are also reports of expropriation of land, private and company cars, and even functioning businesses and shops. Numerous industrial plants and factories have been dismantled and transported to Russia or used for spare parts.

A Russian curriculum has been introduced in schools. Teachers who do not comply face dismissal and persecution. The language of instruction is Russian, and Ukrainian has been completely eliminated from the curriculum. Ukrainian books have been removed from school libraries and universities or destroyed. Ukrainian textbooks on history and Ukrainian literature have been classified as "extremist," and possession of them can be punished with up to five years in prison. Instead, schools receive Russian textbooks, propaganda literature, Russian flags, and portraits of Russian President Putin.

Ukrainian youth are being forcibly indoctrinated in compulsory "patriot trainings" and "information sessions" in schools. The indoctrination continues in their free time, in newly created leisure clubs and associations, during free trips, camps, and competitions. Young people are encouraged to spy on and denounce their classmates, neighbors, and parents.

Russia is using paramilitary organizations (armed units that are not officially part of the army) for young people to prepare Ukrainian children for military service and war against Ukraine. The Young Army ("Yunarmiya" in Russian, see more in Sect. 6.6), the largest paramilitary youth organization in the Russian Federation, alone has an estimated 35,000 members in Russian-occupied territories. According to Russian and Ukrainian reports, numerous former Young Army members from the occupied Ukrainian regions are fighting on the front lines against Ukraine.

In October 2024, the Russian occupation authorities in the Kherson region announced the compulsory conscription of Ukrainian men into the Russian army.

They are being drafted and sent to war against their compatriots. There are documented cases of even 17-year-olds receiving conscription orders.

Uncertainty, arbitrariness on the part of the occupying authorities, and violence prevail in everyday life in the Russian-occupied territories. This affects not only activists or alleged resistance fighters, but also ordinary citizens, especially young women. In multiple reported cases, women have been kidnapped, raped, or abused as (sex) slaves for Russian officers.

Non-Russian religious communities are being persecuted. There are reports of kidnapping, arrest, and murder of Ukrainian priests.

Members of the LGBTIQ community are also being targeted.

In the spring of 2024, presidential elections were held in the Russian Federation. Russian occupation authorities implemented measures in Ukrainian territories to create the appearance of elections. These pseudo-elections are not recognized internationally.

9.3 "New Normality"

The Ukrainian peninsula of Crimea and large parts of the Donetsk and Luhansk regions have been under Russian control since 2014.

Crimea was occupied by Russian forces and annexed to Russia in violation of international law following a sham referendum in March 2014.

In the Donetsk and Luhansk regions, the two fictitious republics "DNR" and "LNR" were initially proclaimed after Russian units invaded in 2014. To the outside world, they presented themselves as "people's republics" of the locals ("Donetsk People's Republic, DNR" and "Luhansk People's Republic, LNR"). However, the key leadership positions were held by Russian citizens under Moscow's control. In 2022, the "DNR" and "LNR" were also illegally annexed to Russia following the sham referendums held back in 2014 and 2022.

The occupation authorities implemented measures similar to those later used in newly occupied territories from 2022 onward, though the intensity varied:

– introduction of a repressive legal system and legal reality of the Russian Federation, with restrictions on freedom of expression, freedom of the press, and freedom of assembly, as well as fabricated court cases against dissidents;
– violence against civilians and arbitrariness by the authorities, human rights violations and persecution of journalists, critics, activists and pro-Ukrainian forces. In Crimea additional persecution of the Crimean Tatars;

- blocking of information from Ukraine and the world (mobile communications, internet, television, newspapers, books) and establishment of Russian propaganda information channels and indoctrination;
- banning the Ukrainian language in schools, universities and the public sector; introduction of the Russian education system with comprehensive indoctrination;
- introduction of Russian passports, compulsory acceptance of Russian citizenship;
- replacing the Ukrainian currency hryvnia with the Russian ruble;
- expropriation, nationalization of the property of local residents and the Ukrainian state;
- settling large numbers of Russian citizens in these territories, filling administrative positions with Russians, and establishing a two-tiered society that privileges Russian settlers while discriminating against local residents.

These measures were accompanied by a decline in population, the closure of Ukrainian and foreign companies, increased unemployment and inflation. From 2018 to 2022, the birth rate in the "DNR" fell by almost 47%. Water supply problems, which existed for years, worsened after 2022. Tap water is rationed and only available for limited hours. Medicines are in short supply, medical care is inadequate, and infectious diseases, especially HIV/AIDS, are on the rise. This led to a massive deterioration in the economic and social situation and in the standard of living of the population in the Russian-controlled areas.

In July 2024, the last Ukrainian church in Crimea was dismantled. Books about the Holodomor, the Soviet-orchestrated famine of 1932–1933, the Crimean Tatars and the Ukrainian resistance as well as books depicting the Ukrainian national emblem Tryzub (= trident) were removed from the libraries on the Ukrainian peninsula.

In 2020, the "DNR" introduced the death penalty. Extrajudicial trials, known as "people's tribunals", were held in the "DNR/LNR" from as early as 2014 and executions were carried out following the corresponding verdicts.

Shortly before the large-scale Russian invasion of Ukraine, the puppet governments of the "DNR"/"LNR" declared a general mobilization (= conscription into the army). Further waves of mobilization followed, including on the Crimean Peninsula. Men of military age were conscripted into the Russian army and sent to fight against Ukraine.

9.4 Resistance Movement

A resistance movement against the occupiers emerged in all Russian-occupied territories.

Their activities ranged from peaceful demonstrations on the Crimean Peninsula in 2014 to poisoning Russian soldiers with pastries offered by locals near Izium (Kharkiv region) in 2022. On the one hand, underground fighters carry out attacks on Russian occupation authorities or destroy their weapons depots. On the other hand, they try to demoralize the occupiers and pass on information to the Ukrainian army. They hang Ukrainian flags, distribute leaflets, spray threats and Ukrainian symbols on walls, and use special apps and chatbots to send photos and coordinates of Russian military equipment to the Ukrainian authorities.

The first acts of resistance took place in Crimea in 2014. On February 26, 2014, at the call of the Mejlis (the highest political body of the Crimean Tatars), around 10,000 to 15,000 residents of the peninsula gathered in front of the regional parliament in the capital Simferopol to protest for the unity of Ukraine. The following night, armed Russian military units without official insignia, known as "little green men," occupied the regional parliament and the Crimean Council of Ministers, paving the way for a sham referendum and Russia's annexation of the peninsula.

Across Crimea, locals, especially Crimean Tatars, demonstrated against the planned sham referendum. Human chains formed as a symbol of inseparability from Ukraine. The initiative "Women of Crimea Stand for Peace" organized rallies with Ukrainian and Crimean Tatar flags.

From the beginning of the occupation, Russia persecuted people with pro-Ukrainian views. Crimean Tatar Reshat Ametov (also Reşat Amet) was abducted in early March 2014 during a peaceful solo protest for Ukraine's territorial integrity in Simferopol's central square, then tortured and killed. At the end of June 2023, Russian snipers killed two 16-year-olds, Tigran Ohannisian and Mykyta Khanhanov, in occupied Berdyansk (Zaporizhzhia region) for their pro-Ukrainian stance. The teenagers had previously been persecuted, arrested, tortured, and harassed by the local occupation authorities for months.

Even seemingly insignificant gestures demonstrate the resistance to the Russian occupation regime, such as a secret reading club of a few teenagers who read Ukrainian books online in secret, or the underpants on the flagpole of a re-education camp, which a Ukrainian boy used to replace the Russian flag during the night.

Several resistance platforms emerged after Russia's full-scale attack on Ukraine in 2022. The best-known nonviolent initiatives are the "Yellow Ribbon" (named after the symbol in the colors of the Ukrainian flag, the yellow ribbon on a blue background, which originated in the then occupied Kherson) and the "Evil Mavka" (women's resistance movement originating in Melitopol, Zaporizhzhia region)—see Fig. 9.2.

The military partisan network Atesh (from the Crimean Tatar word for "fire") consists partly of (forcibly) recruited locals who are attempting to weaken the Russian army from within through acts of sabotage and attacks.

In March 2022, the Ukrainian armed forces set up a website to support resistance fighters and coordinate individual actions. It was initially called "Sprotyv," later "Opir" (both Ukrainian words for resistance).

Fig. 9.2 Natalka Cmoc, Canada's ambassador to Ukraine, posted a photo of her new tattoo featuring the symbol of the "Evil Mavka" on her Instagram account with the accompanying words: "In solidarity with women's resistance in Ukraine's temporarily occupied territories—zla mavka @зла мавка," May 10, 2025. Photo: Natalka Cmoc. Mavka is a forest fairy from Ukrainian mythology. Her character has been artistically adapted in, among other works, the play "The Forest Song" by the most famous female Ukrainian poet and playwright Lesya Ukrainka and in the Ukrainian animated film of the same name "Mavka—Guardian of the Forest," released in 2023

Further Reading

https://www.spiegel.de/ausland/ukraine-krieg-ueberleben-unter-russischer-besatzung-wie-familien-ihre-kinder-verstecken-a-a7457487-ec9a-4586-89b5-a30398ae302e; https://orf.at/stories/3326155/; https://www.dw.com/de/ausl%C3%A4nder-in-der-heimat-leben-im-donbass-unter-russischer-besatzung/a-65442680; https://www.theguardian.com/world/2022/jul/01/moscow-forcing-teachers-in-ukraine-to-sign-up-to-russian-curriculum; https://www.deutschlandfunkkultur.de/ukraine-gefluechtete-100.html; https://www.bpb.de/themen/europa/ukraine-analysen/nr-261/346846/analyse-leben-im-schatten-ueberlebensstrategien-der-menschen-in-der-volksrepublik-donezk/; https://www.dw.com/de/krieg-und-mobilmachung-wie-der-donbass-seine-soldaten-rekrutiert/a-61600170; https://civicmonitoring.org/wp-content/uploads/2023/03/report2022easternUkraine.pdf; https://www.deutschlandfunk.de/die-krim-nach-der-annexion-leben-mit-sanktionen-100.html; https://deportation.org.ua/numbers-and-evidence-of-forcible-deportation-of-ukrainians-to-russia-in-the-russo-ukrainian-war/; https://hromadske.ua/viyna/226746-konfiskatsiia-mayna-na-okupovanykh-terytoriiakh-iak-rosiiany-zabyraiut-bezkhaziayne-zytlo-ta-shcho-robyty-tym-khto-vyyikhav; https://life.nv.ua/ukr/socium/u-mariupoli-rosiyani-prodayut-zruynovani-kvartiri-ukrajinciv-nazivayuchi-jih-razrushkoy-video-50387096.html;https://www.pravda.com.ua/news/2024/06/21/7461843/; https://life.pravda.com.ua/society/rosiyani-katuvali-ta-gvaltuvali-predstavnikiv-lgbtk-na-hersonshchini-cherez-jihnyu-oriyentaciyu-pravozahisn-300766/; https://www.csis.org/analysis/crossing-thresholds-ukrainian-resistance-russian-occupation; https://www.dw.com/uk/vibori-putina-v-okupacii-ak-golosuvali-i-hovalisa-ziteli-zaporizza-i-lugansini/a-68601252; https://www.pravda.com.ua/news/2024/07/22/7466848/; https://life.pravda.com.ua/society/v-okupovanomu-krimu-rosiyani-provodyat-novi-chistki-bibliotek-301233/; https://www.ohchr.org/sites/default/files/2022-08/Ukraine-admin-justice-conflict-related-cases-en.pdf; https://www.tagesschau.de/ausland/europa/ukraine-partisanen-103.html; https://texty.org.ua/articles/115197/zhorstokist-rozlyta-v-rosijskij-kulturi-yak-vyhlyadaye-zhyttya-ukrayinciv-na-okupovanomu-pivdni/; https://suspilne.media/crimea/721956-ponad-35-tisac-ditej-vhodat-v-sklad-unarmii-na-tot-ukraini-almenda/; https://www.radiosvoboda.org/a/skhemy-ukrayinski-dity-yunarmiya-viyna/33203644.html; https://www.ombudsman.gov.ua/storage/app/media/uploaded-files/SpecialReport2025%20-%20ukr.pdf; https://www.theguardian.com/world/2025/mar/22/ukraine-clandestine-book-club-defies-russia-push-rewrite-history; https://www.bpb.de/themen/europa/ukraine-analysen/nr-287/523175/analyse-die-neuen-facetten-der-ukrainischen-zivilgesellschaft/; https://opir.org.ua/

Crime and Accountability in War 10

10.1 War and Law

For a long time in human history, it was assumed that a ruler or a state could start a war to enforce its own interests, i.e., that it had the right to wage war. After the First World War, this approach was increasingly questioned and the use of force (except for the purpose of defense) was outlawed in several treaties, e.g., the Briand-Kellogg Pact of 1928 and, most importantly, the UN Charter of 1945.

Following World War II, the prevailing view became that war is an unacceptable evil, that those who start wars commit the gravest crimes, and that such individuals bear legal responsibility.

Legal responsibility in the context of war takes two forms: civil and criminal.

The basic idea of responsibility in *civil law* states that anyone who has caused damage must make amends or pay for the repair of the damage. The most important objectives of *criminal law* are punishment of offenders, justice for victims, establishment of the legal order and prevention of future crimes.

10.2 War Damages and Civil Law Compensation

The Russian Federation bears overall responsibility for the war against Ukraine. It is therefore obliged to compensate for the destruction, damage, losses, and physical and psychological suffering inflicted on the state of Ukraine, the Ukrainian people, infrastructure, nature, and the economy in the course of the war. This involves compensation for war damage (paid during or after the war) and any reparations (i.e., compensation paid to the victorious state after the end of the war).

In Ukraine, numerous institutions and state authorities are involved in recording and assessing the damage, in particular to provide emergency aid, e.g., in the event of damage to housing, or to repair vital infrastructure.

The official international register of war damage *RD4U* (= *Register of Damage for Ukraine*) was created by decision of the Council of Europe in The Hague, Netherlands. Since April 2024, the damage register has been keeping online records of damage reported by Ukrainian individuals, companies, and government agencies. Building on the work of the damage register, a new international *Claims Commission for Ukraine (INC)* will be established to decide on individual claims for compensation; initial talks on setting up the commission took place at the end of March 2025.

The information and evidence collected will form the basis for possible compensation in the future. A compensation mechanism has not yet been determined.

One of the likely sources of funding for war damage compensation could be the frozen assets of the Russian central bank, sanctioned Russian companies and oligarchs abroad. These include bank funds, real estate, shares, bonds, luxury goods such as yachts, etc., access to which was blocked following corresponding decisions on sanctions by the EU, the USA, Canada, Japan and other countries. As of November 2024, frozen Russian assets amounted to around 300 billion euros worldwide, including around 210 billion euros in the European Union.

10.3 Russian War Crimes

Since the first days of the war, there have been reports from the Russian-occupied Ukrainian territories of crimes committed by members of the Russian army against the local population, abductions, torture and deportations.

On March 16, 2022, a Russian fighter jet dropped a bomb on the theater in Mariupol, Ukraine (Fig. 10.1). The theater served as a shelter for civilians and was marked with the Russian word "children," which was clearly visible from the air. Several hundred people died. The exact number of victims is unknown, as the Russian occupation administration buried the bodies in a mass grave and had the rubble of the building completely cleared away.

At the end of March 2022, when the Russian units were forced to hastily leave the Kyiv suburb of Bucha, they left over 400 civilians dead in mass graves and on the streets of the city. Similar atrocities were uncovered in other Ukrainian cities, including Irpin and Izium.

10.3 Russian War Crimes

Fig. 10.1 Ruins of the Donetsk Academic Regional Drama Theater in Mariupol (Donetsk region) after the Russian bombardment. Photo: Lirhan2016. Source: Wikimedia

Maternity clinics, residential buildings, shopping centers, train stations with hundreds of people, but also churches, museums and schools were targeted by Russian missiles.

Russia has been targeting Ukraine's energy infrastructure since the fall of 2022. Millions of people in Ukraine were left during the winter at times without electricity, water and heating.

Documented Russian war crimes:

- public executions, abuse, rape;
- establishment of torture chambers and illegal prisons, deprivation of liberty without conviction;
- torture, mutilations and killings of Ukrainian prisoners of war;
- operation of *filtration camps;*
- deportations to Russia, in particular abduction and deportation of Ukrainian children;
- militarization, Russification and political indoctrination of Ukrainian children and, as a result, obliteration of their Ukrainian identity;
- looting of private homes, museums, business premises and public property;

- use of banned phosphorus bombs, anti-personnel mines and booby traps;
- systematic attacks on civilian targets, hospitals, energy infrastructure, power plants;
- (deliberate and negligent) destruction of nature;
- destruction of the Kakhovka dam with flooding of the area as a result;
- misuse of the Russian-occupied Zaporizhzhia nuclear power plant as a nuclear threat.

> **Russian filtration camps**
>
> In the filtration camps on Russian-occupied Ukrainian territory, Ukrainian residents are registered and checked. Russian officials collect personal data, conduct an interrogation and scan electronic devices (cell phones, laptops, tablets), sometimes fingerprints are taken, luggage is searched and a physical examination is carried out. Registration is mandatory in order to be able to move freely and continue traveling. Each person must also pass a filtration for voluntary or forced entry into Russia.
>
> People who appear to be pro-Ukraine or critical of Russia are singled out—"filtered out." Their exact fate is often unknown, and many of them are subsequently imprisoned and tortured or even killed.

According to confirmed reports, Russia has abducted at least 20,000 children from the occupied Ukrainian territories. They were given Russian passports, some were adopted in Russia, and others were sent to Russian homes for re-education. Several thousand children were forcibly taken to Belarus. Tracking their whereabouts and returning them to their families is very difficult: often, the abducted children are given new birth certificates with false dates of birth and names, and Russian databases certify that they are of Russian descent.

The Russian Federation has created a camp system for the re-education, indoctrination, Russification, and military training of stolen Ukrainian children. Using satellite imagery, a Canadian-funded international research project found 136 Russian facilities in Russia and Russian-occupied territories where deported children live in prison- or barracks-like conditions. In numerous documented cases, children were abused, beaten, inadequately fed, or received poor medical care. At least six of these facilities are linked to Russia's paramilitary Young Army.

10.3 Russian War Crimes

The Kremlin leadership planned the targeted forced removal of Ukrainian children during the preparation for the large-scale invasion, with the first deportations from the occupied Ukrainian territories taking place in mid-February 2022. Experts see different motives behind this: on the one hand, to improve the poor demographic situation and compensate for low birth rates in the Russian Federation, on the other hand, to replenish the Russian army with young recruits for deployment against Ukraine, as well as to physically reduce the number of people who identify themselves as Ukrainians, i.e., genocidal intent.

In the war of aggression against Ukraine, Russia is deliberately using torture and abuse, including rape and sexual violence by Russian soldiers as a weapon of war.

> This is not random, aberrant behavior. This is orchestrated as part of state policy to intimidate, instill fear or punish to extract information and confessions.
> Alice Jill Edwards, the UN Special Rapporteur on Torture and Other Cruel, Inhuman or Degrading Treatment or Punishment, on September 10, 2023 after her week-long visit to Ukraine.

A number of videos in Russian networks made a new inhumane method known in autumn 2024. In the areas close to the front, especially in the large city of Kherson, which was liberated from Russian occupation in 2023, Russian drones are tracking and attacking Ukrainian civilians, civilian vehicles and buildings. This action, referred to in the media as a "human safari," serves to terrorize the population, deter international aid workers and as training for Russian drone pilots.

Ukrainian army personnel experience particular brutality in Russian captivity. Up to 90% of all returned prisoners of war report systematic and extensive torture and sexual abuse, starvation and inadequate medical care. According to reports, prison doctors also occasionally take part in torture.

Since 2024, there has been an increase in cases of Russian executions of Ukrainian prisoners of war by the Russian army. Observers suspect that this is a deliberate strategy to intimidate Ukrainian defenders.

Many of the bodies of soldiers handed over to Ukraine by Russia show signs of torture, and some are returned without internal organs, which raises suspicions of illegal organ trafficking by Russian authorities.

Russian authorities treat civilian prisoners in a similar manner. Since the start of Russia's military operations in 2014, the Russians have abducted and imprisoned an estimated 16,000 Ukrainian civilians. Since they are not prisoners of war and are mostly deprived of their liberty without legal grounds, Russian authorities refuse to release them as part of prisoner exchanges.

Russia has established a network of torture prisons where Ukrainian civilians are mistreated and tortured and held without charge, without lawyers, and without access to the outside world. Ukrainian journalist Viktoria Roshchyna investigated this on site in Russia in 2023. However, she herself was imprisoned, tortured, and finally killed in September 2024. Months later, Russian authorities handed over Viktoria Roshchyna's body to Ukraine bearing signs of torture and with several body parts missing. Her investigative work on Russian torture prisons was continued by journalists from 12 international media outlets as part of the "Viktoria Project," an initiative launched by the investigative network Forbidden Stories.

Russia denies international organizations access to Ukrainian prisoners of war, which means that most of the data comes from interviews with affected individuals after their return.

In contrast, UN representatives are regularly granted access to Russian prisoners of war on Ukrainian territory. They confirm that they are being treated in accordance with the standards of international humanitarian law, even if there are isolated cases of abuse.

10.4 War Crimes Under International Criminal Law

International criminal law, which deals with war crimes as part of international law, distinguishes between four criminal offenses related to war:

- *Crime of aggression*—a war of aggression. Use of armed forces by a state against the sovereignty, territorial integrity or political independence of another state in manifest violation of the Charter of the United Nations. The crime of aggression can only be committed by a state's highest political and military leadership.
- *War crimes* in the narrow sense. According to the general international understanding, certain rules must be observed even in wars so that human suffering and damage to material assets and cultural property are kept to an unavoidable minimum. These rules are called *international humanitarian law*. Violations of these rules are war crimes, such as violence, mistreatment and killing of civilians, prisoners and medical personnel, targeted shelling of civilian objects, use of chemical or biological weapons and cluster munitions, etc.
- *Crimes against humanity*. Serious crimes committed as part of an *extensive and systematic attack against the civilian population*. These crimes can take place during an armed conflict or even without one.
- *Genocide*. Serious crimes committed with the *intent to destroy a national, ethnic or religious group* in whole or in part.

These criminal offenses are laid down in international treaties such as the Rome Statute of the *International Criminal Court (ICC)* of 1998 and the *Geneva Conventions* of 1949 (consisting of four treaties and three additional protocols) and are expressly enshrined in the national criminal law of many states.

10.5 Documentation of War Crimes

In the period between February 2022 and May 2025, Ukrainian investigative authorities have collected evidence of over 167,000 Russian war crimes.

With the support of the European Union, a *Joint Investigation Team (JIT)* consisting of the International Criminal Court, Europol (= EU Police Office), Ukraine, Lithuania, Poland, Estonia, Latvia, Slovakia and Romania was set up in 2022 to document Russian war crimes and collect evidence.

In July 2023, the *International Center for the Prosecution of the Crime of Aggression against Ukraine (ICPA)* began its work. It consists of selected national prosecutors who are already involved in the Joint Investigation Team, JIT. The ICPA is tasked with analyzing the evidence collected since the start of Russia's war of aggression. The new center is based in The Hague, within the European Union Agency for Criminal Justice Cooperation (Eurojust).

The *Core International Crimes Evidence Database (CICED)*, which records data on war crimes, including in Russia's war of aggression against Ukraine, was also set up at Eurojust in 2023.

The UN Human Rights Council has set up a commission of inquiry. Several NGOs are also involved in documenting alleged Russian war crimes.

10.6 Prosecution of War Crimes

Several institutions may be responsible for the prosecution of Russian war crimes:

- Ukrainian courts under national jurisdiction,
- courts in other countries under universal jurisdiction,
- existing international courts, in particular the International Criminal Court, ICC in The Hague,
- newly created special tribunals, so-called ad hoc criminal courts.

By its own account, Ukraine has already passed dozens of war crime convictions. According to Ukrainian Justice Minister Denys Maliuska (2019–2024), the Ukrainian authorities intend to focus on two main charges in the future: crime of aggression and genocide.

More than 20 countries, including the USA, Germany, Romania and Argentina, are investigating Russian President Putin and other responsible politicians, commanders and soldiers for war crimes. *Universal jurisdiction* allows any country to prosecute war crimes, even without a direct national connection. Direct national connection means that the perpetrator or victim resides in the state, is a citizen of the state or the crime was committed on the territory of the state.

The investigations are running in several directions: there are investigations into war crimes committed by individual Russian military personnel as well as crimes against humanity, genocide and crime of aggression committed by Russia's highest political and military leadership, including its President Putin.

In mid-March 2023, the International Criminal Court, based in The Hague in the Netherlands, issued an arrest warrant for Russian President Vladimir Putin and the Russian Commissioner for Children's Rights Maria Lvova-Belova. They are accused of organizing the abduction and deportation of thousands of Ukrainian children from Russian-occupied territories to Russia. The abduction of children for the purpose of indoctrination or re-education constitutes genocide.

Additional four arrest warrants were issued by the ICC in 2024 against former Russian Defense Minister Sergei Shoigu, Army Chief Valery Gerasimov and two senior Russian officers Sergei Kobylash and Viktor Sokolov. The defendants are accused of deliberately firing missiles at the Ukrainian energy infrastructure and thereby causing great suffering to the Ukrainian civilian population. They are therefore accused of alleged war crimes and crimes against humanity.

The arrest warrant means that the 125 member states of the ICC are contractually obliged to arrest Putin and other suspects after entering their territory. In particular, this restricts the Russian president's freedom to travel.

In September 2024, Vladimir Putin traveled to Mongolia, which is a member of the ICC. However, the country did not have the Russian president arrested. Mongolia argued that the international arrest warrant was ignored due to its dependence on Russian energy sources.

ICC members
All states of the European Union have signed or ratified the Statute of the International Criminal Court (ICC)—the so-called Rome Statute—and are therefore members of the ICC.
Like the USA, China, India, Israel and Turkey, Russia is not a member of the ICC and is therefore not subject to its jurisdicvtion.
Ukraine ratified the Rome Statute in August 2024 and became the 125th member of the ICC effective as of January 1, 2025.

The Statute of the International Criminal Court stipulates that the ICC may investigate war crimes (in the narrow sense) as soon as one side of the conflict agrees. Since Ukraine is subject to the jurisdiction of the ICC, the ICC can take action here.

However, the ICC may only prosecute crimes of aggression (= war of aggression) if both warring parties—the attacking and the attacked state—agree to the investigations. Such consent is not to be expected from Russia.

The EU and a number of states therefore advocated the establishment of a special tribunal for Russian war crimes. Examples of such special tribunals in the past include the Nuremberg Tribunal and the Tokyo Trials after the Second World War, the International Criminal Tribunal for the former Yugoslavia and the International Criminal Tribunal for Rwanda.

In February 2025, the Council of Europe announced that a so-called Core Group of experts from around 40 countries had reached a basic agreement on an ad hoc criminal court within the framework of the Council of Europe for the Russian crime of aggression. The Council of Europe is a European international organization founded in 1949, comprising 46 states with a population of almost 700 million. On June 25, 2025, Ukraine's President Volodymyr Zelensky and the Secretary General of the Council of Europe, Alain Berset, signed an agreement on the establishment of a *Special Tribunal for the Crime of Aggression against Ukraine*, including the Statute of the Special Tribunal. The new body will be based in The Hague, Netherlands, alongside the ICC.

10.7 Addressing Accountability in Russian Society

The assessment of Russian crimes in the war against Ukraine is not only about the legal aspects of criminal prosecution, but also about political, social and moral responsibility.

Documenting the Russian crimes and convicting the guilty in fair trials means justice for the victims and deterrence for potential perpetrators. This would also allow Russian society to process the events and move forward.

The crimes committed by the Russian army in the wars in Transnistria (Republic of Moldova), Chechnya, Georgia and Syria, as well as atrocities committed long ago by the communist leadership in the Soviet Union and the war crimes of the Red Army during the Second World War have still not been dealt with in a critical manner in Russia, nor has the Hitler-Stalin Pact.

The popular idea of "Russkiy mir"/"Russian world" in Russia thrives, among other things, on the feeling of one's own impunity and superiority over the law and the international order. In the Russian collective memory, the Second World War in particular is closely linked to the idea that wars are worthwhile in the end, despite great suffering. The Russian-dominated Soviet Union ended the Second World War with territorial gains. It conquered western Ukraine, western Belarus, parts of Romania (Bessarabia), Latvia, Lithuania, Estonia and Kaliningrad (Königsberg). Violence is still perceived and accepted in Russian society as a legitimate and inevitable means to an end.

Critical analysis of the historical accountability of one's own country and a corresponding culture of history and remembrance, as was implemented and promoted in Germany after 1945, can hardly be found in Russia. The NGO Memorial was an exception, but it was banned in Russia in December 2021.

Feeling a sense of responsibility for the state and for collective action would be important for a vibrant civil society and for the future democratization of Russia.

Further Reading

https://www.rnd.de/politik/russland-un-beobachterin-sieht-folter-als-teil-der-kriegspolitik-JWP6GU63UJKFTHQVS76KKSCETI.html; https://laender-analysen.de/russland-analysen/427/filtration-system-ablauf-und-ziele/; https://www.rnd.de/politik/russische-filtrationslager-in-der-ukraine-gesinnungscheck-und-folter-FBXUPJUR6REBRNF7S3OYR3GRZE.html; https://www.lpb-bw.de/ukraine-kriegsverbrechen#c88612; https://ec.europa.eu/commission/presscorner/detail/de/ip_23_3606; https://rd4u.coe.int; https://www.dw.com/uk/vijna-rf-proti-ukraini-ak-rozsliduut-voenni-zlocini/a-65460543; https://www.reuters.com/world/ukraine-mans-torture-case-against-russians-seeks-justice-argentina-2024-04-16/; https://www.theglobeandmail.com/world/article-satellite-data-sheds-light-on-russias-modern-day-gulags-for-ukrainian/; https://de.euronews.com/2024/12/06/inhaftiert-deportiert-und-einer-gehirnwasche-unterzogen-wie-moskau-ukrainische-kinder-russ; https://detector.media/infospace/article/240993/2025-05-18-v-ukraini-zafiksuvaly-ponad-167-tysyach-rosiyskykh-voiennykh-zlochyniv-za-chas-povnomasshtabnoi-viyny-lubinets/

Geopolitical Aspects 11

11.1 Global Peace Architecture After World War II

After the Second World War, the international community endeavored to create a world order that would prevent future wars. The *United Nations Organization* (UNO/United Nations/UN) was founded on 24 October 1945 with the aim of securing global peace. Over time, it has united 193 of the world's currently 195 recognized states.

In Europe, the newly established *Coal and Steel Community*, the forerunner of today's *European Union*, aimed to secure peace by controlling industries relevant to warfare at the time, namely coal and steel.

The fundamental principles of the new international order laid down in the UN Charter (= the founding document of the United Nations Organization) were: renunciation of the use of force as a means of international politics, equality of peoples, and the obligation to respect the independence, sovereignty (= self-determination) and territorial integrity of all states. After World War II, this international order was referred to as the "*global peace architecture.*"

11.2 Geopolitics

The word *geopolitics* is often used in socio-political debates to describe the world order, intergovernmental relations and foreign policy strategies of individual countries. It combines the words "geography" and "politics" and has no clearly defined meaning. Geopolitics is often mentioned when states attempt to assert their own interests outside their territory and consolidate their power in the world.

Some people claim that geopolitics involves much more, namely that states even have a right to pressure others in order to pursue their own interests as they see fit. These people view events in international relations as a competition between the big powerful states—the "superpowers," the smaller states are seen as "spheres of influence" of the larger ones.

This view contradicts the principle of sovereign equality of states and the prohibition of violence as outlined in the UN Charter.

11.3 Pacifism

Just as geopolitics is sometimes understood as the right of individual states to use force, pacifism is sometimes understood as the duty of individual states or other actors to refrain from violence at all costs.

- **Pacifism**, also known as the peace movement (from the Latin pacificus—"peace-loving"), is a world view that rejects violence and war. The aim of pacifism is also disarmament, i.e., the destruction and prohibition of weapons, based on the belief that without weapons, there can be no war.

Extreme pacifists oppose the use of weapons, even in self-defense. With regard to Russia's aggression against Ukraine, they advocate that Ukraine end its armed resistance against Russia and that the West stop supplying weapons to Ukraine and maintain peaceful relations with Russia.

This approach contradicts the UN Charter, Article 51 of which stipulates "the inherent right of individual or collective self-defense" in the event of an armed attack against a member of the United Nations.

A strong peace movement emerged on German soil in the late 1970s—early 1980s in the Federal Republic of Germany (= FRG, "West Germany") after the Soviet Union deployed nuclear missiles targeted at Europe. The peace movement in the FRG aimed to prevent the deployment of US missiles in response to the deployment of Soviet missiles.

In addition to Christian, feminist and environmental activist groups, pro-Soviet and communist factions were also very active in the West German pacifist movement. The influence of the SED (= Socialist Unity Party of Germany, the ruling party in the Soviet-controlled German Democratic Republic GDR, "East Germany"), the Stasi (secret service of the GDR) and the KGB (secret service of the USSR) on the peace movement is also well documented.

The activists of the peace movement, also referred to as "peace struggle" called for world peace and disarmament in Europe and criticized the USA, whose policies they described as imperialist. Criticism of the totalitarian imperialist regime of the Soviet Union and its military buildup was not part of the German peace movement's agenda.

There were similar movements in other Western countries.

Doctrinaire pacifists who oppose the support of Ukraine with Western weapons in the current Russian-Ukrainian war repeatedly mention the peace movement of the 1980s as their role model or as a desirable point of reference.

Peace movements in Western countries have long been considered ideologically left-wing. Since the beginning of Russia's aggression against Ukraine in 2014, and to a greater extent since Russia's large-scale invasion in 2022, many right-wing and far-right networks and politicians have been making similar pacifist demands. These include calls for Ukraine to give up its resistance to the Russian war and for foreign governments to end their support for Ukraine.

At events labeled as peace demonstrations, it is not uncommon to find representatives of both left- and right-wing ideologies, followers of conspiracy theories, vaccine skeptics, deniers of COVID-19 and climate change, and supporters of Russia's war against Ukraine. In this context, in the German speaking countries the terms "Querfront" (= "cross-front") or "Querdenker" (= "lateral thinkers"), meaning a mix that cuts across various ideologies and confusions, are used.

11.4 Principles of the Peace Architecture

The international peace architecture after World War II was based on the assumption that the following principles are universally valid in world politics:

- *Law*. Treaties are respected. The entirety of international organizations, international law and interstate economic relations operate based on trust in the binding power of written agreements. As soon as an agreement is contractually notarized, it should be upheld.
- *Trade*. Trade brings peace. Interstate economic relations, free movement of capital and goods and economic interdependence reduce tensions between states.
- *Diplomacy*. There is always goodwill. Every leader, organization or state has legitimate interests and is solution-oriented. The key is to listen, negotiate, and be willing to compromise, in other words, to act diplomatically.
- *Humanism*. Human life is the highest value. Every state aims to protect the lives of the people in its country and ensure the common good.

11.5 Zeitenwende: Historical Turning Point

After the Second World War, there were several challenges to the international order, ranging from smaller armed conflicts to larger wars. The Russian war against Ukraine has made it particularly clear that law, trade, diplomacy and humanism are not laws of nature, but human imperatives. They only work if everyone abides by them.

With the large-scale invasion, Russian President Putin has broken numerous treaties, some of which he personally signed (= blatant disregard for the law). The Russian economy is closely intertwined with the global market, especially with Ukraine. However, this did not prevent the war. Quite the opposite: Putin uses the one-sided dependency he has strategically created, such as in the energy sector, to blackmail (= trade does not necessarily bring peace).

Russian representatives used diplomatic channels to conceal war preparations and deny military intentions. They use obviously false claims in their argumentation of war (= abuse of diplomacy). Russian soldiers are poorly equipped and inadequately trained, the number of Russian military personnel killed and wounded is excessively high. Furthermore, the Kremlin is employing war tactics deliberately designed to cause high human losses (= blatant disregard for human life, even within their own ranks).

The Russian war against Ukraine has undoubtedly become the greatest challenge to the international order and the global peace architecture since the Second World War.

At a special session of the German Bundestag, Germany's lower house of parliament, on February 27, 2022, German Chancellor Olaf Scholz delivered his so-called *Zeitenwende speech* (German Zeitenwende—"times-turn", a historical turning point, watershed era). Scholz declared: "We are experiencing a Zeitenwende. And that means that the world after is no longer the same as the world before."

This means that trust in the power of law, trade, diplomacy and humanism and the conviction of pacifism and neutrality do not protect against aggression.

11.6 International Organizations

The network of international institutions, in particular the United Nations, the OSCE (the Organization for Security and Co-operation in Europe) and the Council of Europe, were unable to avert the war in Ukraine. Some of them turned out to be largely ineffective in the face of the war.

Russia repeatedly blocked decisions made by international organizations or refused to recognize their authority. This is possible because Russian representatives hold a veto right in the decision-making bodies of numerous organizations.

As one of the five permanent members of the UN Security Council (alongside the USA, France, the UK and China), Russia has a particularly strong influence on the Council's resolutions. According to Article 24 of the UN Charter, the UN member states delegate to the Security Council "primary responsibility for the maintenance of international peace and security." The fact that Russia is allowed to co-decide and even temporarily chair this body (as was the case in April 2023 and July 2024) while waging a war of aggression is a glaring contradiction in terms.

The Russian Federation can also withdraw from organizations at any time. For example, in March 2022, Russia left the Council of Europe to preempt its impending expulsion from the organization.

In July 2024, the Russian parliament announced that it would no longer participate in the work of the Parliamentary Assembly of the OSCE. Even before this, Russia had largely suspended its financial contributions to the OSCE.

According to the findings of Western intelligence services, Russia has repeatedly used international organizations for espionage or to provide its intelligence service employees with legends (= disguised identities).

The infiltration and paralysis of numerous international organizations by the Kremlin in the recent past has fueled the debate on new mechanisms and systems for the global peace architecture. The palpable need for reforms prompted the UN in particular to adopt the so-called "Pact for the Future" at the end of September 2024.

11.7 The Multipolar World and Its Centers of Power

In his incendiary speech at the 43rd Munich Conference on Security Policy in February 2007, Russian President Putin publicly criticized the West, NATO and the USA in harsh terms for the first time. In his speech, he called for a new multipolar world order. According to him, there are several centers of power in such a multipolar world, and Russia is one of them, that actively influence other countries or have the right to do so.

Putin has repeated these ideas on many occasions and elaborated on them in several essays. However, he has also made contradictory statements at times.

Experts on Putin and Russian communication culture emphasize that the simultaneous delivery of contradictory messages is a well-known rhetorical technique in Russian political debate. When Putin praises world peace, human rights, democracy, international order and the self-determination of peoples, his motives vary depending on the situation: to mislead friends and foes; to demonstrate his own power or the privilege of being able to lie without consequences; to be polite in communication with Western partners.

Putin's "new world order" reflects old ideas of great world powers—"superpowers"—and their "spheres of influence," which the UN Charter sought to overcome in 1945 with the principle of equal rights and sovereignty of all states.

Some countries are openly showing interest in this "new old model" of intergovernmental relations.

The People's Republic of China (PRC or China for short) has been striving for political and economic influence around the world for years. To this end, the Chinese government, or Chinese companies with the support of the government, are purchasing critical infrastructure facilities, raw material mining licenses and important companies in Europe, the USA and worldwide. As part of the so-called "New Silk Road," China is building European-Asian and intercontinental trade and transportation networks under its own control and is seeking relationships with other countries that will increase their dependence on China.

China would like to extend its influence to the island of Taiwan as well, which the Chinese government views as part of its own national territory and whose "reunification" by military force it does not rule out.

China and Taiwan
The People's Republic of China (with its capital in Beijing) and the Republic of China (Taiwan's official name, with its capital in Taipei) have developed separately since 1949. At that time, during the civil war, the Communists under Mao Zedong won control of mainland China, and the nationalist Kuomintang government retreated to the island of Taiwan. Since then, the island's legal status under international law has remained unresolved. However, Taiwan, which operates under democratic principles, seeks to preserve its de facto independence and refuses to place its democracy under the control of the autocratic regime in Beijing.

The mullah regime in the Islamic Republic of Iran (IRI or Iran for short), with its declared goal of destroying Israel, seeks to establish its dominance in the Middle East and invests heavily in developing nuclear weapons. It is one of Putin's closest allies.

11.8 Trump and the End of the Existing Peace Architecture

Throughout its history, the United States of America (USA) has alternated between two approaches to foreign and security policy: isolationism (focusing on domestic issues and interests, closing itself off from the outside world) and internationalism (engaging with global issues and situations in other countries).

The phases of internationalism in the twentieth century brought the USA both great recognition worldwide (for its contribution to the defeat of Hitler's Germany in World War II and to the reconstruction of Europe through the Marshall Plan after the war) and great criticism and hatred (e.g., for the intervention in the war in Vietnam and for wars alike in other countries).

Since entering WWII, the USA has consistently pursued an internationalist foreign policy and played a special role in the global peace architecture after the war. As the counterweight to the totalitarian Soviet empire during the Cold War, the USA saw itself as the protector of Western democratic liberal values and global order and security, as the "leader of the free world."

Even after the collapse of the Soviet Union and the end of the Cold War, foreign policy experts in the USA, now the most powerful country militarily and the largest economy on the planet, believed that liberal internationalism would best serve US national interests.

For decades, the transatlantic (or Euro-Atlantic) partnership was part of the US self-image. This was understood to mean, on the one hand, a friendly relationship and strategic cooperation with Europe and, on the other hand, the so-called "nuclear umbrella" or nuclear deterrence, i.e., the US promise to use nuclear weapons to defend European NATO members in case of emergency (in fulfillment of its obligation to provide assistance under Article 5 of the NATO Treaty).

Critics, however, accused the United States of not fully adhering to its own declared values (= hypocrisy and double standards) and of interfering in the affairs of other countries or seeking to subject them to its own values and power (= imperialism).

Regardless of the complex and often controversial policies, the US leadership elite, above all US presidents, consistently and publicly committed themselves to value-based politics, the protection of Western values, and the existing peace architecture over the past 80 years.

The Republican US President Donald Trump, newly elected at the end of 2024, has made a decisive change of course.

With his slogan "America first" and his promise to focus primarily on domestic interests and concerns, Trump is taking a clear isolationist stance. With the words "I wouldn't protect you (Europe—ed.), I would even encourage them (Russia—ed.) to do whatever they want," he distanced himself from Europe and from the promise to protect Europe as early as February 2024.

Regarding Russia's aggression towards Ukraine, Donald Trump avoided clearly condemning the actions of the Russian Federation and pledging unequivocal support to Ukraine. He calls for an end to the war, even if this means forcing Ukraine to surrender (more on peace talks in Chap. 16). Trump repeatedly affirms his respect for Putin.

The first months of Trump's second term (he already held this office from 2016 to 2020) after his inauguration in January 2025 were marked by the following tendencies:

- "Deal making," i.e., (personal) profit or gain as the primary guiding principle.
  Values, moral considerations, realism, consistent action, applicable laws, and politeness are not considered decisive, but are used as a means to an end depending on the situation. President Trump's statements often stand out for their clear falsehoods and errors. On his own social media platform, "Truth Social," Trump repeatedly shares fake news and conspiracy theories. In June 2025, he reposted a message from another user claiming that his predecessor Joe Biden had already been executed in 2020 and replaced by a clone or robot.
- Power politics and the law of the strongest: division of the world into "superior" and "inferior" parties, granting special rights to the "superior"—the "stronger"—parties, and striving for power at any price.
  According to this way of thinking, pressure and threats are acceptable instruments of interpersonal and intergovernmental relations, and enlarging one's own territory at the expense of other, "weaker" states is a desirable goal.
  President Donald Trump has repeatedly expressed his intention to incorporate Canada as the 51st state of the USA and to take control of Greenland (an autonomous territory belonging to Denmark) as well as the Panama Canal (owned by Panama).
  Trump repeatedly pressured Ukrainian President Zelensky and insulted him in order to force concessions to Russia. At the same time, Trump often spoke mildly and sympathetically about Russian President Putin.
- Distrust or disregard for the state, established institutions, science, the press, and diplomacy. Fight against the "establishment," i.e., against existing systems. Trump dissolved numerous government institutions, including the US Department of Education, and dismissed tens of thousands of civil servants. He ended US membership in the World Health Organization (WHO), the Paris

Climate Agreement, and the UN Human Rights Council. He imposed tariffs and protectionist policies contrary to the free trade rules of the World Trade Organization (WTO).

The US president cut or reduced funding for foreign aid via USAID (United States Agency for International Development) and for the state-run foreign radio stations Radio Free Europe/Radio Liberty (RFE/RL) and Voice of America. He targeted independent media with lawsuits, threats, and targeted manipulation, and attacked US universities, especially Harvard University, verbally and then by threatening to cut funding. Some of these measures, which were carried out bypassing the US Congress or existing US laws, were blocked by the courts.

- Unconditional (albeit temporary) personal loyalty as a decision-making criterion.

President Trump appointed numerous individuals with no relevant experience to top US offices on the basis of their demonstrated loyalty or his personal preference. Trump entrusted Elon Musk, entrepreneur, tech billionaire, and major sponsor of his election campaign, with the task of reducing government spending. The Department of Government Efficiency (DOGE), created for this purpose and headed by Musk, employed mostly young people with a tech background and no government experience, had broad powers and access to secret, highly sensitive data, operated without transparency or external oversight, and showed little success in cost optimization. At the end of May 2025, Musk ended his work for DOGE.

- Xenophobia.

Trump has repeatedly made disparaging remarks about foreigners, ended the protection program for hundreds of thousands of migrants, and banned students from multiple countries from entering the US.

- Exaggerated, emotional, often vulgar language (expressions used by Trump such as "big beautiful bill" or "kissing my ass" or "f***").

Many of the measures taken followed the so-called "Project 2025" plan of the right-wing conservative think tank "Heritage Foundation." This think tank strongly supported Donald Trump in his election campaign movement under the slogan "Make America Great Again," abbreviated MAGA. Experts describe the contents of "Project 2025" as a guide for the transformation of the state into an autocracy, with the weakening of democratic institutions and the concentration of power in the hands of the president. It remains to be seen how far this restructuring will go.

The United States of America is experiencing a turnaround in several respects during Donald Trump's new term in office: on the one hand, a return to isolationism and a departure from Euro-Atlantic cooperation; on the other hand, a departure from its commitment to Western values and peaceful coexistence based on the UN Charter.

Russia's large-scale war of aggression against Ukraine heralded a turning point, and with Donald Trump's second presidency, the era of the previous peace architecture has now finally come to an end.

Countries that do not (want to) participate in international geopolitical games, especially smaller states without a strong military apparatus, were dependent on the existing international order, in which the law of treaties and not the law of the strongest prevails.

Since the end of World War II, there have been numerous hotspots around the world that have not escalated into major armed conflicts solely because the parties involved feared negative consequences. It is therefore very important that Russia's military force does not achieve its goals and that the war does not bring any other advantages for Russia.

The course of the Russian-Ukrainian war will play a significant role in determining what the future world order will actually look like.

Further Reading

https://www.youtube.com/watch?v=YHN43mEWza8; https://www.derstandard.at/story/3000000185023/spionage-und-sabotage-wie-russland-die-osze-unterwandert-und-lahmlegt; https://politik.watson.de/politik/analyse/812558853-project-2025-in-der-zusammenfassung-die-ziele-und-die-rolle-von-donald-trump

Dealing With War in the World   12

12.1 Interests

Relatively early in the war, three fundamental attitudes toward the Russian-Ukrainian war emerged: on the one hand, pro-Western/pro-democratic/pro-Ukrainian; on the other hand, authoritarian/pro-Russian; and in between, vacillating/self-serving.

Despite regional differences and individual cases, the following pattern emerges: the more a country's socio-political mood is characterized by democracy, human rights, liberal freedoms, and—in Europe—pro-European sentiment, the more decisive that country's support for Ukraine is.

When the mood in a country changes, so does its attitude toward Ukraine. The more autocratic, *populist*, or extreme a movement, party, or person appears, the more likely they are to take a sympathetic stance toward Russia and a critical stance toward Ukraine.

- **Populism** (from the Latin populus, meaning "people") is an approach used by politicians who seek immediate approval from voters by offering supposedly simple and quick, but not necessarily correct, solutions to complex issues. "Populist" means "in line with the wishes of the people."

On March 2, 2022, the United Nations General Assembly voted on UN Resolution A/ES-11/L.1 in its 11th emergency session, condemning Russia's invasion of Ukraine and calling for its immediate end and full Russian withdrawal. 141 of 193 UN members voted in favor of the resolution, 5 (Russia, Belarus, North

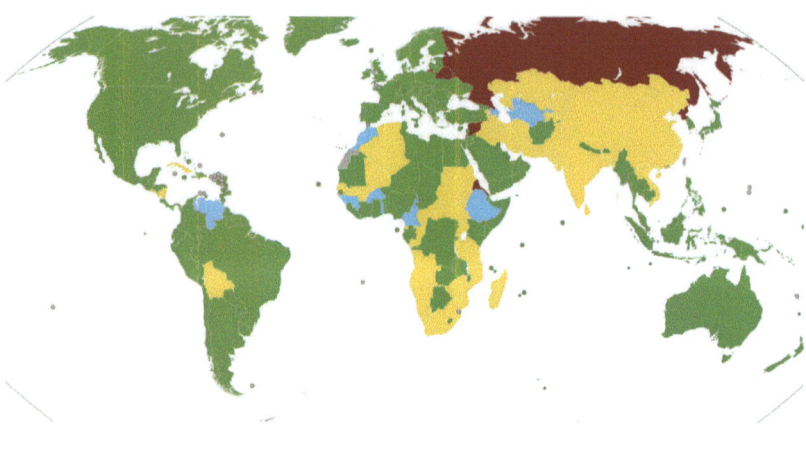

■ in favour ■ against ■ abstentions ■ absent ■ non member

Resolution A/ES-11/L.1 of the UN General Assembly
on March 2, 2022

Fig. 12.1 Voting results on Resolution A/ES-11/L.1 of the United Nations General Assembly in the 11th emergency session, condemning Russia's invasion of Ukraine, on March 2, 2022. (Chart: Jurta. Source: Wikipedia)

Korea, Syria, Eritrea) voted against it, and 35 (including Iran, China, India, Pakistan, Cuba, and others) abstained (Fig. 12.1).

Many countries condemned Russia's large-scale invasion of Ukraine in 2022 from the very beginning and offered Ukraine their support. These include, in particular, the Western countries like the UK, the USA, Poland, the Baltic states of Estonia, Latvia, and Lithuania, as well as Germany, France, Italy, and other EU countries, but also Canada, Australia, and Japan.

The European countries Finland and Sweden, which had previously been neutral, decided against neutrality and in favor of applying for NATO membership, and pledged comprehensive assistance, including military aid, to Ukraine. Other neutral states like Switzerland and Austria are maintaining their neutrality.

Even governments of European countries that were under strong Russian influence before the war or had particularly good relations with Russia, such as Hungary, Serbia, Bulgaria, Greece, and Austria, condemned Russia's invasion of Ukraine. However, some continue to express reservations about certain sanctions against Russia or measures to support Ukraine.

12.1 Interests

Unlike the other EU member states, the six countries of Slovakia, Hungary, Austria, Bulgaria, Malta, and Cyprus have not concluded a security agreement with Ukrainian by the end of 2024.

In the Christian Orthodox countries of Serbia, Bulgaria, and Greece, Russian propaganda is reinforced by the influence of the loyal to the government Russian Orthodox Church. Pro-Russian demonstrations took place in these countries (but also in Germany, which has a large Russian-speaking minority). However, they were smaller overall than the protests and rallies against the Russian invasion and in support of Ukraine.

Only a few countries have shown explicit support for Russia, including Belarus, North Korea, and Syria, or rather the Syrian dictator Bashar al-Assad, until he was overthrown in December 2024.

Iran and China provide the Russian Federation with a wide range of support, but repeatedly deny doing so.

The authoritarian mullah regime in Iran supplies Russia with various weapons, such as combat drones, in particular the Shahed-136 type, and the corresponding technology.

In 2024, joint Russian-Chinese, Belarusian-Chinese, and Russian-Chinese-Iranian military maneuvers took place.

The attitude of other countries toward Russia ranges from condemnation of the acts of war to partial understanding for the Kremlin and a neutral or opportunistic position.

- **Opportunism** – behavior that adapts to different situations in order to gain an advantage.

African countries and most South American countries view the war as a matter of little concern to them. Russia maintained close relations with many of them during the Soviet era and fueled anti-American and anti-Western sentiment in their countries, recalling their colonial past.

In the states that were formerly part of the Soviet Union, such as Kazakhstan, Armenia, and Azerbaijan, there is strong support for Ukraine among the population. People remember Russian oppression during the Soviet era. They see the war as a struggle by Ukrainians against Moscow's imperialist attacks. However, their governments are acting cautiously, as they are often dependent on Russia in many ways. The governments of the Baltic states of Estonia, Latvia, and Lithuania, on the other hand, are supporting Ukraine with all their power.

Russia has long been trying to win over the BRICS countries to its war against Ukraine. But the shows no interest in doing so.

> BRICS—a group consisting of Brazil, Russia, India, China and South Africa (the name comes from their first letters), founded in 2006. Iran, Egypt, Ethiopia and the United Arab Emirates were added at the beginning of 2024, as well as Indonesia in 2025, which is why the association is also referred to as BRICS plus. Russia and China are endeavoring to shape BRICS as an anti-Western alliance, which contradicts the interests of India and Brazil in particular, who are not seeking confrontation, but even deeper relations with the West. For the time being, BRICS remains a loose organization of unequal members without unified goals or positions.

Selected countries, regions, and actors are presented in detail below. Chapter 13 is devoted to Ukraine's most active supporters.

12.2 Democracies Are Moving Closer Together

The term "collective West" encompasses a number of countries that adhere to the "Western values" of liberal democracy and respect for human rights. They are united in numerous organizations and alliances. When referring to "Western support" for Ukraine, this usually means the European Union, NATO, and the G7 (Fig. 12.2) or most of their members.

Russia's attack on Ukraine was intended to weaken the democratic West. However, in response to the war, the EU and NATO have strengthened their cooperation, taken an active stance, and are regularly coordinating their approach. Japan, Australia, and South Korea also support the joint measures in response to Russia's war.

The countries of Europe have deepened their cooperation in the field of defense.

In October 2022, the *European Sky Shield Initiative (ESSI)* was launched, which aims to build an improved European air defense system and comprises 17 European countries (including non-NATO members Switzerland and Austria); four other countries have expressed their interest.

At the end of 2023, the neutral states of Switzerland, Austria, Malta and Ireland proposed an expanded partnership in a joint letter to NATO. They would like to participate in joint exercises with NATO and, in particular, increase interoperability (which is achieved when military systems are coordinated with each other). Switzerland has already started to implement some measures to increase interoper-

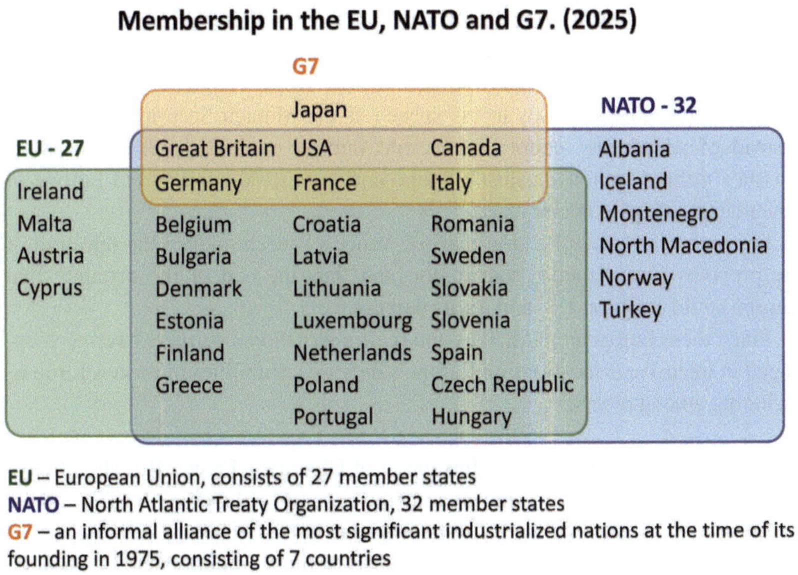

Membership in the EU, NATO and G7. (2025)

EU - 27	G7			NATO - 32
	Japan			
Ireland	Great Britain	USA	Canada	Albania
Malta	Germany	France	Italy	Iceland
Austria	Belgium	Croatia	Romania	Montenegro
Cyprus	Bulgaria	Latvia	Sweden	North Macedonia
	Denmark	Lithuania	Slovakia	Norway
	Estonia	Luxembourg	Slovenia	Turkey
	Finland	Netherlands	Spain	
	Greece	Poland	Czech Republic	
		Portugal	Hungary	

EU – European Union, consists of 27 member states
NATO – North Atlantic Treaty Organization, 32 member states
G7 – an informal alliance of the most significant industrialized nations at the time of its founding in 1975, consisting of 7 countries

Fig. 12.2 Membership of the EU, NATO, and G7. June 2025. (Graphic: Oksana Stavrou)

ability and, for example, completed joint military exercises with the NATO member state Italy in September 2024.

In October 2024, Germany and the United Kingdom (UK) signed an agreement on closer cooperation in defense and security policy.

In numerous European countries, such as Germany, Sweden, Croatia, and Serbia, a discussion began about reintroducing compulsory military service or reforming military service.

Multiple countries worldwide increased their defense and military spending after Russia's full-scale invasion of Ukraine.

In the European Union, plans for a common foreign and defense policy came back into focus. In March 2024, the European Commission presented the first *European Defense Industrial Strategy (EDIS)*, which also includes Ukraine.

The European Union has resumed the enlargement process and launched accession talks with Ukraine and the Republic of Moldova in 2024, as well as has taken further steps in accession negotiations with Albania and Bosnia and Herzegovina.

Relations between Europe and the USA initially intensified with the start of Russia's full-scale war. However, Donald Trump, elected president of the USA in

2024, distanced himself from US security guarantees within NATO and demanded that (European) NATO members invest in their own defense.

In February 2025, US Vice President and close Trump confidant J.D. Vance also sharply criticized Europeans in his speech at the Munich Security Conference. Instead of addressing security issues and threats, particularly those posed by Russia's military actions against Ukraine and Europe, Vance accused Europe of misunderstanding democracy.

For many European decision-makers, Vance's speech marked the rejection of the previous Euro-Atlantic cooperation and thus the end of the certainty that Europe could count on US help for its defense.

Since then, European politicians and their international partners have been engaged in intensive discussions on Europe's defense capabilities in various formats, including among others:

- the "Coalition of the Willing" in support of Ukraine: a French-British initiative involving more than 30 countries and representatives of the EU, NATO, and the European Council, convened for the first time in November 2024;
- E3: an informal foreign policy and security cooperation arrangement between the UK, Germany and France, established in 2003;
- the "Group of Five," E5: an informal cooperation of the Defense Ministers of the UK, Germany, France, Italy and Poland for support of Ukraine, meeting for the first time in November 2024;
- the "Nordic-Baltic Eight," NB8: an alliance founded in 1992 and consisting of the Nordic countries of Denmark, Finland, Iceland, Norway and Sweden, and the Baltic countries of Estonia, Latvia and Lithuania. NB8 has emerged since 2022 as a pioneer in the debate on advanced defense concepts and support for Ukraine.

Discussions about the future of Western security policy are moving in the following directions:

- Strengthening support for Ukraine so that Russia can be stopped in Ukraine and prevented from attacking European or other countries.
- Investing in the military and expanding national armies.
In March 2025, the European Commission and the EU High Representative for Foreign Affairs and Security Policy, Kaja Kallas, presented a plan to increase defense capabilities in EU countries called *Readiness 2030*" (also known as "reArm Europe"). The plan creates a new program called *Security Action for Europe (SAFE)* for the joint procurement of weapons and ammunition with the

12.2 Democracies Are Moving Closer Together

help of low-interest loans totaling €150 billion and provides incentives for EU member states to invest more in defense.

At the NATO summit on June 25, 2025, NATO defense ministers decided to gradually increase member countries' defense spending. While the target since 2014 has been to spend at least 2% of GDP on national defense, NATO countries are now expected to reach 5% of GDP by 2035 at the latest.

– Knowledge and technology transfer from Ukraine.

In the face of hybrid and military threats during the war, Ukraine has developed innovative, forward-looking technologies and solutions that would also significantly strengthen the defense capabilities of the collective West. In joint projects, Western partners have now begun to learn from Ukrainian experience, so that both sides benefit from the cooperation.

As part of the "Interflex" military training program for Ukrainian soldiers in the UK, Ukraine is reportedly sending drone experts to train British military personnel in the latest Russian drone tactics.

The Ukrainian military software DELTA for real-time monitoring of events on the battlefield attracted the interest of a NATO country in 2025.

In May 2025, Lithuanian Defense Minister Dovilė Šakalienė outlined the "1 + 1" initiative for the production of the Ukrainian surface drone "Magura" in her country: one drone for Ukraine, one for Lithuania, both financed by Lithuania.

Further cooperation with Ukraine in the field of military research and production was initiated by defense companies such as Rheinmetall (Germany), Weibel Scientific (Denmark), Thales International SAS (France), Baykar (Turkey), Atlas Aerospace (Latvia), Northrop Grumman (USA), and Česká zbrojovka (Czech Republic).

– Creation of a (UN) peacekeeping mission for Ukraine. In theory, joint EU forces or an EU army.

French President Emmanuel Macron first floated the idea of an international troop deployment in Ukraine in early 2024. In the months that followed, representatives from several countries said they'd think about sending their own military personnel to Ukraine, maybe as part of a peacekeeping mission. These include France, the United Kingdom, Germany, Switzerland, Australia, Denmark, Sweden, Estonia, Lithuania, and Austria. No specific initiatives have been announced yet.

– Nuclear umbrella provided by France and the United Kingdom.

In Belgium, Germany, Italy, the Netherlands, and Turkey, there are a total of around 100–150 US nuclear warheads owned by the USA, which can only be delivered to their targets by air. In Europe, only France and the UK possess nuclear missiles. In March 2025, French President Emmanuel Macron indicated his willingness to make nuclear deterrence available to European partners. Active engagement by European politicians is widely supported by EU citizens. The regular Eurobarometer survey conducted in April 2025 showed the highest level of trust in the EU in 18 years (52%). More than three-quarters of the European population (76%) are in favor of providing financial and humanitarian aid to Ukraine, while 59% support military assistance.

12.3 Hungary and Slovakia

Hungary is the only EU member state classified as "partly free" by the NGO Freedom House. Under the long-standing leadership of right-wing conservative Prime Minister Viktor Orban since 2010, democratic institutions have been systematically weakened, press freedom and the independence of the judiciary restricted, and the activities of the opposition, NGOs, and journalists hindered. Due to violations of the rule of law and a lack of reforms, the country lost over €1 billion in EU funding at the end of 2024, after it had already been frozen in 2022.

Orban and Hungarian Foreign Minister Peter Szijjarto continue to maintain good relations with the Kremlin. In 3 years of full-scale Russian war against Ukraine, Szijjarto visited the Russian Federation 13 times, while visiting Ukraine only once in January 2024 (according to official figures). During the war, the Hungarian prime minister attempted to delay and weaken EU sanctions against Russia, block financial and military aid to Ukraine, halt Ukraine's accession negotiations with the EU, and obstruct Sweden's accession to NATO. He has spoken out a number of times against Ukraine's accession to the EU and NATO.

In 2024, Hungary eased visa requirements for Russians and Belarusians, which was criticized as potentially facilitating Russian espionage in the EU.

In May 2025, Ukraine announced that it had captured two suspected Hungarian spies who had allegedly been spying on military facilities in Ukraine. This raised suspicions that the information obtained was intended for Russia, as Hungary itself has no interest in such data. Hungary responded by expelling two Ukrainian diplomats, to which Ukraine reacted by expelling two Hungarian diplomats.

The left-wing populist Prime Minister of Slovakia, Robert Fico, also pursues a pro-Russian policy. Unlike its southern neighbor Hungary, his country has so far supported all EU aid packages for Ukraine and all sanctions against Russia without exception. However, like Orban, Fico has repeatedly attracted attention with negative comments about the European Union and NATO's policy toward Ukraine. Alongside Orban and Austrian Chancellor Karl Nehammer (2021–2025), Fico is one of the few European leaders to have visited Russian President Vladimir Putin since Russia's invasion of Ukraine.

When protests against the government broke out in Slovakia in early 2025, Fico accused Ukraine of orchestrating them.

12.4 Austria

The Austrian Neutrality Act of 1955 prohibits Austria from joining military alliances and allowing foreign countries to establish military bases on its territory. Neutrality was a condition demanded by the Soviet Union in exchange for withdrawing its troops from Austria in 1955.

Citing its legally established neutrality, Austria is not providing Ukraine with any support in the area of defense, but is supporting the country and Ukrainians displaced by the war financially, with relief supplies, services, and aid initiatives. In addition, Vienna has financed demining equipment for Ukraine and participated in the "Grain from Ukraine" food initiative, which purchases Ukrainian grain for countries in Africa and Asia.

Austria has long maintained close political, economic, and cultural ties with Russia. Several former Austrian politicians have been given jobs at Russian state-affiliated companies, Austria's dependence on Russian gas has increased over time, and Russian disinformation and anti-Western propaganda have spread in Austria via social media, Austrian newspaper forums, and conspiracy theory platforms and associations.

When Ukrainian President Volodymyr Zelensky delivered a speech to the Austrian parliament via video link in the spring of 2023, the members of the right-wing populist Freedom Party of Austria (FPÖ) walked out of the plenary chamber in protest, and more than half of the members of the Social Democratic Party of Austria (SPÖ) were not even present.

Over the years, the Alpine republic has developed a strong dependence on Russian gas, which it has increased since the start of Russia's aggression against Ukraine in 2014 – to over 90% of imported gas in 2023.

The Austrian oil and gas company OMV, which is 31.5% state-owned, signed gas supply contracts with the Russian company Gazprom in 2018 and kept them secret. It only terminated the contracts in December 2024, after Ukraine did not extend the gas transit agreement with Russia via its territory for 2025 and after Russia's Gazprom stopped gas deliveries to OMV in November 2024 due to payment disputes.

Dependence on Russian gas was one of the reasons why the British weekly magazine *The Economist* ranked Austria second after Hungary in its list of "Putin's useful idiots" in July 2023.

The legal and political situation in Austria allows for extensive Russian espionage activities against Western countries. Austrian law does not prohibit espionage as long as it is not directed against Austria.

As early as 2018, information leaked that European intelligence services were withholding highly sensitive information from their Austrian colleagues for fear that it would be passed on to Russia. With influence from Russia, including via Russian agent and Austrian entrepreneur Jan Marsalek, and with the involvement of the FPÖ, the Austrian Federal Office for the Protection of the Constitution and Counterterrorism (BVT) was subsequently dismantled.

A Bulgarian woman from the Russian agent network surrounding Marsalek was exposed in 2025. She carried out anti-Ukrainian influence operations, stuck stickers portraying Ukraine as a right-wing extremist country, and incited hatred against Ukraine using fake accounts in online forums.

The extent of Russian influence and infiltration in Austrian institutions is unknown; it is hardly monitored or combated. The Austrian far-right party FPÖ signed a friendship agreement with Putin's party "United Russia" in 2016 and consistently displays a pro-Russian stance.

With an aggressive campaign on TikTok and Telegram, the FPÖ achieved first place in the Austrian parliament for the first time in October 2024. The Chinese-controlled TikTok and Telegram, founded by a Russian, are heavily criticized for spreading pro-Russian and anti-Western propaganda, hate speech, and conspiracy narratives, and for promoting them through algorithms.

At the beginning of March 2025, a three-party coalition consisting of the conservative Austrian People's Party (ÖVP), SPÖ, and NEOS took over the reins of government without the FPÖ. The new foreign minister, Beate Meinl-Reisinger from the pro-European liberal NEOS party, affirmed Austria's support for Ukraine and paid her second official visit to Kyiv in this function. The Austrian foreign minister's consistent stance repeatedly triggers hostility from pro-Russian and right-wing populist forces.

In June 2025, Ukrainian President Volodymyr Zelensky visited Austria for the first time since the Russian invasion, accompanied by his wife Olena Zelenska, and met with Austrian President Alexander Van der Bellen (Fig. 12.3) and Chancellor Christian Stocker (ÖVP).

Fig. 12.3 Ukrainian President Volodymyr Zelensky and First Lady Olena Zelenska (both in the middle) with Austrian President Alexander Van der Bellen and First Lady Doris Schmidauer during the official visit in Vienna, Austria on June 16, 2025. (Photo: Stefan Schocher)

12.5 Belarus

The history of Belarus dates back more than a thousand years. The city of Polotsk, first mentioned in writing in the ninth century, was the center of the Polotsk Principality, which later became part of Kyivan Rus. Over the centuries, today's Belarusian territories came under the control of the Grand Duchy of Lithuania, the Polish-Lithuanian Commonwealth and the Russian Tsarist Empire. After the collapse of the Russian Empire, the Belarusians founded the independent Belarusian People's Republic in 1918. Like the Ukrainian People's Republic, this was crushed by the Russian Bolsheviks and incorporated into the newly founded Soviet Union as the Belarusian Soviet Republic. In 1991, Belarus declared its independence.

In 1994, Alyaksandr Lukashenka (Russian modification: Alexander Lukashenko) was elected President of Belarus. He has built an authoritarian, repressive, pro-Russian regime and has clung to power ever since. Lukashenka pursued a policy of close alignment with Russia and made the country dependent on Russia in many ways. After widespread electoral fraud during the Belarusian presidential election in 2020, massive protests against Lukashenka's regime erupted across the country. The demonstrations were brutally suppressed.

Belarus has 9.4 million inhabitants. Centuries of Russification have almost completely pushed the Belarusian language out of public life. Although today both Russian and Belarusian are official languages in Belarus, Russian dominates official communication, the media and everyday life.

The Belarusian government is supporting Russia in the war against Ukraine. Lukashenka enabled the Russian army to attack Ukraine from Belarusian territory although Belarusian army itself does not fight in Ukraine.

After the attempted uprising at the end of June 2023 by the Wagner paramilitary group, which was fighting in Ukraine on Russia's side, Lukashenka allowed the Wagner mercenaries and their leader Yevgeny Prigozhin to relocate to Belarus.

Belarus regularly conducts joint military exercises with Russia. In July 2024, joint Belarusian-Chinese military drills took place near the Polish border.

Reports also indicate that several thousand Ukrainian children were forcibly taken to Belarus.

The EU, the USA, the UK, Japan, Canada and numerous other countries imposed sanctions on Belarus.

During the war in Ukraine, an anti-war movement emerged in Belarus. Belarusian opponents of the war repeatedly carried out attacks, e.g., on Belarusian military airfields and railroad lines used to support Russian military operations and supply routes in Ukraine.

12.6 North Korea

In September 2023, the dictator of communist North Korea (officially known as the Democratic People's Republic of Korea), Kim Jong Un, visited Moscow. In June 2024, Russian President Putin paid a return visit to the North Korean capital Pyongyang, during which Kim Jong Un and Putin signed a treaty on comprehensive strategic partnership and mutual military assistance. Thus, North Korea supplies the Kremlin with artillery ammunition, missiles, and other military goods.

Ships began transporting hundreds of containers from the North Korean port of Rajin to Russia as early as September 2023, according to research by the Reuters news agency. Estimates suggest that North Korea delivered at least four million artillery shells to Russia by May 2025. The deliveries represent the most significant direct military aid for Russia's war effort.

Since October 2024, approximately 11,000 North Korean soldiers have been stationed on the front lines in the Kursk region of Russia. According to a South

Korean security source, North Korea sent another 3000 soldiers by mid-February 2025. According to a report by the British Ministry of Defense, approximately 6000 North Korean soldiers were killed or wounded in fighting against Ukrainian forces by June 2025.

12.7 Syria

Since 1970, Syria has been ruled by an authoritarian regime under the presidency of Hafiz al-Assad, and after his death in 2000 under the leadership of his son Bashar al-Assad as president. In 2011, Assad violently suppressed the initially peaceful protests demanding political freedoms during the so-called "Arab Spring," which then triggered a civil war in Syria.

Russia, Iran, the Iranian-backed Lebanese Hezbollah militia and China supported Assad's government. Terrorist Islamist groups such as the Islamic State (abbreviated to IS or ISIS) and others claimed to rule Syria.

The USA, France and the UK supported opposition forces fighting against the Assad regime and the Islamists. Turkey supported opposition members loyal to it, with the exception of Kurdish groups, as it wanted to prevent the Kurds from gaining influence.

Moscow already maintained close contacts with the Syrian regime during the Soviet era. Russian mercenaries from the shadow army "Wagner Group" worked for Assad. When forces loyal to the government lost almost all of Syria's territory in 2015, Russia flew massive airstrikes, mainly against opposition forces, helping Assad to re-establish control. The Russian bombing of the city of Aleppo in 2016 and again in 2024 became infamous. The attacks and the brutality of war forced tens of thousands of Syrians to flee, including to Europe.

The Russian airstrikes in Syria regularly led to high casualty figures among the Syrian population, mainly targeting civilian infrastructure such as hospitals, water supply companies and grocery stores.

In Syria, Moscow also developed the "double tap" tactic (= double strike). This involves striking a target twice in succession, with the second strike delayed to hit first responders and rescue teams rushing to the scene, thus maximizing casualties and injuries. Moscow now often uses this method against Ukraine.

In 2024, Ukraine supported the Syrian opposition forces with drones; in September 2024, Ukrainian intelligence services attacked a Russian military base near Aleppo.

On November 27, 2024, the rebels opposing Assad's rule, led by the Hai'at Tahrir ash-Sham (HTS) and the Turkish-backed Free Syrian Army, launched a major offensive. Within 12 days, they captured large parts of the country, including the capital Damascus, leading to the fall of the Assad regime on the night of December 7–8, 2024. Assad fled to Moscow. The Russian military began withdrawing its forces from the Hmeimim military airport near Latakia and the Tartus naval base.

The fall of the Assad regime in Syria was a major setback for Russia, complicating its operations in African countries, especially its logistics, weapons supplies and personnel rotations of the Russian military units of the Africa Corps.

Since the end of Assad's rule, the new government has been working to rebuild the country and establish closer ties with the international community.

12.8 China

The People's Republic of China, which has been ruled authoritatively by the Chinese Communist Party since the mid-twentieth century, was described by NATO in July 2024 as a "key enabler" of Russia's war against Ukraine. A good half of all goods that are important for the Russian economy or military industry come from the People's Republic. These include electrical appliances, vehicles, raw materials and, above all, so-called dual-use goods, i.e., products that can be used for civilian and military purposes, such as machine tools, microelectronics and chemicals that are essential for the production of ammunition and rocket fuels. In 2025, Ukraine reported reliable information from its intelligence services that China was directly supplying at least 20 Russian arms factories with gunpowder and components.

China's actions are helping the Russian Federation to circumvent Western sanctions. The majority of imported technology and components in Russian weapons originate in the West and are passed on to Russia by Chinese intermediaries. After Russia's invasion of Ukraine, China increased imports of Russian gas and oil, albeit at discounted prices, and is providing necessary services to ships in Russia's shadow fleet (see Sect. 15.2). In this way, the People's Republic is partially compensating Russia for the profits it has lost due to Western sanctions.

There are indications that Chinese companies are testing combat drones in Russia and exporting them there, that they are producing some weapons locally in Russia, and that China is supplying some types of weapons (assault rifles and a laser weapon system) to Russia. The exact veracity of such reports is still unclear.

Satellite images show that China provided a berth for at least one Russian cargo ship delivering North Korean weapons to Russia.

At the same time, the People's Republic is trying to present itself as neutral, avoiding direct confrontation with the West and obvious violations of Western sanctions. Its strategy aims to expand its influence in Russia and around the world by strengthening economic dependence.

On the last day of 2024, Chinese President Xi Jinping reaffirmed China's good relations with Russia and his desire to further deepen them in his New Year's message to Russian President Vladimir Putin. The People's Republic and the Russian Federation would "move forward hand in hand on the right path," Xi said, according to the state news agency Xinhua. In May 2025, he took part in the parade in Moscow marking "Victory Day," as the anniversary of the end of World War II is known in Russia.

12.9 The Republic of Türkiye (Turkey)

Turkey has condemned Moscow's attack on Ukraine and has even provided Ukraine with some support on several occasions. Bayraktar drones made in Türkiye played an important role for Ukraine's defense in the spring of 2022. On the other hand, Turkey is one of the NATO countries with the closest ties to Russia. Turkish President Recep Tayyip Erdogan has a close relationship with Putin and speaks with him regularly on the phone; Putin and Erdogan have both been in power for more than two decades and rule in an authoritarian way.

In the war between Russia and Ukraine, Erdogan is attempting to mediate—similar to the case of the grain agreement, which Turkey negotiated together with the United Nations in 2022 and which is now considered to have failed. The major Turkish city of Istanbul served as the venue for peace talks between Russia and Ukraine in the spring of 2022 and the spring of 2025.

At the same time, the Turkish government has spoken out in favor of closer economic ties with Russia, has not joined Western sanctions against Russia, and is benefiting from increased trade with Russia, especially cheap Russian energy supplies.

In March 2025, Turkish Foreign Minister Hakan Fidan stated that Turkey was prepared to send its peacekeeping forces to Ukraine, but only with the consent of Russia and Ukraine.

12.10 Israel—Hamas—Iran

On October 7, 2023, fighters from the Palestinian radical Islamist terrorist organization Hamas and other terrorist groups attacked several kibbutzim (= communal settlements) and an open-air music festival in southern Israel from the Palestinian autonomous territory of the Gaza Strip. The attack began with a massive rocket attack on Israel by Hamas. The terrorists brutally murdered over a thousand people, wounded several thousand, raped and killed many women and girls, and kidnapped several hundred people as hostages, including babies.

As a result, a war broke out marking a new level of escalation in the *Middle East conflict*.

The Middle East conflict

The Middle East conflict is the dispute between Jews and Arabs over the territory of Israel and Palestine. It arose at the beginning of the twentieth century and repeatedly led to wars between the state of Israel, founded in 1948, and some of its neighboring states, as well as to numerous armed conflicts between Israelis and Palestinians.

The Middle East conflict has always polarized societies and politics, as its legal, political, historical, religious and moral assessments often contradict each other.

The state of Israel is accused in particular of occupying and settling areas claimed by Palestinians, such as Gaza, the West Bank and the Golan Heights, and of building fences and barriers in these areas, as well as denying the return of descendants of Palestinian refugees and imposing a blockade on the Gaza Strip, thereby exacerbating the humanitarian situation.

Legitimate criticism of Hamas focuses, in particular, on the denial of Israel's right to exist and its declared goal of wiping out Israel; authoritarian Islamist rule, terrorist attacks and the use of excessive violence, including against civilians; disregard for human rights, the oppression of women and children, and the abuse of civilians as shields (construction of military installations in civilian facilities such as hospitals and schools).

The Israel-Hamas war marked a dividing line between democratically governed states and authoritarian forces. Israel was supported to varying degrees by the USA, Germany, but also by the UK, France, and other Western countries. On the other side were Islamist militias such as the Palestinian Hamas and Islamic Jihad, the Lebanese Hezbollah, the Yemeni Houthis, and the authoritarian states of Iran, Syria under the regime of Bashar al-Assad, Russia, North Korea, and China. They support each other in the war against Israel in various ways.

12.10 Israel—Hamas—Iran

> If Russia had not invaded Ukraine, Hamas would in all probability not have launched such an attack against Israel.
>
> Giorgia Meloni, Prime Minister of Italy in an interview for il Giornale on February 27, 2024

One of Hamas' biggest supporters in the war against Israel is the Islamist regime in Iran. The regime does not recognize the State of Israel's right to exist. Iran's Supreme Leader, Ayatollah Ali Khamenei, declared in 2015 that Israel would not survive another 25 years. In 2017, a large digital clock was erected in "Palestine Square" in the center of the Iranian capital Tehran, counting down the days until the planned destruction of Israel in 2040.

On June 13, 2025, Israel launched a major missile attack on Iran's nuclear facilities and military infrastructure, killing numerous top Iranian military officials and at least six nuclear scientists with the help of drones. Israel justified its action by saying that Iran's nuclear program posed an existential threat to Israel; Tehran was pursuing a secret program to build nuclear weapons and had enough material to manufacture a dozen nuclear bombs that could be used against Israel.

The hostilities between Israel and Iran sparked a war in the Middle East, with the involvement of the USA and also fought on the territory of other states.

Relations between Israel and Ukraine are largely kept out of the public eye but are based on informal cooperation. Relations between Israel and Russia are marked by tensions. The Russian Federation supported regimes hostile to the State of Israel: the mullah regime in Iran and the regime of Bashar al-Assad in Syria (until its fall at the end of 2024). A few days after October 7, 2023, the Hamas leadership was invited to Moscow, which Israel also regarded as support for terrorism. In June 2025, 9 days after the start of Israel's offensive against Iran's nuclear program, President Putin received Iranian Foreign Minister Abbas Araqhchi in the Kremlin.

Given Russia's strong role in the Middle East, Israel is trying to maintain a balance in its communications with the Russian Federation so as not to further jeopardize its own security. Officially, Israel is not providing military aid to Ukraine and has not imposed sanctions on Russia.

However, Michael Brodsky, Israel's ambassador to Ukraine since 2021, hinted at communication channels between the secret services of both countries in 2025. Experts pointed out the similarity between the Israeli drone attack on Iranian military personnel and nuclear physicists on June 13 and the Ukrainian operation "Pavutyna" on June 1, 2025. In any case, it shows the direction in which modern warfare is moving.

According to Brodsky, Israel handed over components for an early warning system to Ukraine and promised American Patriot air defense systems that it no longer needed itself. A Patriot system was sent to the USA for scheduled modernization, but according to President Zelensky, it had not arrived in Ukraine by June 2025.

12.11 African Countries

Russia has massively expanded its influence in Africa in recent years, primarily with the help of shadow armies such as the private military company Wagner Group under the leadership of Yevgeny Prigozhin. Wagner mercenaries have carried out missions in Syria, Ukraine, Venezuela, and other countries. Since their arrival in Sudan in 2017 at the invitation of the country's dictator, Wagner mercenaries have spread their presence across the entire African continent through a mixture of military, economic, and political activities.

In the Central African Republic, Libya, and Equatorial Guinea, the Wagner Group has taken on various tasks for local leaders, such as reinforcing the local army, providing security services, and conducting military training.

The Democratic Republic of Congo and the small island state of São Tomé and Príncipe have signed military agreements with Russia.

In Mali, Burkina Faso, and Niger, they provide military support to dictatorial regimes. In 2023, the three military juntas founded the Alliance of Sahel States (AES), within which they intend to pursue a common security and foreign policy, create their own investment bank, and launch a large number of joint infrastructure projects. Their most important new partner is Russia, with which they have signed agreements on cooperation in areas such as the military, agriculture, and education. After 50 years, the countries left the Economic Community of West African States (ECOWAS).

According to reports, Russian mercenaries have committed serious human rights violations in a number of African countries, particularly in the Central African Republic, including torture, mass rape, executions, mutilation, destruction of homes, kidnappings, human trafficking, and the murder of journalists. The July 2023 resolution of the Organization for Security and Co-operation in Europe, OSCE, classified the Wagner Group as a terrorist organization.

The Wagner Group was soon followed by subsidiaries such as Meroe Gold (Sudan), Kraoma Mining (Madagascar), and Lobaye Invest (ZAR) to mine natural resources such as uranium, gold, and diamonds, among others. Experts estimate the turnover of companies linked to Russia in African countries at several billion

12.11 African Countries

dollars per year. These funds flow directly or indirectly into the Russian state budget and finance, among other things, the war against Ukraine.

After an unsuccessful protest against the Russian military leadership in Ukraine, Wagner leader Prigozhin was killed in a plane crash in Russia in August 2023. In 2024, mercenaries from the Wagner Group were incorporated into a military unit called the Africa Corps, which is directly subordinate to the Russian Ministry of Defense. Austrian Jan Marsalek, the former head of the German payment service Wirecard, who built up a Russian spy network in Europe, worked on creating a globally functioning financial structure for the Wagner militia and the new Africa force.

In addition to paramilitary activities, Russia used so-called soft power to influence African countries.

Russia developed political activities in countries such as the Democratic Republic of Congo, Equatorial Guinea, South Africa, and Zimbabwe. In Madagascar, Moscow financed political campaigns through the Wagner Group. Authorities in Chad received "political consulting services" from Putin's presidential administration. In 2023, Russia donated 20,000 tons of fertilizer to Malawi with the request that it oppose international sanctions against Russia.

For missionary work, the Russian Orthodox Church founded the Patriarchal Exarchate of Africa at the end of 2021. In the 3 years since 2022, the Russians have opened around 350 Russian Orthodox churches on the African continent, compared to four previously.

In 2023, the Russian propaganda media platform "African Initiative" was created in connection with the Wagner Group. Its headquarters are in Moscow, with branches in Mali and Burkina Faso. It produces content in English, French, Arabic, and Russian, with a high proportion of disinformation and pro-Russian and anti-Western narratives.

In February 2025, Sputnik, the Russian state news agency for an international audience, banned in the EU for spreading Russian propaganda, opened a new office in the Ethiopian capital Addis Ababa. Similar plans exist for South Africa and Tanzania. In addition to English, French, and Amharic (the official language of Ethiopia), these stations will also broadcast in Hausa and Swahili—the most widely spoken languages in West and East Africa.

Since 2024, new state-funded "Russian Houses" have been promoting so-called "friendship lessons" in schools in Burkina Faso and the Central African Republic, where children are taught the Russian language, culture, and history. Russia offers educational programs for students, as well as trips to Moscow and the Russian-occupied territories of Ukraine for journalists from Africa.

Observers criticize the Russian Federation's approach, namely the combination of (para-)military force, resource extraction, and proselytizing, as neo-imperialist.

Until 2022, Ukraine had only 10 diplomatic missions in the 54 African countries. The vast majority of African ambassadors to Ukraine are also accredited as ambassadors to Russia, with their seats in Russia. This complicates communication, especially with regard to Russian aggression. In order to deepen African-Ukrainian relations and counter anti-Ukrainian sentiment in African countries, Ukraine opened 10 new diplomatic missions in Africa in 3 years since 2022.

In August 2024, Niger and Mali broke off diplomatic relations with Ukraine over alleged support from Ukrainian intelligence services for Tuareg rebels. Shortly before, the rebels had killed dozens of Wagner mercenaries and Malian army soldiers and then posed for photos with the Ukrainian flag.

Further Reading

https://www.dw.com/de/medien-russland-liefert-luftabwehrsysteme-an-den-iran/a-69865911; https://www.welt.de/politik/ausland/article254047628/Netanjahu-Interview-Russland-soll-die-Hisbollah-mit-Waffen-beliefern.html; https://www.spiegel.de/ausland/israel-gaza-krieg-nordkorea-beliefert-hamas-laut-bericht-mit-waffen-offenbar-erneut-tote-bei-luftschlag-im-suedlibanon-a-7adeb5ff-c492-4e2b-8de1-13b3b1507987; https://www.ilgiornale.it/news/governo/ucraina-gaza-e-loccidente-mia-idea-pace-2288075.html; https://www.washingtonpost.com/opinions/2024/12/10/ukraine-syria-russia-war/; https://www.dw.com/de/partisanenbewegung-in-belarus-gegen-russisches-milit%C3%A4r/a-64844888; https://www.theguardian.com/commentisfree/2025/jun/09/nordic-baltic-eight-europe-western-resolve; https://techukraine.org/2025/04/30/ukraines-battle-forged-delta-system-catches-nato-eye-export-talks-underway-for-advanced-situational-awareness-platform/; https://www.youtube.com/watch?v=HOYh7XKtlu0; https://www.bpb.de/themen/europa/ukraine-analysen/nr-312/560844/analyse-wir-koennen-mehr-tun-wovon-die-ukrainische-ruestungsindustrie-lebt-und-was-ihr-wachstum-behindert/; https://www.reuters.com/graphics/UKRAINE-CRISIS/NORTHKOREA-RUSSIA/lgvdxqjwbvo/; https://www.radiosvoboda.org/a/posol-izrayilyu-brodskyy-khamas-rosiya-ukrayina/33290212.html; https://www.youtube.com/watch?v=09vyQNsc6eM; https://www.bbc.com/news/articles/c30pjv8vp8o; https://www.t-online.de/nachrichten/ausland/internationale-politik/id_100757588/wagner-russische-soeldnertruppe-will-mali-verlassen.html; https://www.theguardian.com/global-development/article/2024/jul/23/central-african-republic-women-girls-rape-sexual-violence-conflict-food-security-wagner-russian-mercenaries-un; https://adf-magazine.com/2023/03/new-report-examines-russian-wagner-groups-expansion-across-africa/; https://www.n-tv.de/politik/Die-Gruppe-Wagner-heisst-jetzt-Afrikakorps-article24713963.html; https://www.voanews.com/a/is-russia-courting-malawi-support-on-ukraine-/6994321.html

Support for Ukraine 13

13.1 Why Support Ukraine?

At the beginning of the war, many thought that Ukraine would capitulate within a few hours or days under Russian military pressure. The Russian army was considered to be the second strongest in the world after the USA. Russia is the largest country in the world in terms of territory and almost thirty times larger than Ukraine. However, the military successes and the resistance of the Ukrainians have persuaded the world to support the country in its defense against the aggressor.

The following considerations speak in favor of supporting Ukraine in its war against Russia:

- The will and ability of Ukrainians to defend their country, as evident in their strong resistance to Russian aggression.
- Liberal values. Ukrainians are defending their democratic state and their freedom – the fundamental values of the free world, especially Europe – against the authoritarian Russian regime and its allied authoritarian forces. For many states, this is a battle between democracy and authoritarianism.
- International law. One of the most important principles of international law is: no shifting of borders by force. If Russia were to defeat Ukraine, this would destroy trust in international law and the validity of written agreements. It would send a strong negative signal that the law of the jungle now prevails in international relations.
- Ethical reasons. The particular brutality of Russian warfare, numerous atrocities committed by the Russian army and the enormous suffering of the Ukrainian

population triggered a wave of outrage and solidarity with Ukraine in many countries.
- Self-protection. The Baltic countries Estonia, Latvia, Lithuania, the Eastern European countries Poland, the Czech Republic, Slovakia and the Republic of Moldova see themselves as the next potential victims of Russian aggression. They fear that Putin's Russia seeks to bring them under its control, as it did during the Soviet Union. Russia's hybrid war tactics against several Western countries have shown that Russia will also directly endanger Western societies if it is not stopped.
- Fears of a third world war. Experts have expressed the belief that Moscow would attack other countries if it were to succeed in Ukraine. In any case, it would be more sensible—and, from a cost perspective, more economical—to push back against Russia's aggression in Ukraine than to allow the destabilization of other states by the Russian Federation, which would require defending those territories and risk triggering a world war. This is especially concerning as the Kremlin uses men from occupied regions for its wars and militarizes children.
- Humanitarian reasons. The Russian war caused the largest movement of refugees since the Second World War. If Russia were to occupy even larger areas, this would displace even more people.
- Economic reasons. Ukraine supplies a number of countries with food. Europe has an urgent interest in the stable economic development of Ukraine but the Ukrainian economy is suffering greatly from the Russian war.
- Historical parallels with the Second World War. Historians note similarities between Hitler's and Putin's policies of aggression, though without equating the regimes directly.

Similarities Between Hitler's and Putin's Policy of Aggression

- The failure of the *appeasement policy* (= concessions and accommodation towards the aggressor) in Europe towards Hitler in the run-up to the Second World War can be compared with the weak response to the Russian annexation of Crimea and occupation of the eastern Ukrainian territories in 2014, which only encouraged Russia in its actions.
- The destruction of democracy. Both regimes came to power through democratic elections and subsequently restricted or abolished democracy.
- Spreading hatred and defamation of certain groups fueled by state propaganda. Once the population becomes accustomed to a designated enemy image, the inhibition to physically attack that group decreases. The insults

and defamation of Ukrainians as "Nazis," drug addicts, corrupt, and inferior people strongly resemble the Nazi rhetoric used against Jews, Poles, Roma, and Sinti.
- The claim to have been humiliated as a country. Hitler saw Germany treated unfairly after the First World War. Putin uses similar rhetoric, accusing Europe and the USA of treating Russia unfairly and not respecting Russia's greatness and importance.
- A cult of military strength and a strong militarization (= arming) of the country and the formation of numerous paramilitary groups, with a particular focus on children and teenagers, such as the Hitler Youth in Nazi Germany and the Young Army (see Sect. 6.6) in the Russian Federation.
- Invoking allegedly threatened minorities. Hitler justified his claim to the Sudetenland, part of the Czech Republic, with the alleged threat to the German-speaking population living there at the time. Putin is laying claim to the South and East of Ukraine under the pretext of a "threat to Russian speakers."

13.2 Overview

Ukraine is receiving a wide range of support from abroad in its resistance to Russian aggression. This includes measures and funds for Ukrainian military defense, such as the provision of weapons, military equipment, and ammunition, as well as training for Ukrainian soldiers in the EU.

Decisions and actions by international actors are also important, which

- directly or indirectly increase the resilience of Ukraine and Ukrainians: financial and humanitarian aid, trade facilitation (e.g., suspension of import duties by Canada), admission of war refugees, demining of Ukrainian territories, reconstruction of destroyed infrastructure, and delivery of energy equipment;
- make it more difficult for Russia and its allies to wage war: sanctions (see Sect. 14.1) and prosecution of war crimes (see Chap. 10);
- show Ukrainians a way forward: the process of getting closer to NATO (see Sect. 5.3), starting talks to join the European Union in June 2024, and different agreements on security between Ukraine and more than 20 countries.

Since February 2022, Ukraine has received aid from approximately 50 countries around the world, particularly from Europe and North America, as well as from international organizations such as the EU and NATO. The European Union has pledged a total of €251 billion in aid through April 2025, of which €156 billion has been provided. The US has pledged €119 billion over the same period, of which €114 billion has actually been provided.

The Kiel-based Institute for the World Economy (IfW) project, Ukraine Support Tracker, records the aid that governments or government organizations from 41 countries have promised and provided to Ukraine since February 2022. These include the EU member states, other members of the G7 as well as Australia, South Korea, Turkey, Norway, New Zealand, Switzerland, China, Taiwan, India and Iceland. Private donations or commitments from international organizations such as the Red Cross are not included.

Looking at the financial amount of bilateral aid (= between two parties, i.e., from state to state) to Ukraine in relation to the economic output or GDP of the respective country, the seven largest supporters of Ukraine are Estonia, Denmark, Lithuania, Latvia, Sweden, Finland, and the Netherlands. See top 7 supporters of Ukraine by GDP share in Fig. 13.1.

The highest bilateral aid in absolute terms, excluding shares within the EU, was provided in the period February 2022-April 2025 by seven countries: the USA (€114.63 billion), the UK (€19.27 billion), Germany (€15.92 billion), Japan (€10.74 billion), Canada (€10.36 billion), Denmark (€9.54 billion), and the Netherlands (€8.42 billion). See top 7 supporters of Ukraine in absolute terms, excluding EU aid, in Fig. 13.2.

EU countries provided additional aid under joint EU aid programs for Ukraine, so that, taking EU aid into account, the top 7 supporters of Ukraine in absolute figures include the USA, Germany, the United Kingdom, France, the Netherlands, Denmark and Japan (in descending order).

Ranked by GDP share of aid to Ukraine excluding EU aid, Poland ranks 9th, the UK ranks 10th, Canada 12th, the USA 14th, Germany 15th, France 20th, and Japan 21st.

The following subchapters portray Ukraine's biggest supporters from three top-7 categories: by GDP share; in absolute figures, excluding EU aid; in absolute figures, including EU aid; as well as Poland due to its high spendings for Ukrainian refugees. The ranking is based on the amount of aid provided to Ukraine in relation to the economic output (GDP) of the respective country, excluding EU aid, as this representation most accurately reflects the active commitment to Ukraine's resistance against Russian aggression.

In 2024, the EU agreed that profits from frozen Russian assets would be used to finance aid.

13.2 Overview

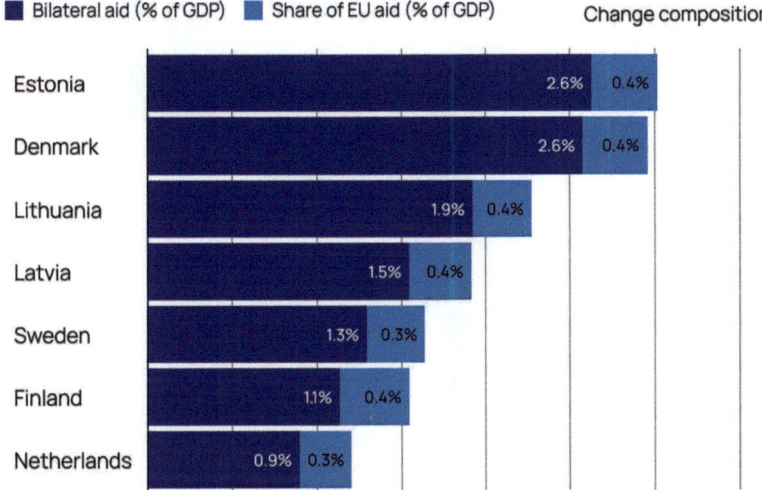

Fig. 13.1 Government aid to Ukraine from the seven largest donor countries in relation to their economic output (% of GDP). Data includes aid between January 24, 2022 and April 30, 2025. (Source: Trebesch et al. (2023) "The Ukraine Support Tracker" Kiel WP)

The USA and the European Union initially responded hesitantly to the Ukrainian government's requests for weapons and military equipment. However, as Russian fighting continued, with large-scale missile and drone strikes on Ukrainian cities and energy infrastructure, and in view of the Russian army's extreme brutality towards civilians, there was growing willingness to supply Ukraine with more sophisticated and modern military equipment.

Throughout the war, bevor and after February 2022, the amount of foreign weapons and ammunition promised was much lower than what Ukraine requested or needed to effectively fight the Russian army. Observers see this as a political calculation, primarily on the part of the USA and Germany, which, fearing escalation, provided just enough aid to prevent Ukraine from losing completely, but not enough to enable it to push Russia out of Ukraine.

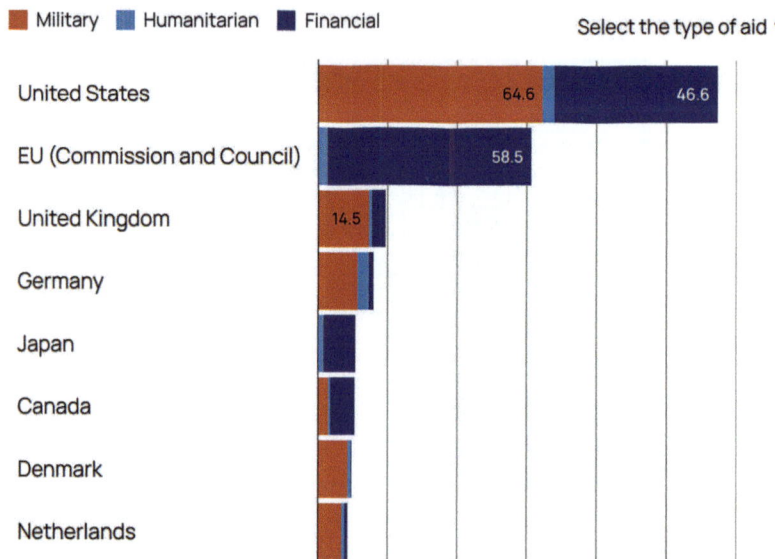

Fig. 13.2 Government aid for Ukraine from the seven largest donor countries and aid from the European Union in absolute figures. Data includes direct aid and EU contributions from January 24, 2022 to April 30, 2025. (Source: Trebesch et al. (2023) "The Ukraine Support Tracker" Kiel WP)

At the end of 2023 and the beginning of 2024, the Ukraine aid package of around $60 billion was blocked for several months by Republicans in the US Congress, which increasingly worsened the military situation for the Ukrainian army.

Since President Trump took office in January 2025, the United States has decided to stop providing aid to Ukraine. However, the Nordic countries and the United Kingdom have been able to fill the gap in payments with increased aid contributions. In March 2025, Sweden provided Ukraine with €1.6 billion, and Norway provided €670 million in April. In addition, Norway delivered more F-16 fighter jets than promised by mid-2025—14 aircraft instead of the promised 6.

13.2 Overview

According to reports, Russia continues to maintain its artillery advantage on the front lines. In the winter of 2023–2024, this advantage was 1:10, depending on the section of the front, and in October 2024 it was still 1:3. This means that for every three Russian artillery shells, the Ukrainian army could respond with only one, making it very difficult for Ukraine to defend its territory.

Due to bureaucratic hurdles and logistical delays on the part of donor countries, even military equipment that has been promised is arriving late or not at all. For example, Ukraine waited 6 months for the NASAMS air defense systems requested in June 2022, 9 months for the German battle tanks requested at the same time, and 18 months for the combat aircraft. The Ukrainian counteroffensive in 2023 started much later than planned and ended without success, at least partly because the promised Western weapons systems had not arrived on time. The delay allowed the Russians, in the winter of 2022–2023, to build large fortifications with trenches and tank barriers along the entire front line, making future Ukrainian offensives much more difficult.

The failure to deliver the promised air defense systems to Ukraine enabled Russia to carry out targeted attacks on Ukrainian energy infrastructure, causing widespread damage due to poor protection. The lack of equipment promised by Western partners to Ukrainian army units weakens morale and makes it more difficult to mobilize additional soldiers.

Western support is subject to numerous restrictions. For example, the EU and the UK are training Ukrainian soldiers, but not on the ground in Ukraine. Western political elites reject the deployment of Western troops (from the EU, NATO, or individual countries), and even a peacekeeping mission to secure a potential cease-fire remains an unformulated idea in 2025.

The USA and other countries have consistently rejected Ukraine's request to shoot down Russian drones and missiles over Ukrainian territory due to its lack of adequate air defense. This earned them accusations of double standards after the USA, Britain, and France shot down Iranian missiles headed for Israel in April 2024. Like Germany, these countries had also prohibited Ukraine from using the weapons they supplied to attack military targets in Russia. They only relaxed the ban after the Russian assault on Kharkiv in May and the increasing Russian attacks on the whole of Ukraine in November 2024.

In the early stages of the Russian full-scale invasion, Ukraine received Western-made weapons. As the war progressed and Ukraine developed its own weapons and boosted production capacities, the focus shifted toward investing directly in military equipment and ammunition manufacturing within Ukraine. In 2024, Denmark used interest from frozen Russian assets in the EU to finance the production of Ukrainian "Bohdana" howitzers in Ukraine for the first time. Norway, Sweden, Lithuania, and the Netherlands are following this "Danish model."

In April 2022, at the initiative of the USA, a contact group for coordinating military and civilian support for Ukraine (*Ukraine Defense Contact Group, UDCG*) met for the first time at the US base in Ramstein, Germany. Since then, the group has also been referred to as the "Ramstein Group" or "*Ramstein Format*" and includes representatives from more than 50 countries. The group's monthly meetings were held at the invitation of and under the leadership of US Secretary of Defense Lloyd Austin until September 2024.

After US President Donald Trump took office, the United States largely withdrew from the contact group. The subsequent meetings of the group were then chaired by the United Kingdom alone or jointly with Germany.

Within the Ramstein format, the so-called *coalitions* of states organized themselves in the areas of artillery, air force, air defense, tanks, drones, demining, and IT/cyber defense.

In addition to military aid, many countries around the world are providing humanitarian and financial support and taking in Ukrainian war refugees. Of the approximately five million registered Ukrainian war refugees in Europe in 2022, Poland has taken in the highest number of refugees—more than 1.5 million. Germany took in the second highest number, approximately one million war refugees. In relation to its size, Poland has taken in the highest proportion of Ukrainian war refugees, along with the Czech Republic, the Baltic states, and the Republic of Moldova.

Fundraising campaigns around the world, organized by celebrities, institutions, companies, and charities, have brought millions in aid to Ukraine.

Psychological services for traumatized individuals on site, treatment of Ukrainian wounded in foreign hospitals, scholarships for Ukrainian researchers, students, and scientists, as well as funding, performance, and publication opportunities for Ukrainian artists and cultural figures represent valuable assistance for Ukraine from abroad.

13.3 Estonia

Estonia provides the largest support to Ukraine in terms of economic output—2.63% of Estonian GDP went to Ukraine aid between 2022 and 2025. The Estonian people and government stand united behind Ukraine in multiple ways. Estonia was one of the first countries to condemn the Russian invasion of Crimea in 2014. The state was one of the first to deliver defensive weapons to Ukraine even before the Russian full-scale invasion in 2022. Estonia proposed to NATO members that in future at least 0.25% of GDP should be dedicated to military aid to Ukraine each year.

The coalition of numerous countries, the so-called "Tallinn Mechanism," named after the Estonian capital, is coordinating measures to strengthen cyber defense/IT in Ukraine.

EU High Representative for Foreign Affairs Kaja Kallas, Estonian Prime Minister 2021–2024, visited the Ukrainian capital Kyiv together with EU Council President António Costa on the very first day of her term of office on December 1, 2024.

Like Latvia and Lithuania, Estonia came under the rule of the Moscow Tsarist Empire in the eighteenth century and founded an independent state after its collapse in 1918. In 1940, the Soviet Union occupied the three Baltic states. They only regained their independence in 1991. The Baltic states therefore have a deep understanding of the mechanisms of Russian rule (including mass deportations), propaganda and hybrid warfare.

13.4 Denmark

The Kingdom of Denmark, consisting of three constituent territories Denmark, the Faroe Islands, and Greenland, has been one of Ukraine's strongest financial, military, humanitarian and political supporters since the beginning of Russia's war of aggression. The country, with a population of just under six million, has supplied the Ukrainian armed forces with a disproportionately large amount of military equipment, gear, and ammunition, with no restrictions on their use. In absolute terms, in military aid Denmark ranks fourth after the USA, the UK, and Germany, having transferred €8.6 billion to Ukraine.

In particular, in 2024–2025 Copenhagen provided Ukraine with 19 F-16 aircraft, tanks, and other heavy weapons. In view of the dramatic shortage of artillery ammunition on the front lines in the spring of 2024, the Danish government handed over its entire stockpile of artillery shells to Ukraine.

In 2024, Denmark invested directly in the Ukrainian arms industry for the first time, providing approximately €50 million to finance the production of Ukrainian "Bohdana" howitzers locally in Ukraine. To fund this effective and cost-efficient "Danish model," the country is also using the interest on frozen Russian assets. The Ukrainian side of the project is called "ZBROYARI: manufacturing Freedom" and in 2025 included eight other countries that are having equipment for Ukraine produced in Ukraine following the "Danish model."

The Danish government is working hard to strengthen the country's defense. In March 2024, Danish Prime Minister Mette Frederiksen announced that military service would be longer in the future and apply equally to women and men. Who gets called up for military service in Denmark is decided by lottery.

Denmark also plays an active role in the search for global responses to food security, energy supply, and economic crises. The Danish Prime Minister Frederiksen was appointed by the UN Secretary-General as one of six "Global Champions" for the "Global Crisis Response Group on Food, Energy, and Finance," which analyzes the consequences of the war in Ukraine and makes recommendations on how to deal with its aftermath.

The Kingdom has no special historical or other ties to Ukraine. For the Danish people and government, supporting Ukraine is a matter of values, and a willingness to help, and foreign aid projects are firmly established in socio-political practice. According to a report by the National Bank of Ukraine, donations to the Ukrainian army's special account in the first 6 weeks of 2025 (approx. $360 million) almost reached the donation level for the entire year 2024 (approx. $385 million). The Ukrainian National Bank informally explained the sharp rise as "payments made by a legal entity in Denmark."

13.5 Lithuania

Lithuania supports Ukraine on multiple levels. In addition to military, humanitarian, and financial aid, Lithuania, together with the other Baltic states, is strongly committed to Ukraine's accession to NATO and the EU. Together with Denmark, Sweden, and the EU, the country has been financing the EU integration assistance program "Ukraine2EU" since 2025.

In the fall of 2024, the government in Vilnius announced its intention to invest in the production of the newly developed Ukrainian missile-drone "Palianytsia" on site in Ukraine.

At the end of 2023, Lithuania and Iceland launched a coalition for demining Ukraine.

A Lithuanian fundraising initiative collected €14 million for radar equipment for Ukraine in February 2023. Lithuanian institutions had already begun rebuilding destroyed urban infrastructure, such as Ukrainian kindergartens, and constructing air-raid shelters in Ukrainian schools in the summer of 2022.

Andrius Kubilius, Lithuania's former prime minister, who became EU Commissioner for Defense and Space in December 2024, is calling for higher investment in the European defense industry in light of Russian aggression.

In May 2025, plans for the "1 + 1" production of the Ukrainian surface drone "Magura" in Lithuania were made public: Lithuania is financing the production, with one drone going to Ukraine and one remaining for the Lithuanian Navy.

Lithuania and Ukraine are historically intertwined. The medieval Grand Duchy of Lithuania (thirteenth to eighteenth centuries) also extended in part over the territory of present-day Ukraine and the former territories of Kyivan Rus. The official language of the Grand Duchy of Lithuania was the evolved language of Rus (the predecessor of the Ukrainian and Belarusian languages) until it was replaced by Polish in the seventeenth century.

13.6 Latvia

Similar to Lithuania and Estonia, there is a consensus between the population and the government in Latvia that the successful defense of Ukraine from Russian aggression is the highest priority for their national and European security. Accordingly, Latvia is making a major contribution to supporting Ukraine.

The collective memory of the horrors of Russian rule during the Soviet Union since the occupation of the country in 1940, the liberation struggle, Russification policies and repression against local elites makes the country less receptive to Russian narratives.

In August 2022, the Latvian parliament was one of the first to declare Russia a "state sponsor of terrorism," whose actions in Ukraine constitute "targeted genocide against the Ukrainian people."

Latvia has consistently called for the establishment of a special tribunal for Russia for the crime of aggression. In May 2022, the country joined the Joint Investigation Team (JIT), which was formed by Ukraine, Lithuania and Poland and also includes representatives from Estonia, Slovakia, Romania and the EU.

Latvia, which has the longest border with Russia of the three Baltic states, has taken on a pioneering role in the development and production of new drones, primarily in support of Ukraine. At the end of 2023, Riga initiated the founding of the so-called drone coalition, which now includes a dozen countries.

13.7 Sweden

The Kingdom of Sweden had a long 200-year tradition of neutrality. In response to Russia's invasion of Ukraine in 2022, the country, under the leadership of Prime Minister Magdalena Andersson, submitted its NATO membership application simultaneously with Finland.

Swedish society and politicians agree that the Kremlin's imperialist claims pose a threat to European security and the international rules-based order. Swedish Prime Minister Ulf Kristersson explained his country's decision at the press conference in February 2024 with the words: "We are joining NATO to even better defend what we are and what we believe in: our freedom and our democracy."

The kingdom has invested 1.3% of its GDP in supporting Ukraine in 2022–2025 and is one of the top 10 supporters of Ukraine in this respect. The Scandinavian country contributed financially to the "Grain from Ukraine" program, under which various countries and institutions purchase Ukrainian grain for countries in Asia and Africa threatened by hunger.

In May 2024, the Swedish government decided on a framework for military support for Ukraine amounting to the equivalent of around €6 billion for the years 2024–2026.

13.8 Finland

For centuries, the relationship between Finland and Russia was characterized by Russian attempts to dominate Finland. Finland has always tried to distance itself from Russian influence and build a peaceful relationship with its neighbors.

The Hitler-Stalin Pact placed Finland in a Soviet sphere of interest. As a result, the Soviet Union attacked Finland in 1939. Finland was able to defend itself, but was forced to cede around 10% of its territory to the USSR. With the aim of avoiding the continuing threat from the Soviet Union, the government in Helsinki always took the interests and wishes of the Kremlin into account and remained strictly neutral. The German politician Franz Josef Strauss coined the term "Finlandization" to describe this policy of anticipatory obedience.

Shortly after the collapse of the Soviet Union, Finland joined the European Union. After the Russian full-scale invasion of Ukraine in 2022, the country declared its solidarity with Ukraine under the leadership of Prime Minister Sanna Marin, rejected neutrality (which it had chosen in order to escape Soviet pressure after World War II) and joined the NATO defense alliance in 2023.

When asked about a potential neutral status similar to that of Finland as a possible way out of the war between Russia and Ukraine, the Finns firmly reject such a "Finlandization of Ukraine."

Finland's particular strength lies in its successful education system and the population's high level of media literacy. In various rankings in the areas of freedom of the press, gender equality, social justice, transparency, happiness and education (e.g., Pisa study), the country with its approx. 5.5 million inhabitants occupies top positions from 1 to 4 worldwide.

The country has resisted propaganda campaigns from Moscow for decades. When Russia annexed Crimea in 2014 and started the war in the Ukrainian East, Finland saw through the information war that Russia was waging against Ukraine and the West. In response, the country developed programs to strengthen media literacy, identify disinformation and carry out fact checks and established them at various levels, starting as early as kindergarten.

Finland is one of Ukraine's staunchest supporters. It has so far spent 1.1% of its economic output on direct aid, primarily in the areas of defense, development cooperation and humanitarian aid.

13.9 The Netherlands

Together with several islands in the Caribbean, the Netherlands forms the Kingdom of the Netherlands. Amsterdam is the country's capital. However, the Dutch government and parliament are based in The Hague. The city of The Hague is also home to numerous international institutions, including the International Court of Justice, the International Criminal Court and Europol.

The Netherlands is the fifth largest contributor to Ukraine's defense (after the US, the UK, Germany, and Denmark). In particular, the Netherlands supplied heavy weapons and, in the summer of 2024, delivered the first F-16 fighter jets to the front lines. The country handed over a total of 24 aircraft to Ukraine by May 2025, after they had been decommissioned or replaced by newer F-35As.

The Netherlands is particularly committed to investigating war crimes in Ukraine and prosecuting the perpetrators. It has provided funding to the *International Commission on Missing Persons (ICMP)* in The Hague so that it can use DNA analyses to find and identify missing and deceased persons in Ukraine more quickly. The Human Rights Fund of the Dutch Embassy in Kyiv finances local NGO projects in the field of human rights and the fight against impunity.

In April 2024, the Netherlands, Ukraine and the European Commission co-hosted the international conference "Restoring Justice for Ukraine" at the World Forum in The Hague.

For the Netherlands, it is indisputable that Russia has been waging war against Ukraine since 2014. On July 17, 2014, Russian-controlled fighters shot down the Malaysia Airlines Boeing 777 traveling from Amsterdam to Kuala Lumpur in the Donetsk region with a Russian BUK missile. All 298 people on board died, 192 of whom were Dutch citizens. A Dutch member of parliament and his family were also among the victims.

In November 2022, a criminal court in Amsterdam found two Russian ex-army members and a Ukrainian collaborator guilty of murder in absentia for launching the missile that brought down Flight MH17.

The court ruled that the Russian Federation had full control over the so-called "DNR—Donetsk People's Republic" by May 2014 at the latest, and thus an "international armed conflict" was taking place on Ukrainian territory.

Former Prime Minister of the Netherlands Mark Rutte took over as Secretary General of NATO in October 2024.

13.10 Poland

Poland and Ukraine share a long, complex, and at times very dramatic history. In various historical periods, Polish territories were under the control of Kyiv and Ukrainian territories were under the control of Warsaw (in the Middle Ages during the time of Kyivan Rus, the Grand Duchy of Lithuania and Poland-Lithuania or Rzeczpospolita); both countries were under the rule of other states or empires (above all the Austro-Hungarian Monarchy and the Moscow Tsarist Empire); they fought with each other against a common enemy but also fought against each other (from the First to the end of the Second World War).

This made the process of understanding and reconciliation all the more important, especially after the collapse of the Soviet empire in 1991, when Poland became the first state in the world to recognize Ukraine's independence in December 1991. The basis of this process was always the mutual recognition of existing state borders and state sovereignty as well as shared respect for international law. Over the past 30 years, the two nations have built a close and friendly neighborly relationship, strong enough to withstand occasional conflicts.

Poland was one of the biggest supporters of Ukraine in the EU and NATO even before Russia's full-scale invasion. After its outbreak, the country consistently condemned Russian aggression against Ukraine.

After the start of the large-scale Russian war in 2022, Poland took in most of the war displaced persons from Ukraine—around 1.5 million people. Due to linguistic affinity (Ukrainian and Polish are both Slavic languages and are more similar to each other than, for example, Ukrainian and Russian), many Ukrainians were able to find a job and integrate into society.

In 2024, there were almost one million Ukrainian war refugees living in Poland. According to a Deloitte report for the UN refugee agency UNHCR, 69% of those of working age were in employment (compared to 75% of Polish citizens) and contributed 2.7% to the country's GDP. The economic integration of Ukrainians has brought an increase in employment and productivity to the Polish labor market.

Poland acts as a hub through which Western arms supply for Ukraine is processed. Warsaw itself supplied Ukraine with various weapons and ammunition, organized the training of Ukrainian soldiers and facilitated the maintenance of Western military equipment, delivered several thousand Starlink devices for internet communication, etc.

Starting in January 2025, the newly established JATEC (Joint Analysis, Training, and Education Centre) in Bydgoszcz, Poland, is aimed at enhancing military cooperation between NATO and Ukraine.

There are differences of opinion between Ukraine and Poland on a number of issues, e.g., regarding the interpretation of certain events in their shared history, but also on contemporary matters. For instance, Warsaw continues to reject the request from Kyiv to shoot down Russian drones headed toward Poland while still in Ukrainian airspace.

Certain aspects are being exploited by some politicians in Poland to such an extent that they are also affecting Ukrainian-Polish relations.

In 2022, Ukrainian agricultural companies moved their grain shipments overland through Poland due to the Russian blockade of the Black Sea. Due to faulty management, some of it ended up on the Polish market. Fearing economic losses, Polish farmers protested by blocking the Polish-Ukrainian border with trucks from late 2022 to early 2023, disrupting both aid deliveries and passenger traffic. Pro-Russian posters occasionally appeared during these protests. In the period before the elections, politicians did not want to lift the blockade and tolerated it until a political solution was found.

While the Polish population's support for Ukraine was unanimous at the beginning of the full-scale Russian war, the social mood changed significantly with the rise of right-wing nationalist sentiments in Poland. In June 2025, the country elected right-wing populist Karol Nawrocki as president. He sympathizes with US President Trump and rejects Ukraine's accession to the European Union and NATO, which represents a prominent change in Poland's stance.

13.11 The United Kingdom of Great Britain and Northern Ireland

On February 20, 2022, 2 days before Russia's full-scale invasion of Ukraine, British Prime Minister Boris Johnson (2019–2022) warned at the annual security conference in Munich that Russia was "planning the biggest war since 1945." The UK's intelligence services assumed that a Russian invasion from the east, south and Belarusian territory in the north with the aim of encircling the capital Kyiv was imminent.

Boris Johnson had previously tried unsuccessfully to dissuade Putin from his invasion plans in a telephone conversation. When the Russian armed forces attacked Ukraine on February 24, 2022, the United Kingdom, together with Poland and the Baltic states, was the quickest to respond with military support, weapons and tanks for Ukraine, some of which had already been delivered before February 24. Throughout the war, London has maintained its leadership role in supporting Ukraine.

Boris Johnson was the first Western European head of government to visit Volodymyr Zelenskyi in Kyiv on April 9, 2022. London helped to train Ukrainian soldiers. The success of the British program helped convince the EU to launch a similar initiative.

In January 2024, London signed a 10-year security agreement with Kyiv, pledging the UK support in areas such as cyber defense, intelligence sharing, military training and cooperation in the defense sector. The agreement had a major symbolic impact, prompting other countries to follow suit.

The UK's all-encompassing support for Ukraine spans military, financial, humanitarian and political areas and continues to be highly regarded across all walks of life, political parties and governments. By April 2025, it had reached the equivalent of €19 billion—the second largest after the USA in terms of direct bilateral aid.

British intelligence services played a crucial role in the run-up to the full-scale Russian invasion and throughout the course of the war. The USA and the UK took the unusual step of leaking intelligence information about Kremlin's attack plans months in advance to warn decision-makers and the global public. This move undermined the Kremlin's claims that it was merely reacting to alleged Ukrainian provocations. The close cooperation and secret data from Washington and London contributed to the success of the Ukrainian counteroffensive in autumn 2022. The daily intelligence updates from the British Ministry of Defense on the situation in Ukraine counter Russian disinformation, an area where the EU still has room for improvement.

In 2022–2024, Britons experienced high inflation rates and rising heating and living costs. However, unlike in many continental European countries, no British political party has called for an end to the UK support for Ukraine to ease the crisis. Polls show that the public supports sanctions against Russia and is against pressuring Ukraine into ceding territory.

In January 2025, the United Kingdom, led by Keir Starmer (Prime Minister since July 2024), and Ukraine signed a 100-year partnership agreement. The agreement aims to further develop military, economic, and cultural relations.

The UK views Russia's aggressive regime as one of the greatest threats to Europe, alongside climate change and China. The large-scale attacks on peaceful

Ukrainian towns and villages by Russian missiles and drones evoke associations with the massive bombing of Great Britain by Nazi Germany during the Second World War.

Over the past decade, the country has gained sufficient experience with Russian hybrid warfare and hostile actions from Moscow. These include, in particular, the poisoning of former Russian intelligence officer Sergei Skripal in Salisbury in 2018, suspected Russian interference in the 2016 Brexit referendum and cyberattacks on British healthcare infrastructure, businesses and institutions.

13.12 Canada

Ukraine and Canada have long enjoyed good and stable relations, supported by the people, political forces, and governments of both countries.

Canada has the second largest Ukrainian diaspora in the world (after the Russian Federation). In the 2016 census, approximately 1.2 million Canadians identified themselves as being of Ukrainian descent, which represents approximately 4% of the Canadian population. Since the first wave of immigration at the end of the nineteenth century, Ukrainians have played an active role in the social, cultural, economic, and political life of this North American country. Many prominent Canadian figures have Ukrainian roots, such as Canadian Deputy Prime Minister Chrystia Freeland (2019–2024), whose mother was born in Germany to a family of Ukrainian refugees who later emigrated to Canada.

Canada, together with Poland, was the first country to recognize Ukraine's independence from the Soviet Union in 1991 (on the same day, December 2, but Poland's announcement arrived hours earlier).

After the start of Russian aggression against Ukraine in 2014, the government in Ottawa was one of the first countries to impose sanctions on Russia. Although Canada did not send weapons, it did send equipment to the Ukrainian army. In 2015, Canada launched Operation UNIFIER, in which trainers from Canada, in coordination with other countries (Lithuania, the USA, the UK, etc.), provided training for Ukrainian armed forces on the ground in Ukraine. Twelve days before the full Russian invasion in 2022, Canadian personnel were withdrawn from Ukraine. In August 2022, Canadian forces resumed training for the Ukrainian army outside Ukraine as part of the British Operation Interflex.

In 2022, Canada condemned Russia's full-scale war of aggression against Ukraine, imposed further sanctions, including against Russian propaganda channels Russia Today (RT) and RT France, and in July 2022 became the first G7 member to pass legislation allowing for the possible confiscation (= expropriation without compensation) of frozen Russian assets. In 2025, the Canadian authorities took legal action to permanently confiscate the seized Antonov AN-124 aircraft belonging to a sanctioned Russian company and to hand it over to Ukraine.

The Canadian government led by Justin Trudeau (Prime Minister of Canada 2015–2025) of the Liberal Party had been providing military, financial, and humanitarian support to Ukraine since 2022. The country also supplied weapons for the first time and in 2024 signed an Agreement on Security Cooperation with Ukraine. However, Trudeau's hesitant approach to aid for Ukraine, especially arms deliveries, was repeatedly criticized as "too little too late" within the Liberal Party and by Canada's other major party, the Conservatives.

In 2024 and early 2025, a domestic political crisis intensified in Canada. It was accompanied by accusations of facilitating drug smuggling, threats of punitive tariffs and mocking Canada as the "51st state of the US" voiced by Donald Trump, the new president of the country which Canada had previously considered a close strategic partner.

After early parliamentary elections, Mark Carney of the Liberal Party was sworn in as the new prime minister in March 2025. His policies were clearly defined: rejecting US threats and demands; intensifying cooperation with the European Union; building up defense capabilities at home and internationally, e.g., within NATO; and increasing support for Ukraine.

Carney's first foreign visit 3 days after taking office was to Europe. At the end of June 2025, the EU-Canada Summit took place, during which deeper cooperation between the European Union and Canada was agreed upon, particularly in the area of defense.

In March 2025, Canada increased its contribution to Ukraine's Energy Fund for the restoration of Ukraine's destroyed energy infrastructure in order to compensate for the funding gap created by the United States' withdrawal of USAID aid.

In June 2025, Mark Carney pledged $4.3 billion in new funding for military equipment and the reconstruction of Ukraine during a meeting with Volodymyr Zelensky at a G7 meeting.

13.13 The USA: The United States of America

Under the presidency of Joe Biden of the Democratic Party in 2020–2024, the United States of America (USA) was the largest supplier of weapons and military equipment and thus the most important supporter of Ukraine's defense against Russian aggression. This was accompanied by substantial humanitarian and financial aid.

13.13 The USA: The United States of America

The United States plays a decisive role in the Russian-Ukrainian war in many respects:

- the US aid provided is difficult to replace in the short term, particularly in three areas: the Patriot air defense systems, intelligence data, and spare parts for US military equipment;
- as the country with the greatest military strength in the NATO defense alliance, the USA has a decisive influence on NATO policy in the war, especially with regard to Ukraine's accession to NATO;
- as the world's largest economy, they possess enormous economic power; their sanctions to contain Russia's war, as well as tariffs, have a noticeable impact;
- the USA is an important and active player on the world stage. Its reactions and actions in international politics set the tone for many countries.

Some parts of the Republican Party and its representatives, especially President Donald Trump, who was elected in November 2024 (first time in office from 2016 to 2020), are critical of support for Ukraine. In the winter of 2023–2024, Republicans in Congress, the US parliament, blocked a $60 billion aid package for Ukraine for 6 months. Since January 2025, the USA has not approved any new aid for the Ukrainian resistance against Russian aggression, and aid measures that had already been decided upon have been repeatedly delayed or withheld.

Before taking office in January 2025, Trump promised to end the Russian-Ukrainian war within a very short time, in his words "within 24 hours." Since then, the intensive peace efforts of the US leadership have largely consisted of putting pressure on Ukraine (more on peace talks in Sect. 16.2).

President Trump acts in conflicts according to the logic of strength and power, outside of ethical considerations and with a focus on potential profits. His approach seems to be based on the assumption that a conflict or war between a "strong" and a "weak" party ends when the stronger party is strengthened and the weaker party is weakened.

During a heated exchange in the Oval Office of the White House (the seat of the US president) in February 2025, Trump and his Vice President, J.D. Vance, tried to persuade Ukrainian President Volodymyr Zelensky to give in to Russia, arguing that he had "no cards" to play, meaning that Ukraine had no strengths vis-à-vis Russia.

The following major and minor steps taken by the US government since early 2025 have more or less weakened Ukraine's position:

- No new aid for Ukraine was approved.
- Trump denied the possibility of Ukraine joining NATO; expressed an intention to recognize the occupied Ukrainian peninsula of Crimea as Russian territory;

suggested that Russia should keep the occupied Ukrainian territories; and imposed no new sanctions on Russia.
- As part of massive cuts to US foreign aid (USAID), the United States ended its aid to Ukraine in the areas of energy security, healthcare, press freedom, etc., in particular US support for the restoration of Ukraine's power grid after Russian shelling (January-February).
- Trump called Zelensky a "dictator" but refused to use the same term for Putin. Trump later toned down his statement (February).
- The KleptoCapture task force, a law enforcement unit within the Department of Justice responsible for enforcing sanctions and export restrictions against Russia, was disbanded (February).
- The USA suspended for a few days the delivery of aid to Ukraine that had been promised under Joe Biden's presidency, including aid that was already en-route, as well as the transfer of intelligence information and commercial satellite images from Maxar, resulting in direct losses for Ukraine on the front lines (early March).
- Government working groups on countering Russian hybrid actions, sabotage, disinformation, and cyberattacks ended their work (March).
- Keith Kellogg, the US special envoy for Ukraine, floated the idea of dividing Ukraine into several control zones, similar to Nazi Germany after its defeat by the Allies in World War II (April).
- The USA refused to condemn Russia's acts of war on several occasions, among others by voting alongside Russia, Belarus, North Korea, etc., against UN Resolution A/ES-11/L.10 condemning Russian aggression (February) and blocking G7 resolutions on Ukraine (April and June).
- Trump imposed trade tariffs on multiple countries around the world, including Ukraine, but not on Russia (from April).
- US authorities scaled back investigations into Russian war crimes. For example, the USA withdrew from the International Centre for the Prosecution of the Crime of Aggression against Ukraine (ICPA), an international investigative group looking into Russian war crimes in Ukraine (April). Trump cut the funding of the project to search for abducted Ukrainian children *The Ukraine Conflict Observatory* at Yale University's Humanitarian Research Lab.
- The US largely withdrew from the Ukraine Defense Contact Group (UDCG), known as the "Ramstein format." US Defense Secretary Pete Hegseth was absent from the Ramstein Group meeting in early June, the first time since its establishment in April 2022 on the initiative of then-US Defense Secretary Lloyd Austin.

The US President Trump has not granted direct aid to the Russian Federation, he even extended the sanctions against Russia decided under the leadership of his predecessor Joe Biden until April 2025. The US Secretary of State Marco Rubio also confirmed that he did not intend to provide military aid to Russia. At the same time, Trump and high-ranking US officials often showed a benevolent or understanding attitude toward Russia and Russian President Putin.

After several visits to Moscow, US Special Envoy Steve Witkoff praised the friendship that had developed with the Russian president. In an interview with right-wing podcast host Tucker Carlson, the envoy said he didn't regard Putin as a "bad guy," and that the Russian president was a "great" leader seeking to end Moscow's deadly 3-year war with Kyiv which Putin had unleashed.

In June 2025, Secretary of State Rubio congratulated Russia on its national holiday and affirmed the United States' commitment to "supporting the Russian people as they continue to build on their aspirations for a brighter future."

The USA sees China as the greatest threat to the country. Its efforts are aimed at persuading Russia to stop cooperating with China by making concessions. Personal ties of the US government representatives to Russian President Putin facilitate this approach.

Trump initially demanded that Ukraine compensate for the non-repayable aid already provided and add a massive surplus on top. To this end, he drew on the idea from Ukrainian President Zelensky's so-called "Victory Plan" (more on the victory plan in Sect. 16.2) of using Ukraine's rich deposits of rare earths. Without such a "deal," it was nearly impossible for Ukraine to acquire US military goods or services—even for payment—since the beginning of Trump's presidency.

After several months of turbulent negotiations, the USA and Ukraine signed a raw materials agreement on April 30, 2025: in return for future military aid, the USA would receive a share of the profits from the joint exploitation of Ukrainian mineral resources.

Subsequently, the US State Department approved the possible sale of training and maintenance for F-16 fighter jets to Ukraine for $310 million.

13.14 Germany

Germany is the third largest donor country for Ukraine after the USA and the UK in terms of overall aid in absolute figures excluding EU aid and the second largest after the USA including EU aid. In 3 years of war, the German government has provided Ukraine with bilateral funds totaling around €15.92 billion. This is roughly 1.7 times the direct aid provided by Denmark, while Germany's GDP is around 9 times larger than Denmark's and Germany's population is almost 15 times larger than Denmark's.

In addition, there are German contributions within the framework of EU programs as well as expenditure for Ukrainian war displaced persons and support from federal states, municipalities, private initiatives and companies.

Prior to 2022, support for Ukraine was not an issue in Germany's political debate. German foreign policy over the past two decades has largely taken into account the alleged Russian interests and the Russian point of view.

For example, former German Chancellor Gerhard Schröder of the Social Democratic Party of Germany, SPD (in office 1998–2005) has been a close friend of Russian President Putin for years. After his political career in Germany, Schröder held positions in Russian state-owned companies, including as chairman of the supervisory board of the Russian state-owned oil company Rosneft. In 2005, Gerhard Schröder became chairman of the supervisory board of Nord Stream AG, the operator of the Nord Stream 1 gas pipeline from Russia to Germany.

His successor Angela Merkel of the Christian Democratic Union of Germany, CDU (Chancellor 2005–2021) repeatedly showed understanding for Putin's policies. Together with the then President of France, Nicolas Sarkozy, she voted against the start of the NATO accession process for Ukraine and Georgia in 2008 out of consideration for Putin's wishes.

Following Russia's unlawful annexation of Ukraine's Crimean Peninsula in 2014, the Merkel government ruled out arms deliveries to Ukraine. In 2018, Germany approved the construction of the Nord Stream 2 gas pipeline for Russian gas, bypassing Ukraine.

A number of European countries and the USA have repeatedly criticized Germany's policy towards Russia for being too lenient or too hesitant. In Germany, there was a lack of understanding among the population and political elites of the possible consequences of the Ukrainian defeat for security and peace in Germany and Europe.

The German Federal Intelligence Service stopped its counter-intelligence activities against Russia more than a decades ago and, according to a report in the German newspaper *Der Spiegel*, only attempted to rebuild it in 2018. The warnings from the US and British intelligence services about Russia's imminent large-scale attack on Ukraine received little attention in Germany until February 24, 2022.

At that time, numerous German media companies did not maintain foreign offices in Ukraine or closed them and only opened new local offices as the war progressed.

Just a few weeks before the Russian full-scale invasion of Ukraine in 2022, Germany had refused to supply weapons at Ukraine's request.

13.14 Germany

On the third day of the war, German Chancellor Olaf Scholz (SPD, in office 2021–2025) started his speech in front of the Bundestag, Germany's lower house of parliament, with the words: "February 24, 2022 marks a Zeitenwende (= "times-turn," a historical turning point) in the history of our continent." He promised to provide Ukraine with weapons—anti-tank systems and Stinger missiles—for the first time in history.

However, a thorough review of past German Russia policies and misjudgments has taken place only to a limited extent.

At the urging of the German government, the EU had to weaken the planned 14th sanctions package in June 2024. The package was intended to prevent the circumvention of previously imposed sanctions against Russia and, in particular, to prevent the resale of European war-related goods to Russia. Germany argued based on its own economic interests.

With regard to arms deliveries, Chancellor Scholz pursued a hesitant, wait-and-see strategy. As a rule, concrete commitments regarding German war equipment were only made once similar commitments from other countries had already been forthcoming.

Until the coalition government collapsed in November 2024, Scholz refused to supply the Taurus cruise missiles urgently needed and requested by Ukraine. Despite repeated requests from Ukraine, the German government only partially allowed the use of German weapons to target Russian territory after massive Russian attacks on Kharkiv in the spring and on Ukraine as a whole in the fall of 2024.

After the snap federal election, a governing coalition of the CDU/CSU and SPD was formed in early May 2025, led by Chancellor Friedrich Merz of the CDU. The new chancellor is actively promoting the strengthening of European defense, more intensive support of, and a just peace for Ukraine. To this end, he is relying on consultations in various formats, such as the so-called "Coalition of the Willing" (approx. 30 countries), E3 (Germany, France, Great Britain), Group of Five (Germany, France, UK, Italy, Poland), etc.

On his third day in office, he traveled by train to Kyiv with French President Emmanuel Macron, British Prime Minister Keir Starmer, and Polish Prime Minister Donald Tusk for a joint meeting with Ukrainian President Volodymyr Zelensky. During Zelensky's visit to Berlin at the end of May, Merz pledged further military aid and expanded cooperation with Ukraine, without revealing any details for strategic reasons.

Merz sees Ukraine as a member of the EU and NATO in the long term, but has spoken out against its early accession.

13.15 France

France is a presidential republic in which the president traditionally holds significant powers. The current French President Emmanuel Macron was elected to office in 2017 and re-elected in April 2022. His stance has been instrumental in shaping France's policy toward Ukraine and Russia.

For a long time, there was little knowledge of and interest in Ukraine in France. Even a decade after the break-up of the Soviet Union into multiple states, recognition and attention in the country was primarily focused on the Russian Federation. In 2008, French President Nicolas Sarkozy (in office 2007–2012), together with German Chancellor Angela Merkel, rejected NATO membership for Ukraine and Georgia.

Following the annexation of Crimea and the Russian occupation of the Ukrainian East in 2014, France and Germany took part in the so-called "Minsk Peace Process." The corresponding contact group, which also included the presidents of Russia and Ukraine, became known as the "Normandy Format." However, the Minsk agreements lacked realistic implementation strategies from the outset and were never effectively enforced.

From 2021 to early 2022, Emmanuel Macron was in close contact with Russian President Putin, spoke to him regularly on the phone and visited him in Moscow on February 7, 2022 in the hope of preventing the full-scale Russian attack on Ukraine through diplomacy.

After the large-scale Russian invasion began, Macron's tactics, often labeled as "telephone diplomacy" or "appeasement," gradually lost relevance. By February 2024, Macron had shifted his approach toward the Kremlin, stating that no options should be ruled out in the war. He notably suggested the possibility of sending Western troops to Ukraine, and in December 2024, he further developed his idea of an international peacekeeping mission.

After the French government admitted errors in its assessment of Russia, French society also started a discussion about reassessing its previous policy on Russia.

At the beginning of Russia's large-scale war against Ukraine, the majority of the French population was in favor of aid to Ukraine. As the war continued, criticism of Ukraine and pro-Russian sentiments grew louder, particularly among right-wing and left-wing political factions. This intensified after the strong performance of the left-wing electoral alliance Nouveau Front Populaire (NFP) and the right-wing populist Rassemblement National (RN) in the early parliamentary elections in summer 2024.

Additionally, France has growing concerns over Russia's increasing influence in its former African colonies. Russia is skillfully exploiting anti-French sentiment in the region and reinforcing it with massive disinformation and anti-Western propaganda. Under the guise of fighting colonialism, Moscow supports military coups and dictatorship regimes in Mali, Burkina Faso, Niger, the Central African Republic (CAR) and Guinea with mercenary armies, such as the Wagner Group. France has recently decided to withdraw its military bases from Senegal, Chad, Mali, Burkina Faso, and Niger.

In Africa, dependence on France is increasingly being replaced by dependence on Russia and, in economic terms, on China. For more information on relations between African states and Russia, see Sect. 12.11.

As far as European issues are concerned, President Macron often takes the initiative and acts as a key proponent of new ideas. In 2022, he proposed a new form of political cooperation between European countries, including Ukraine, as a *European Political Community*; he advocates a strong European defense force independent of the USA; he is pushing the idea of creating a European army and sees France in a leading military role in Europe.

Since the start of the full-scale invasion, Paris has supplied Ukraine with military aid worth around €6 billion. This is the seventh highest contribution in the defense of Ukraine after the USA, the United Kingdom, Germany, Denmark, the Netherlands and Sweden.

During the first half of 2022, France held the presidency of the European Union and played a key role in securing Ukraine's EU candidate status in June 2022. The French government remains open to Ukraine's NATO membership and actively supports Ukrainian President Volodymyr Zelensky's so-called "Victory Plan."

13.16 Japan

Article 9 of Japan's 1946 constitution, which is considered "pacifist," renounces the state's right to wage war. Its initial interpretation as a strict limitation on military capabilities—up to and including a ban on having an army—has changed significantly over time. The country now has so-called Self-Defense Forces and a defense industry geared toward defense, but not offensive operations.

2014 and especially 2022 were turning points in Japan's history. In 2022, Japanese Prime Minister Fumio Kishida (in office 2021–2024) spoke of "the most difficult and complex security environment since the end of World War II" and warned of new hotbeds of conflict: "What is Ukraine today could be East Asia tomorrow."

Previously, Japan only considered North Korea a threat. The communist regime regularly fires ballistic missiles toward South Korea and Japan. At the latest with Russia's full-scale war of aggression against Ukraine, Tokyo realized that Russia and China also pose a real threat to peace in the region.

The revealed Russian plans from 2013 to 2014 showed that Moscow was seriously preparing for a local military conflict with Japan and South Korea and had drawn up lists of potential targets for civilian infrastructure, including nuclear power plants. According to a Russian intelligence source, there were also concrete considerations in the Kremlin in 2021 to start a war with Japan.

After Russia's invasion of Ukraine, tensions intensified around the Northern Territories/the South Kuril Islands.

> **Dispute over the Northern Territories/the South Kuril Islands**
> In 1945, Moscow, then the capital of the Soviet Union, occupied the islands of Etorofu, Kunashiri, Shikotan, and the Habomai group of islands and expelled the Japanese population living there. They belong to the chain of islands between the Japanese island of Hokkaido and the Russian peninsula of Kamchatka, which separates the Sea of Okhotsk from the open Pacific Ocean. In Japan, these areas are referred to as the Northern Territories, while in Russia they are known as the South Kuril Islands.
>
> Since then, Japan has been seeking the return of the islands through diplomatic channels, but Russia has no interest in reaching an agreement. The dispute over the Northern Territories/South Kuril Islands explains why there is still no peace treaty formally ending World War II between Japan and the Russian Federation.

There are also tensions between Japan and the People's Republic of China, on the one hand, because of unresolved territorial disputes over the Senkaku Islands, and on the other, because of China's increasingly vocal claims to the island of Taiwan (details in Sect. 11.7).

Since the start of Russia's large-scale invasion of Ukraine in 2022, Japan has strongly supported Ukrainian resistance to the war. The country imposed sanctions on the Russian Federation, supplied the Ukrainian armed forces with non-lethal military equipment, agreed on a security agreement with Ukraine, and provided substantial financial and humanitarian aid. Among other things, the government in Tokyo is participating in the demining and IT coalitions within the Ramstein format.

In March 2023, Japanese Prime Minister Fumio Kishida visited Ukrainian President Zelensky in Kyiv for the first time during the war. The joint statement by the heads of state on the special global partnership between the countries emphasizes that Russian aggression poses a threat to peace and security not only in Europe but also in the Indo-Pacific region, and that the violent annexation of territories and the violent change of the status quo (= "existing state" from Latin) must be resisted.

Japan strives for a world order based on rules and principles and rejects the use of force in international relations in light of its own pacifist constitution and painful experiences in World War II. Some voices argue that existing restrictions on arms deliveries by Japan should not extend to states that are victims of aggression.

The Japanese people perceived Russian nuclear threats particularly negatively. Prime Minister Kishida comes from Hiroshima, where his family members were killed in the atomic bombing in 1945.

After the US briefly halted the transfer of intelligence data to Ukraine in March 2025, Japan signed an information security agreement with Ukraine in April. Under the agreement, the Japanese satellite operator iQPS (Institute for Q-shu Pioneers of Space), based at Kyushu University, will provide satellite images for geolocation to the Ukrainian military intelligence service GUR. Japan has similar agreements only with NATO, France, Germany, the UK, Italy, Australia, India, and South Korea.

The new Japanese Prime Minister Shigeru Ishiba (since October 2024) assured Ukrainian President Volodymyr Zelensky of Japan's continued support during the G7 meeting in June 2025.

Further Reading

https://www.ifw-kiel.de/de/themendossiers/krieg-gegen-die-ukraine/ukraine-support-tracker/; https://edition.cnn.com/interactive/2019/05/europe/finland-fake-news-intl/; https://www.reuters.com/world/europe/hungary-set-ratify-swedens-nato-accession-clearing-last-hurdle-2024-02-26/; https://www.regeringen.se/pressmeddelanden/2024/05/75-miljarder-kronor-i-militart-stod-till-ukraina/; https://www.government.nl/topics/russia-and-ukraine/dutch-aid-for-ukraine; https://www.t-online.de/nachrichten/ukraine/id_100538750/-daenisches-modell-darum-produzieren-ukrainische-firmen-waffen-fuer-europa.html; https://www.courtmh17.com/en/summaries-and-news/news/transcript-of-the-mh17-judgment-hearing.htm; https://www.bbc.co.uk/news/uk-politics-60448162; https://www.nzz.ch/english/why-britains-support-for-ukraine-is-so-strong-ld.1821436; https://www.stern.de/politik/ausland/ukraine-krieg%2D%2Dwelche-rolle-westliche-geheimdienste-im-spielen-32786220.html; https://www.sn.at/politik/weltpolitik/russland-setzt-frankreich-in-afrika-unterdruck-134719444; https://www.zbroyari.gov.ua/en; https://epravda.com.ua/finances/htozadonativ-milyardi-griven-na-specrahunok-nbu-u-sichni-803296/; https://www.deloitte.com/pl/pl/services/consulting/research/raport-analiza-wplywu-uchodzcow-z-Ukrainy-na-gospodarke-Polski.html; https://www.canada.ca/en/department-national-defence/services/operations/military-operations/current-operations/operation-unifier.html; https://prismua.org/ukraine-canada/; https://www.nbcnews.com/politics/state-department-terminates-us-support-ukraine-energy-grid-restoration-rcna194259; https://truthsocial.com/@realDonaldTrump/posts/114031332924234939; https://www.washingtonpost.com/national-security/2025/04/22/trump-russia-war-crimes-intelligence-ukraine/; https://www.msn.com/en-us/news/world/yale-project-tracking-stolen-ukrainian-children-shuts-down-after-trump-cuts-funding/ar-AA1GySm9; https://www.merkur.de/politik/russland-japan-ukraine-krieg-geheimdienst-whistleblower-kreml-fsb-kurilen-angriff-91939950.html; https://www.bbc.com/ukrainian/articles/c6pqmn92g3lo

Economic Impact of the War 14

14.1 Sanctions

Since Russia's annexation of Crimea in 2014, there have been isolated sanctions imposed by the EU and some other countries, such as the USA. In direct response to the Russian invasion on February 24, 2022, many countries imposed or tightened sanctions against Russia. Additional sanctions followed as the war progressed.

> Various countries and international organizations imposed sanctions of varying degrees of severity on the Russian state, its organizations and individuals. These include the EU and other European countries such as Switzerland, Norway and the UK; the USA and Canada on the American continent; Japan, South Korea and Taiwan in Asia as well as Australia.

The objectives of the sanctions are:

- to prevent Russia from purchasing weapons and their components abroad. This is achieved through military goods embargo (= ban on trading military goods);
- to cut Russia off from the international financial system so that it cannot use its foreign currency (like euros or US dollars) to finance the war. This is being done by excluding many Russian banks from the SWIFT payment system, banning loans to Russian state-owned companies and banning Russian state-owned companies from trading on the stock exchange;

- to weaken certain sectors of the Russian economy so that less money is available for the war effort. This includes restrictions on trade in Russian oil and gas, oil embargoes (= ban on trade in Russian oil), limited access for Russia to ports abroad, and a ban on imports of luxury goods and technology to Russia;
- to target individuals close to the regime and responsible for the war, making the war tangible for them—through travel bans, freezing of foreign assets, and banning economic relations;
- to secure frozen Russian assets for future compensation and for the rebuilding of Ukraine;
- to prevent Russia from manipulating and unsettling people abroad through targeted disinformation. For this reason, the Russian state-owned broadcasters RT (Russia Today) and Sputnik are banned in the European Union;
- to prevent other countries, such as Iran, Belarus and China, from supporting Russia's war of aggression through targeted sanctions.

The Russian Federation sometimes manages to circumvent some sanctions with the help of third countries such as Turkey, China, the United Arab Emirates, the Maldives, etc. For example, downed Russian drones and missiles also contain Western-made components that Russia is not allowed to buy directly. Russian oil and gas also sometimes reach European and other countries under sanction via detours. The sanctioning countries are therefore working to tighten existing sanctions and improve their enforcement.

Over 1000 companies have restricted or terminated their business activities in Russia since the Russian invasion of Ukraine, partly due to the sanctions, partly in protest against the Russian war.

> The following brands have withdrawn from Russia due to the war: Adidas, Amazon, Audi, Asos, BMW, Chanel, Coca-Cola, IKEA, Levis, Mango, McDonald's, Mercedes-Benz, Netflix, OBI, Samsung, Shell, Sony, Spotify, Starbucks.

Western companies that continue to operate in Russia are criticized for using their taxes to co-finance the Russian state and thus the war of aggression. Supporters of remaining argue that a withdrawal from Russia could lead to significant financial losses for these companies.

The largest taxpayers among foreign corporations in Russia are US companies (led by Philip Morris, Procter & Gamble, and Pepsico) and companies from Germany, such as the Metro retail group. Despite the war, around two-thirds of German companies remained in Russia in 2023. Nestlé (Switzerland), Auchan (France), Raiffeisen Bank International, RBI (Austria) also continued their activities in Russia despite its criminal war of aggression.

14.2 Russian Gas in Europe

The European Union was Russia's largest single market (= largest buyer) for Russian energy until 2022. Almost three quarters of exports of Russian natural gas and almost half of exports of Russian crude oil and oil products went to European countries in 2021.

The energy business is an important source of financing for the Russian state. Until 2022, the state-owned gas company Gazprom contributed around 10% of the Russian state budget revenue through customs duties, consumption taxes and profit taxes alone. Oil revenues normally accounted for a further 30% of budget income.

In 2021, the 27 EU member states obtained 23% of their energy from natural gas and 34% from crude oil.

The EU imports more than half of its energy from abroad. In the years before the Russian full-scale invasion of Ukraine, the EU slightly reduced its dependence on energy imports. At the same time, the share of Russian gas in gas imports rose from 26% in 2010 to 44% in 2021 despite reduced imported energy volumes.

Gas consumption in individual countries varies greatly, while overall EU consumption has remained at a similar level for years.

In 2021, Russian gas reached Europe from three directions:

- the "Soyuz" and "Yamal" gas pipelines run via Ukraine and Belarus via Poland and Slovakia towards Western Europe;
- Nord Stream underwater pipeline across the Baltic Sea to Germany;
- TurkStream via Turkey towards Bulgaria, Hungary, Romania, Moldova, Serbia, and Greece.

Following the annexation of Crimea and the start of Russian hostilities in the East of Ukraine in 2014, some countries reduced their dependence on Russian gas, particularly Poland, Italy and the Baltic states of Estonia, Latvia and Lithuania. They built liquefied natural gas terminals (LNG terminals) and pushed ahead with pipeline projects to supply gas from alternative sources.

In contrast, countries such as Hungary, Austria and Germany significantly increased the volume of gas imported from Russia after 2014.

Germany increased the Russian share of imported natural gas to 55% in 2021. Together with the Russian company Gazprom and co-financed by energy companies from Germany, France, the UK, the Netherlands and Austria, Germany built the Nord Stream 1 underwater pipeline in the Baltic Sea (started operating in 2011), and approved the construction of a second pipeline, Nord Stream 2, by Russia (never started operating).

The aim of Nord Stream was to import Russian gas bypassing Ukraine. Germany was criticized for this by the EU institutions, as well as Poland, Sweden, the Baltic countries, the USA and Ukraine. They warned of a security risk by bypassing Ukraine, as Russia no longer needed it for the transit of gas to Europe, as well as an increase in energy dependence on Russia. In 2021, Ukrainian President Volodymyr Zelensky described the Nord Stream project as a weapon against Ukraine.

> During the so-called *"gas wars"* in 2005–2006, 2007–2008 and 2008–2009, Russia cut the amount of gas supplied to Europe in order to obtain favorable conditions for itself. Experts spoke of "blackmail with gas."

Over the course of 2021 and 2022, Russia reduced the volume of gas to Europe several times and shut down the Nord Stream pipelines in the summer of 2022. In September 2022, unknown persons damaged both strings of Nord Stream 1 and one string of Nord Stream 2 in an explosion. The gas pipelines were not repaired.

Afterwards, at least 19 companies from 11 European countries filed lawsuits against Gazprom for breach of contract or non-delivery of gas amounting to more than €18 billion and were partially successful. In June 2024, an arbitration tribunal awarded the German energy group Uniper alone €13 billion in compensation, while the Austrian group OMV was awarded €230 million.

In December 2024, the agreement between Ukraine and Russia on the transit of Russian gas through Ukrainian territory to Europe expired. Ukraine refused to extend the transit agreement.

With the loss of other gas pipelines, gas volumes from Russia via TurkStream rose sharply.

Since 2022, numerous EU countries have been taking measures to reduce their dependence on Russian gas. In May 2022, the European Union launched the *REPowerEU* plan to phase out imports of Russian fossil fuels. To this end, floating

14.2 Russian Gas in Europe

LNG terminals were built off the European coast and investments in alternative energy sources, including renewables, were accelerated.

The United Kingdom took decisive action and gradually banned imports of Russian energy sources: coal in August 2022, crude oil and oil products in December 2022, and liquefied natural gas in January 2023. However, in the 3 years since Russia's full-scale invasion, around 76% of LNG shipments of Russian gas were carried out by ships owned or insured in the UK.

In 2023, Norway, the USA, Qatar, and North African countries were the largest LNG gas suppliers to Europe. However, Russian LNG gas deliveries to Europe also increased. Russian gas from the pipeline (main recipients Austria, Slovakia, the Czech Republic, Hungary, and Italy) accounted for 8% of EU gas imports. Including LNG, purchased mainly by France, Spain, and Belgium, Russian gas accounted for 15% of total EU imports in 2023 and as much as 19% in 2024—see Fig. 14.1.

According to estimates by the Finnish research institute Centre for Research on Energy and Clean Air (CREA), Russia has generated approximately €870 billion in revenue from fossil fuel exports since the start of the full-scale invasion in 2022 until April 2025. Despite a noticeable reduction, the countries of the European Union have purchased approximately €208 billion worth of fossil fuels. During the same period, the EU allocated approximately €131 billion in aid to Ukraine.

In May 2025, the EU presented a *roadmap for the REPowerEU* plan dating back to 2022 with the aim of completely phasing out imports of Russian gas by the end of 2027, minimizing imports of Russian oil, stepping up the fight against Russia's shadow fleet, and significantly reducing dependence on Russia in the nuclear sector, in particular by restricting supplies of enriched uranium. Hungary and Slovakia expressed their opposition to the plan.

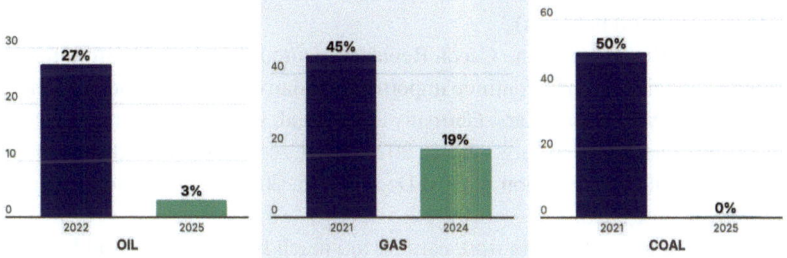

Fig. 14.1 Energy imports from Russia to the EU in 2021–2022 vs. 2024–2025. (Source: European Commission)

After the collapse of European revenues from pipeline gas exports, Russia was able to increase liquefied gas exports. From 2023, the USA imposed sanctions on some companies and ships working on Russian LNG projects. Prior to this, Japan announced the withdrawal of employees from a planned Russian LNG project. In summer 2024, the EU banned the transshipment and servicing of Russian LNG ships in EU ports as part of the 14th EU sanctions package. The UK sanctioned numerous Russian LNG ships in October 2024.

These measures had an impact: in the fall of 2024, Russia's Arctic LNG 2 gas export terminal suspended operations, and two other projects under construction—Murmansk LNG and OB LNG—were halted.

The Russian energy company Gazprom reported a massive loss of $6.1 billion for 2023, its first since 1999, and in 2024 the loss was even greater at $12.89 billion. This significantly reduced Gazprom's contribution to the Russian Federation's budget and thus to the financing of Russia's war of aggression.

14.3 Russian Crude Oil

Shortly after the start of the Russia's full-scale invasion of Ukraine in 2022, the USA and the UK announced a ban on Russian oil imports. Canada has even stopped importing Russian crude oil since the end of 2019.

Europe was the largest buyer of Russian crude oil until 2022. Overall, the EU countries accounted for 47% of the 230 million tons of Russian crude oil exported in 2021–108.1 million tons worth $50.9 billion.

In 2021, the EU covered around 34% of its energy needs from crude oil, of which Russia supplied around a quarter. One third of Russian crude oil comes to Europe via the "Druzhba" pipeline ("Druzhba"—Russian word for friendship) and two thirds by sea in tankers. In May 2022, the EU decided on a ban on oil imports from Russia, which came into force in December 2022 (for crude oil) and May 2023 (for crude oil products).

Slovakia, Hungary and the Czech Republic secured an exemption from the oil embargo allowing them to continue importing Russian crude oil via the "Druzhba" pipeline for several more years. Germany and Poland, which are also connected to this oil pipeline, chose to forgo this in 2022. The Czech Republic did not request an extension of the exemption beyond December 5, 2024, and thus stopped using Russian oil as of 2025.

In order to prevent Russia from earning too much from the global oil business and thus financing the war chest, the European Union, the G7 and Australia decided at the end of 2022 to impose a so-called "price cap" on Russian crude oil of

14.3 Russian Crude Oil

$60 per barrel (= approx. 159 L, a historical unit for crude oil that is still in use today).

> The price cap means a maximum price for oil transported in tankers to third countries. Most shipping companies that operate oil tankers were based or insured in the EU or G7 in 2025 (over 60% and 70%, respectively). The principle of the price cap is that shipments of Russian oil are only permitted if the price of the transported oil does not exceed $60 (approx. €57). The same rule applies to services such as insurance, technical assistance, financing and brokerage services for oil transportation.

Despite these sanctions, Russian oil exports remained at a high level but Russian profits decreased. The non-participation of India, China and Turkey prevented the sanctions from taking full effect. After the EU import ban came into force in 2023, Turkey doubled its imports of oil from Russia and at the same time doubled its exports of oil to the EU, meaning that Russian oil is probably flowing into the EU without being declared as such.

India, which became the largest buyer of Russian crude oil in 2024, processes and sells it to Europe as Indian oil products, among other things. India's exports of fuel to the EU reached several times the pre-war level in 2024.

By 2024, Russia had also built up a so-called "shadow fleet" to circumvent the sanctions with an estimated 500 tankers that use illegal techniques to transport Russian oil to India, China, Turkey and other countries. They manipulate their position data, rename themselves, switch off transmitters, reload the transported oil or mix it with other oil. This disguises where the oil comes from and at what price it was traded.

These "ghost ships" of the "shadow fleet" often sail under the flags of countries that do not have strict shipping regulations, such as Panama, Liberia, and the Marshall Islands. The owners of such ships have little contact with US or EU authorities, making it difficult to enforce sanctions. The oil tankers are usually very old and in poor technical condition, which has already led to a number of shipping accidents and oil spills at sea. In January 2025, for example, the ship "Eventin," fully loaded with Russian oil, drifted for hours in the Baltic Sea off the German island of Rügen, unable to maneuver, and had to be seized by German authorities.

There have been some successful efforts to improve monitoring of existing sanctions and introduce new targeted sanctions against the shadow fleet. In 2025, with its 17th package of sanctions, the European Union added 189 ships to the sanctions list (in addition to the 79 already specified). The US, under the presidency of Joe Biden until January 2025, and the UK also sanctioned a number of ghost ships. Canada and Australia also imposed sanctions on numerous ships belonging to Russia's "shadow fleet" in 2025.

In response, Panama went along and announced in November 2024 that it would revoke the registration of the four ships sanctioned by the US, with dozens more ships following suit in 2025. Barbados did the same. Time and again, some businesses from third countries also forego Russian oil in consideration of the sanctions.

Ukraine recognized the importance of Russian energy exports for the war and increasingly attacked Russian gas and oil industry facilities with drones, with over 60 such attacks in 2024 alone.

14.4 Grain

Ukraine, with its fertile black soil, has always been considered the "breadbasket of Europe" and supplies many countries with food. Globally, prior to 2022 the country ranked number one in sunflower oil production, number five in corn, and number six in wheat. In 2021, Ukraine accounted for 10% of global wheat exports, 15% of corn and barley exports and 50% of sunflower exports. At that time, agriculture accounted for just under 10% of gross domestic product, around 18% of employment and as much as 44% of the value of Ukraine's exported goods.

Rare minerals, iron, steel, wood, parts for the furniture industry and other products are also important export goods of Ukraine.

Countries in Africa and Asia are dependent on agricultural products from Ukraine, which are transported by ship across the Black Sea. After the start of the large-scale invasion, Russia blockaded Ukraine's Black Sea ports, meaning that no agricultural shipments were able to leave Ukraine until summer 2022. The resulting uncertainty and lack of exports triggered a global price increase for grain and other food consumer products and exacerbated food shortages worldwide.

In order to compensate for the loss of the sea route for Ukrainian agricultural exports during the Russian blockade, the European Union has lifted the existing trade restrictions and customs duties for Ukrainian food products, thereby enabling them to use the so-called "solidarity corridor," i.e., the overland route via the EU. The EU let the concessions expire in June 2025.

In July 2022, a so-called "grain agreement" was concluded under the mediation of the United Nations and Turkey, according to which Russia partially lifted its sea blockade for Ukrainian grain ships.

14.4 Grain

Ukraine exported a quarter less grain in 2022 than a year earlier. Some of the yields were destroyed by acts of war, not harvested or harvested and stolen by Russia. Russia reported a record grain harvest for 2022.

> In November 2022, the US space agency NASA announced that Russia had harvested 5.8 million tons of wheat worth $1 billion in the occupied territories of Ukraine judging by satellite images.
> Revelations show that Russia had planned the theft of Ukrainian grain months before the full-scale invasion. The Russian army acquired numerous grain trucks and three grain ships as early as December 2021 and began the coordinated removal of agricultural products in the very first week of the occupation of the Ukrainian territories.
> The main markets for stolen Ukrainian grain in 2024 were Iran and Yemen.

In July 2023, Moskow rejected the extension of the grain agreement. Shortly afterwards, the Russian army began bombing the port infrastructure of the Ukrainian port city of Odesa on the Black Sea. In addition, Russia's drones destroyed grain warehouses containing hundreds of thousands of tons of grain in the Ukrainian Danube port of Izmail on the Romanian border. This led to a renewed rise in grain prices and an increase in Russian food exports, particularly to Africa and Asia.

The European Union criticized the Kremlin for misusing food as a weapon and offering developing countries cheap grain as a substitute for the failed Ukrainian supplies in order to make these countries dependent on Russia.

During the Russia's sea blockade, Ukraine used alternative transportation options by rail and trucks via Europe's land routes and the Danube. Ukraine's neighboring countries had difficulty managing the increased quantities of imported Ukrainian grain, and at the end of 2022—beginning of 2023, farmers protested, especially in Poland. As a result, first the national governments and then the EU itself partially banned the import of Ukrainian agricultural products to Poland, Hungary, Slovakia, Bulgaria and Romania in 2023.

The successful Ukrainian military operations against the Russian Black Sea fleet enabled Ukraine to open up a new transport route across the Black Sea from the end of 2023. The export of Ukrainian food products to Asian and African countries, particularly as part of the "Grain from Ukraine" program, almost reached pre-war levels in 2024. As a result, the Russian Federation intensified attacks on Ukrainian ports and grain storage facilities. Since the summer of 2024, it has been regularly shelling grain ships in the Black Sea. In July–September 2024 alone, Russian attacks hit 22 merchant ships in the Black Sea under the flags of Panama, Turkey, Palau, St. Kitts and Nevis, etc.

Moscow's attacks on food production and transportation are a tactic of war and threaten the food supply of millions of people in Africa and Asia.

14.5 Inflation and Economic Growth

Global prices have been rising since 2021. The problems with disrupted supply chains during the COVID-19 pandemic and the high demand for consumer goods at the end of the pandemic are partly responsible for this. In some countries, inflation rates reached double digits before February 24, 2022.

Irregular energy supplies and the grain blockade by Russia starting in 2022 also fueled rising prices for energy and food worldwide. The average inflation rate in the eurozone was 8.4% in 2022, but fell slightly at the start of 2023. Energy prices also fell back to almost pre-war levels in 2023. In 2024, inflation in the EU stabilized at just over 2%.

Russia's ongoing war against Ukraine has exacerbated economic instability around the world. War-related events such as energy supply cuts and attacks on grain warehouses and merchant ships by Russia are causing price fluctuations and concerns about food supplies.

Despite Russia's war of aggression, the EU economy, i.e., gross domestic product, grew by an average of 3.5% in 2022. In the following years, 2023–2024, economic growth in the EU slowed to below 1%. The global economy also slowed during this period.

The first half of 2025 was dominated by Trump's chaotic economic and customs policy, the resulting turmoil on the stock markets and the fall in oil prices, as well as the rise in oil prices after the outbreak of hostilities between Israel and Iran.

Further Reading

https://thepage.ua/ua/economy/yaki-veliki-inozemni-kompaniyi-pracyuyut-v-ukrayini-ta-u-rf; https://ec.europa.eu/eurostat/web/interactive-publications/energy-2023; https://www.bpb.de/system/files/dokument_pdf/Energieimporte%20der%20EU-27_0.pdf; https://www.diw.de/de/diw_01.c.838366.de/publikationen/diw_aktuell/2022_0081/europa_kann_die_abhaengigkeit_von_russlands_gaslieferungen_durch_diversifikation_und_energiesparen_senken.html; https://www.president.gov.ua/news/intervyu-prezidenta-ukrayini-inozemnim-zmi-69061; https://www.bundesnetzagentur.de/DE/

Further Reading

Gasversorgung/aktuelle_gasversorgung/_svg/Gasimporte/Gasimporte.html; https://reports.omv.com/en/annual-report/2022/directors-report/refining-marketing/business-overview.html; https://www.moment.at/story/osterreich-gas-russland-kritik/; https://www.reuters.com/world/eu-warns-that-russia-aims-create-new-dependencies-with-cheap-grain-2023-08-02/; https://www.dw.com/de/wer-kauft-russisches-gas-wenn-europa-es-nicht-mehr-tut/a-61411898; https://www.consilium.europa.eu/de/infographics/eu-gas-supply/; https://www.epravda.com.ua/news/2024/10/23/720918/; https://www.focus.de/finanzen/news/europa-kauft-weiter-gas-ohne-ende-aus-russland-das-sind-die-gruende_id_259902424.html; https://www.merkur.de/politik/russland-staatskonzern-problem-putin-nordstream-gazprom-geld-ukraine-krieg-zr-93079205.html; https://www.bloomberg.com/news/articles/2024-10-25/russia-s-arctic-lng-2-plant-halts-amid-tightening-us-sanctions; https://www.kommersant.ru/doc/7179952?from=glavnoe_1; https://de.rbth.com/wirtschaft/86093-in-welche-laender-verkauft-russland-oel; https://www.dw.com/uk/zaborona-tranzitu-lukojla-cerez-ukrainu-so-vidbuvaetsa/a-69755953; https://www.tagesschau.de/wirtschaft/weltwirtschaft/oel-geschaeft-indien-russland-eu-100.html; https://www.amp.gob.pa/noticias/notas-de-prensa/cuatro-naves-sancionadas-por-estados-unidos-estan-en-proceso-de-cancelacion-de-la-bandera-panamena/; https://www.bpb.de/themen/europa/ukraine-analysen/nr-304/552653/analyse-auswirkungen-von-russlands-krieg-auf-die-landwirtschaftliche-produktion-und-den-agrarhandel-der-ukraine/; https://www.independent.co.uk/news/world/europe/putin-grain-theft-ukraine-russia-latest-b2447644.html; https://www.wsj.com/world/how-russia-profits-from-ukraine-invasion-by-selling-stolen-grain-on-a-global-black-market-60cca0a4; https://ces.org.ua/tracker-economy-during-the-war/; https://energyandcleanair.org/publication/insured-complicity-76-of-russias-lng-exports-carried-on-uk-owned-or-insured-vessels/; https://www.russiafossiltracker.com/; https://commission.europa.eu/topics/energy/repowereu_en?prefLang=de#pooling-gas-demand; https://www.moscowtimes.ru/2025/04/23/gazprom-poprosil-snizit-nalogi-posle-ubitka-natrillion-rublei-zagod-a161809

Social Debate 15

15.1 Dealing With Russian Culture

The Russian government under President Putin is using culture for propaganda purposes. Cultural workers and institutions in Russia face a difficult choice: they can support official state policy, in which case they receive funding and opportunities to perform and develop their projects. If they do not support the government and the war against Ukraine, they are suppressed.

The new Russian strategy officially declares culture, science, education, sport and tourism (Russia uses the term "humanitarian sector" for this) to be part of Russia's influence abroad.

> Russian culture is an important part of world culture. As an instrument of 'soft power,' it contributes to strengthening Russia's international authority.
>
> The tasks of the humanitarian policy of the Russian Federation abroad are: […] protection, preservation and promotion of the traditions and ideas of the Russian world.
>
> Support and promotion of the Russian language is an essential part of the educational mission of the Russian Federation abroad.
>
> Excerpts from the "Concept of Humanitarian Policy of the Russian Federation Abroad," approved by presidential decree of the Russian Federation of September 5, 2022.

At the same time, Russia is waging a targeted war against Ukrainian culture. The Russian army is deliberately destroying museums, historical buildings, monuments, theaters, concert halls and libraries.

After February 24, 2022, a debate erupted in Western cultural circles about how to deal with Russian culture. Many cultural institutions in Europe and around the world canceled events involving Russian artists and Russian works of art; they do not want to contribute to the promotion of Russian interests through culture while Russia is destroying Ukrainian culture. Their critics declared that Russian culture remains worth seeing, even if the Russian government misuses it for its own purposes; artists should not be forced to take stance on politics and the war.

At the same time, those interested in culture advocate taking a closer look at Russian culture and literature in particular and questioning the views of Russian authors. The famous Russian poets Aleksandr Pushkin and Mikhail Lermontov as well as the writer Fyodor Dostoyevsky and others held clear imperialist views. They devalued peoples who resisted Moscow's rule, such as Poles, Ukrainians and Caucasian peoples as well as Western Europeans. The influence of such attitudes on Russian society and politics, past and present, should be examined.

Numerous artists and cultural workers from Russia now live abroad. Some condemn the war against Ukraine, others remain silent or continue to support Putin's government.

> Some of the Ukrainian cultural figures who lost their lives in the Russian war: Victoria Amelina, writer; Volodymyr Vakulenko, writer; Olexandr Shapoval, ballet dancer and soloist of the National Opera of Ukraine; Yuriy Kerpatenko, conductor of the Kherson Philharmonic; Rostyslav Yanchyshen, ballet dancer of the Odesa National Opera; Lubov Panchenko, painter; Oksana Shvets, actress; Pavlo Lee, actor; Artem Datsyshyn, singer and soloist of the National Opera of Ukraine; Elizaveta Ochkur and Sonya Amelchikova, two 9-year-old actresses from Mariupol.

15.2 Dealing With Russian Athletes

There is no independent elite sport in Russia. Almost all sports schools, sports associations, sports facilities and sports clubs are directly or indirectly state-owned. Athletes who want a career in Russia must align with the government's politics. "Enhancing Russia's authority on the global sports stage" is the official goal of the Russian Federation in the field of sport.

According to the tradition inherited from the Soviet era, sport and the army are closely linked in Russia. Athletes can do their military service in so-called sports companies of the Russian armed forces. Many professional athletes also sign long-term contracts with the Russian Ministry of Defense. Of the 212 Russian athletes who took part in the 2022 Winter Olympics in Beijing, 34 were military personnel, 15 of whom held officer ranks.

15.2 Dealing With Russian Athletes

In 2025, the Ukrainian Ministry of Youth and Sports listed around 800 Russian and Belarusian athletes and sports officials who support Russia's war of aggression. They include Vladimir Bakin, vice president of the Moscow Region Volleyball Federation, president of the CSKA volleyball club, and general of the Russian army; Nikolai Valuev, member of the Russian State Duma and former world boxing champion, who publicly justified the attacks on Ukraine, and Nikita Nagorny, Russian Olympic and world champion gymnast, leader of the paramilitary youth organization "Yunarmiya" ("Young Army") from 2020 to 2024, which provides military training to children and young people.

In recent years, several cases have come to light in which Russian state sports institutions, with the help of state laboratories, organized systematic doping of athletes. In 2019, the World Anti-Doping Agency (WADA) banned the Russian Federation from participating in the Olympic Games and World Championships due to doping. Russian athletes were only allowed to compete under a neutral flag, not under the Russian state flag.

- **Doping**—the use of illicit substances to enhance athletic performance.

Due to the war against Ukraine, several international sports federations banned athletes from Russia and Belarus in 2022, such as the World Athletics Association (WA), the world federations for cycling, skiing, field hockey, triathlon and badminton, rowing, canoeing and rugby. Russian and Belarusian athletes were also excluded from the UEFA and FIFA soccer competitions taking place in 2023, the European handball and volleyball and the World Figure Skating Championships.

In March 2023, the International Olympic Committee (IOC) spoke out in favor of a partial return of Russian athletes to competitions under certain conditions. Fifteen Russian and 16 Belarusian athletes from the Russian Federation were admitted as "neutrals" to participate in the Olympic Games in Paris in July-August 2024. This decision was criticized as contradicting the "Olympic idea" in the midst of Russia's war.

> The Olympic idea is that sport and sporting competitions such as the Olympic Games should serve to show top sporting performance, to compare it in peaceful competition, to promote friendship and international understanding and to observe the rule of fair play.

Fig. 15.1 Girl with ribbon, graffiti by street artist Banksy in Irpin, a suburb of Kyiv. (Photo: Rasal Hague. Source: Wikimedia)

It is neither fair nor peaceful for Russia to kill Ukrainian athletes and destroy training facilities. According to Ukrainian sources, by August 2024, about 500 Ukrainian athletes had been killed in the war, and over 500 sports facilities had been destroyed.

The world-famous street artist Banksy attempted to capture what sport feels like during the war against one's own country in one of his artworks in Irpin, a suburb of Kyiv (Fig. 15.1). The graffiti depicts a young gymnast with a neck brace and a waving ribbon balancing over a black hole bombed into the wall. Banksy left several works of art in Ukraine in November 2022, mostly on the ruins of houses damaged in the war. Banksy later donated the proceeds from 50 prints of the graffiti to Ukraine.

In early June 2025, the Ukrainian national athletics team came under Russian rocket fire in Lutsk, western Ukraine. A rocket hit the hotel where the team members were staying during the national championships.

Among the Ukrainian athletes killed in the Russian war of aggression against Ukraine are two-time European weightlifting champion Oleksandr Pielieshenko, four-time world kickboxing champion Vitaly Merinov, Ukrainian kickboxing champion and Muay Thai world champion Oleksiy Yanin, Ukrainian national athletics champion Roman Havryliuk, cyclist and national champion Andriy Kutsenko, fencer and multiple national champion Denys Boreyko, figure skater Dmytro Sharpar, biathlete Yevhen Malyshev, track and field athlete Yury Mochulskyi, soccer players Vitalii Sapylo, Dmytro Martynenko, Eleonora Maltseva and Victoria Kotliarova, 9-year-old judoka Victoria Ivashko, Ukrainian national champion in ballroom dancing Daryna Kurdel and many others.

15.3 Westsplaining

For a long time, European countries under Russian influence or control, including Russia itself, were labeled as "Eastern Europe" by Western European countries and North America. This is why, for example, the Czech Republic was referred to as "Eastern European," even though its capital Prague is geographically located further west than "Western" Vienna, the capital of Austria. Until the end of the twentieth century, Eastern European studies at universities and research institutions around the world were mostly concerned with researching Russia.

The Russian state propaganda itself now describes the Czech Republic, Poland, Slovakia, Estonia, Latvia, Lithuania, etc., which sought to break away from Russian influence after the collapse of the Soviet Union in 1991 and which are still often referred to as "Eastern Europe," as part of the "hostile West." Since Russia's war against Ukraine, the term "Westsplaining" has been increasingly used in the social debate. It is based on the word "mansplaining," which emerged a few years ago.

Mansplaining (from the English "Man explaining things to woman") describes the situation when a man lectures a woman about something she knows better herself.

- **Westsplaining**—speaking about the countries of "Eastern Europe" from the perspective of the West, but without sufficient expertise and from a position of authority. The interests and views of Russia are often given greater weight than the interests of other states.

"Westsplaining" is related to the concept of "Eurocentrism." Eurocentrism refers to a perspective on other countries that is based exclusively on European norms, experiences, and values, as well as on their assumed superiority over others. Both patterns of thinking are shaped by (often hidden) biases toward specific countries, peoples, and ethnic groups, and tend to overlook or underestimate the independence and agency of the countries being observed.

In African, Asian and Latin American countries, this approach is also associated with colonialism and imperialism. European countries such as Germany, France, Belgium, the Netherlands and Great Britain, which in past centuries abused other countries around the world as their colonies, as did the USA, were and still are accused of viewing former colonies and other countries as inferior. Yet, the colonial rule of Russia and the Soviet Union in Eastern Europe and Asia is still widely ignored.

In the context of the Russian-Ukrainian war, Westsplaining often means that Ukraine, or the Ukrainian state and the Ukrainian people, are not fully recognized as active historical agents. Instead, they are viewed as objects of decisions made by major powers, with Russian positions given more weight than Ukrainian ones.

The proponents of Westsplaining, whether consciously or unconsciously, view the sovereign decision of former "Eastern Bloc" states to join NATO as a hostile action by the "West" toward Russia; the unjustifiable Russia's attack on Ukraine as a battle "over Ukraine" between the superpowers the USA and Russia; and Russia's plans to occupy all or part of Ukraine as a "reasonable" solution to safeguard Russian security interests and to end the suffering caused by the war.

Such views see the world as made up of large, strong, superior powers on one side and small, weak, inferior buffer zones on the other. This corresponds to the imperialist narrative that the Kremlin wants to impose as the future world order with the help of other authoritarian regimes.

Further Reading

http://www.kremlin.ru/acts/bank/48280; https://pen.org.ua/lyudy-kultury-yakyh-zabrala-vijna-2022-rik; https://usp-ltd.org/zhyttia-myttsiv-ta-mystkyn-spaleni-muzei-i-vykradene-skifske-zoloto-vtraty-ukrainskoi-kultury-cherez-vijnu/; https://history.rayon.in.ua/news/501852-vtrati-istorichnoi-ta-kulturnoi-spadshchini-ukrainipid-chas-viyni; https://www.deutschlandfunkkultur.de/sportkompanien-in-russland-fuer-gold-und-vaterland-100.html; https://www.dw.com/de/ukraines-olympia-starter-zwischen-sport-und-krieg/a-69634356; https://www.rnd.de/sport/jaroslawa-mahutschich-eine-goldmedaille-fuer-alle-getoeteten-sportler-der-ukraine-5CA2G2GSM5HYRCSKO5A27DFADI.html; https://yangoly-sportu.team ukraine.com.ua/?lang=en; https://mms.gov.ua/russian-and-belarusian-athletes-who-support-the-war-in-ukraine; https://cepa.org/article/its-time-to-stop-westsplaining/; https://geschichtedergegenwart.ch/westsplaining/; https://taz.de/Westliche-Arroganz/!5854921/; https://www.falter.at/maily/20220406/westsplaining

What Comes Next 16

16.1 Military Solution?

Three and a half years after the Russian invasion in 2022, the Russian army controls Crimea, which it occupied in 2014, and areas in the Donetsk and Luhansk regions, as well as additional areas in the Zaporizhzhia and Kherson regions.

Fortunately, the brutal warfare and massive war crimes committed by the Russian army have not broken Ukrainian society.

However, Ukraine's ability to defend itself against Russia's military actions, i.e., the success of the resistance, has depended from the outset on support from abroad, especially air defense to protect Ukrainian territory and weapons for effective strikes on the front lines and on Russian territory. Western aid prevented Ukraine from falling under Russian pressure but it was not sufficient to give Ukraine a chance of military victory over Russia, meaning to expel Russian forces from Ukraine.

In the course of Russia's full-scale war since 2022, Ukraine has significantly reduced its dependence on Western arms supplies. In 2025, according to official figures, the country produced 30–40% of the weapons and military equipment it used, with the volume rising from around $1 billion in 2022 to $3 billion in 2023 and $9 billion in 2024 (900% growth in 3 years). In the drone sector, Ukraine covered almost all of its needs through domestic production in 2025.

Out of necessity, Ukrainian state and private, commercial and voluntary actors developed numerous novel technologies for use in warfare.

Some examples of new Ukrainian technological and tactical developments in the military sector are:

- for unmanned warfare: sea drones "Sea Baby" and "Magura V5" (in 2022, they succeeded in sinking a warship, the Russian flagship Moskva; in 2024, they shot down military helicopters and in 2025 combat aircraft—all for the first time in history), mobile land robots such as the "Ravlyk" mobile platform, demining drones with magnetic sensors, FPV drones (first person view—the person controlling the drone sees what is happening through attached cameras), fiber optic drones;
- military equipment: "Bohdana" howitzers, "Khorunzhyi" troop transporters;
- missiles: "Peklo," "Trembita," "Palianytsia" missile drone;
- laser weapons: "Trysub" weapon system (Ukrainian word for trident—main element of the Ukrainian coat of arms);
- ammunition: 2024 saw the first harvest of cotton for domestic gunpowder production; half of all artillery ammunition was "made in Ukraine" in 2024;
- system solutions: "DELTA" military software for real-time monitoring of events on the battlefield, AI-based platform for detecting enemy targets Avengers.

According to official figures, in 2025 the country was working on developing its own air defense missile system similar to the US Patriot system.

Until Ukraine builds up its military production capacity to the necessary level, it will continue to need Western imports.

Throughout the course of the war, the Russian Federation has possessed a much greater quantity of weapons systems and ammunition in virtually every category. However, after gaining ground at the beginning of the full-scale invasion in 2022, the numerically superior Russian army was only able to make minor gains in Ukrainian territory during 2024, but at the cost of massive losses of soldiers.

Ukraine has shown that with fewer resources but more flexibility, willingness to learn, smart strategy, and intelligent warfare, it can stop a larger enemy. Ukrainian intelligence services have taken up the fight against Russia in cyberspace and are now carrying out regular successful cyberattacks on Russia's war infrastructure.

The following four Ukrainian military operations in particular demonstrated the striking power of the attacked country and marked a break with the established concepts and beliefs of modern military science:

- *Sinking of the Russian flagship Moskva* on April 14, 2022, and subsequent expulsion of the Russian Black Sea Fleet from the Black Sea. The lesson learned: it is possible to prevail at sea against a country with a fleet while having virtually no fleet of your own.
- *Kherson counteroffensive* in autumn 2022: it is possible to push back a numerically superior army.

- *Kursk offensive* from August 6, 2024: it is possible to occupy the territories of a nuclear superpower without consequences.
- *Operation "Pavutyna"* ("Spiderweb" in English) on June 1, 2025, during which Ukrainian drones launched from trucks near five military airfields in Russia destroyed or damaged dozens of strategic bombers. The lesson learned: it is possible to destroy a country's nuclear capabilities, even at relatively low cost; there are no targets that cannot be destroyed.

Ukraine's approach to national defense gradually opened up a discussion about whether Ukraine could defeat the Russian Federation if it had a similar amount of weapons at its disposal as the Russian Federation, or whether this would have been the case in the earlier years of the Russia's war.

On June 3, 2025, the print edition of *The Wall Street Journal*, one of the most important and widely read newspapers in the US, published a groundbreaking article by French political intellectual Bernard-Henri Lévy entitled "Ukraine Will Win This War."

16.2 Peace Talks as an Option?

One obvious option for ending the war would be for Russia to withdraw its troops from Ukraine and cease hostilities.

> If Russia stops fighting, the war ends. If Ukraine stops fighting, Ukraine ends.
> US Secretary of State Antony Blinken at the UN Security Council meeting on September 22, 2022

It is unlikely that Moscow will voluntarily end the war in this way.

Russian President Putin and Russian government representatives have repeatedly emphasized that their goal is the subjugation of the entire Ukraine—in Moscow's parlance, the "denazification of Ukraine." As a first step in this direction, they are demanding that Ukraine accepts the annexation of Crimea and the conquest of the four Ukrainian regions of Donetsk, Luhansk, Kherson and Zaporizhzhia, even though they are only partially occupied by Russia.

Moscow is using military force to pressure the Ukrainian leadership to accept its terms. In the first 4 days of the Russian full-scale invasion of Ukraine, the occupying forces conquered large areas and stood outside Kyiv. On February 28, the Russian and Ukrainian delegations met for the first time for peace negotiations in Belarus and subsequently in Istanbul, Turkey.

The Russians demanded Ukraine's surrender, demilitarization and neutrality. Ukraine showed willingness to compromise. But negotiations stalled because no one could guarantee that a neutral Ukraine wouldn't be attacked by Russia again. Ukraine's past experience with the ineffective Budapest Memorandum (see Sect. 1.2) made strong security guarantees essential.

In the meantime, Russian troops suffered huge losses as they advanced, failed to encircle the Ukrainian capital and eventually withdrew, concentrating on the Ukrainian South and East. The extent of Russian crimes and atrocities that became known after the Russian retreat, e.g., in the Kyiv suburb of Bucha, revealed a lack of Russian willingness to make peace. The negotiations finally came to a standstill in April 2022.

> Whether through the special military operation or through negotiations—we have no alternative to achieving our goals. And we will achieve them in any case.
> Kremlin spokesman Dmitry Peskov on July 24, 2024 in response to the offer of talks from Kyiv

Such messages only strengthen Ukrainians' resolve to resist and form a mandate for their political leadership. The Ukrainian government's declared goal is to liberate all Ukrainian territory and people from Russian occupation and restore its internationally recognized borders that existed prior to 2014.

In the fall of 2022, President Volodymyr Zelensky proposed a so-called "Peace Formula" for a just peace, with 10 points: nuclear safety; food security; energy security; release of all prisoners and deportees, return of kidnapped Ukrainian children; adherence to the UN Charter, restoration of Ukraine's territorial integrity and peace architecture; withdrawal of Russian troop and end of hostilities; justice; environmental protection and prevention of ecocide; prevention of escalation; confirmation of the end of the war.

Zelensky named five conditions for the Peace Formula, which he described as non-negotiable:

1. Punishment of Russia for the aggression
2. Protection of life by all permissible means
3. Restoration of security and the territorial integrity of Ukraine
4. Security guarantees for Ukraine
5. Ukrainians' determination to defend themselves

In June 2024, a peace summit was held at Bürgenstock, Switzerland, to which 160 countries were invited. Russia declined to participate in advance and was therefore

16.2 Peace Talks as an Option?

not invited. In order to create the broadest possible support among participating states, only 3 out of 10 areas of the Formula were addressed at the summit, which are intended to form the basis for a peace process: nuclear safety, food security and release of prisoners of war. The final declaration of the summit was signed by 88 delegations.

In the fall of 2024, Zelensky presented the so-called "Victory Plan" based on the Ukrainian Peace Formula. The plan, consisting of 5 points, outlines, on the one hand, measures that would enable Ukraine to win the war: NATO membership, strengthening Ukraine's defenses and deterrence by placing non-nuclear weapons on Ukrainian territory. On the other hand, the Victory Plan describes the benefits for or the offer of Ukraine to the West: inclusion of rich Ukrainian natural resources such as rare earths, metals, titanium, agricultural products, etc., in the European/Western economic processes and contribution to European security through the provision of Ukrainian know-how and the deployment of Ukrainian soldiers for peacekeeping (instead of US forces).

Peace initiatives by third parties, such as the joint proposal by China and Brazil from May 2024, were sometimes ambiguous or include compromises that benefit the Kremlin (such as the ceding Ukrainian territories to the Russian Federation).

The US president elected at the end of 2024, Donald Trump, repeatedly promised during his election campaign to end the Russian-Ukrainian war within 24 hours. Months after his inauguration in January 2025 and after many fruitless talks, phone calls, and meetings, he called his promise "sarcastic" and admitted that immediate peace was not possible. Finally, US representatives warned that they would withdraw from the mediation efforts due to lack of success and indeed showed less interest in continuing them.

Trump's negotiating tactics for a "peace deal," as the US president and his confidants put it, differed significantly in his approach toward Ukraine and toward Russia.

Trump put pressure on Ukrainian President Volodymyr Zelensky, calling him a "dictator," accusing him of ingratitude, demanding concessions in favor of Russia (e.g., the cession of Ukrainian territories) and payment for US aid (under the raw materials agreement), and accused him of not wanting to end the war.

The US government leadership responded to Russia in a mild and conciliatory manner, without condemning its acts of war. Trump's harshest description of Russian President Putin was calling him "absolutely crazy." Trump evasively referred to the Russian missile attack on Sumy, Ukraine, which left 36 people dead in April 2025, as "a mistake."

Ukraine and Russia also responded differently to US initiatives in 2025. Ukraine showed a cooperative stance, engaged with US proposals for an (unconditional) ceasefire, accepted offers for meetings and phone calls, and eventually signed the raw materials agreement after making adjustments.

Moscow pursued a strategy of delay and evasion, changed agreements, kept imposing new conditions, sent delegations of low-ranking participants with no decision-making powers to agreed meetings, failed to uphold the promised ceasefire, and carried out deadly attacks on Ukrainian cities at around the time of important peace meetings, etc.

In the first half of 2025, there was a meeting between Trump and Zelensky in New York (February), there were telephone calls between Trump and Putin, meetings between the US and Ukrainian delegations and between the US and Russian delegations in Riyadh (capital of Saudi Arabia, March), meetings between US Special Envoy Witkoff and Putin in Moscow (March), and between the Ukrainian and Russian delegations in Istanbul (Turkey, May–June).

Meanwhile, Russian military operations continued unabated. There were only shifts in the nature of the attacks, e.g., only few attacks on Ukrainian energy facilities during the so-called "30-day energy sector ceasefire" in March–April, accompanied by increased attacks on other civilian infrastructure in Ukraine.

After another round of negotiations in Istanbul in early June, Dmitry Medvedev, deputy head of the Russian Security Council, confirmed Russia's diversionary tactics on his Telegram channel: the negotiations in Istanbul were not necessary for a "compromise peace," but for Russia's "early victory."

Given the opposing positions of Russia and Ukraine, there is currently little basis for direct peace talks between them.

Another argument against a peace agreement or ceasefire in the near future is that there is no higher authority that could guarantee compliance with any peace agreement reached. An agreement that Russia can break will not bring lasting peace. A ceasefire or peace agreement would not mean an end to aggression and Russian war crimes in the Russian controlled parts of Ukraine, as the illegal annexation of Crimea and the period since 2014 have shown.

For Ukraine, the question therefore remains: who and what will force Russia to comply with the agreements? Until a solution is found, e.g., through Ukraine's admission to NATO or comparable security guarantees from Western countries, a genuine peace process is not possible. Until then, the following principle applies to Ukraine: the war will end when Russia is no longer able to wage war.

16.3 Putin, Red Lines and Nuclear Threats

Russian President Putin launched the large-scale war against Ukraine with the promise to Russian society that Ukraine would be defeated. He also wanted to demonstrate Russia's power and greatness to the world and portray the West as weak. In addition, the war was intended to distract attention from pressing domestic problems and make economic and social maldevelopments in the Russian Federation appear as hostile actions by the West.

Support for Putin from the Russian military and intelligence services, the media, business leaders and society is based on his reputation as a strong man who will bring Russia success. In order to present himself as such, Putin systematically resorts to threats against alleged enemies inside and outside the state. This includes, in particular, the repeated threat to use nuclear weapons if certain "red lines" are crossed.

The Kremlin defined such "red lines" for a possible nuclear strike as the delivery of heavy Western weapons to Ukraine and attacks on Crimea by Ukraine (2022), the deployment of German tanks in Ukraine (2023), attacks on Moscow and St. Petersburg (2023), the deployment of American weapons towards Russia near Kharkiv and the delivery of Western fighter jets to Ukraine (2024).

Every single event has occurred without any significant Russia's reaction. Even the unexpected occupation of Russian territories in the Kursk region by Ukrainian troops in 2024 and the destruction of Russian strategic bombers designed to launch nuclear missiles in the course of Operation "Pavutyna" in 2025 did not bring about a change of direction in Russian war strategy.

The threat of nuclear weapons has so far proved to be a political bluff (= deceptive maneuver, deliberate misdirection), a well-known tactic of Russian politics and psychological warfare to blackmail the other side. It is particularly effective in Germany and the USA, where "escalation" and "nuclear strike" can be considered trigger words in foreign policy debates.

Firing a nuclear missile requires the coordinated action of several bodies and is not technically feasible by a single person, for example the president. A nuclear strike would not give the Russian Federation any advantages in the war against Ukraine. On the other hand, the use of nuclear weapons by Russia would trigger a massive backlash from the West. A direct confrontation with NATO, for example, would only harm Russia and the Russian political elites and jeopardize Putin's position of power.

China has warned Russia several times against the use of nuclear weapons. As Moscow is reliant on Chinese support in the war of aggression against Ukraine, it must abide by such warnings.

The longer the war lasts and the worse the Russian army's military performance is, the more fragile Putin's power in Russia becomes. Various interest groups show their dissatisfaction with Putin's leadership, such as the so-called *siloviki* (from the Russian "sila"—strength, power), the high-ranking members of the military and the secret service. Putin responded with repression and restructuring in his environment. In 2024, Russian Defense Minister Sergei Shoigu was dismissed and dozens of high-ranking members of the Russian military were arrested, according to the official version on corruption charges.

> Yevgeny Prigozhin, head of Russia's largest shadow army, the Wagner Group, which fought in Ukraine since 2014, criticized poor military leadership. At the end of June 2023, Wagner mercenaries occupied the Russian border town of Rostov and some of them marched towards Moscow. After negotiations with the Kremlin, Prigozhin and his fighters retreated to Belarus. He was killed in a plane crash near Moscow at the end of August. The Wagner troops were subsequently integrated into the Russian armed forces.

Speculation continues as to who could succeed the now 72-year-old Putin and in what way. For a long time, Putin has both reflected and reinforced the authoritarian mindsets and power structures of Russian society. Without a radical transformation of Russian society, his successors will have to contend with these structures. What this means for the Russia's war of aggression against Ukraine is not yet clear.

Further Reading

https://www.pravda.com.ua/news/2024/10/1/7477626/; https://orf.at/stories/3364626/; https://tgstat.ru/en/channel/@medvedev_telegram/587; https://news.liga.net/ua/politics/news/oboronka-dala-tretynu-rostu-ukrainskoho-vvp-u-2024-rotsi-smetanin; https://www.pravda.com.ua/news/2025/04/12/7507246/

Rebuilding of Ukraine 17

17.1 Actors and Visions

After 3 years of the Russian invasion of Ukraine, a joint *Rapid Damage and Needs Assessment (RDNA3)* by the Ukrainian government, the World Bank Group, the European Commission and the United Nations estimated in February 2025 that the total cost of reconstruction and rehabilitation in Ukraine over the next 10 years would amount to $524 billion (equivalent to €506 billion).

Planning for the reconstruction of Ukraine began just few weeks after the Russian invasion of Ukraine. It deals firstly with reconstruction during the war and secondly with rebuilding after the end of the war.

On the one hand, the infrastructure destroyed by Russia is to be continuously repaired to ensure the survival of the Ukrainian population. This maintains the functionality of the Ukrainian state and supports the Ukrainian resistance. This reconstruction in Ukraine is partly financed by international aid and partly by the country's own efforts.

The so-called "Klitschko Bridge" (Fig. 17.1) is an example of ongoing repairs. The 212-m-long bridge in the center of Kyiv was opened in 2019 under Mayor Vitali Klitschko. Because of its glass components, it is also popularly known as the "Glass Bridge." On October 10, 2022, a Russian missile struck the bridge, destroying numerous glass elements. However, the structure itself remained intact. After repairs, the "Klitschko Bridge" was reopened to pedestrians and cyclists on November 17, 2022.

Fig. 17.1 Pedestrian and bicycle bridge in Kyiv, also known as the "Klitschko Bridge," repaired and reopened after being hit by a Russian missile. (Photo: Kyiv City Administration, kyivcity.gov.ua)

On the other hand, post-war reconstruction aims to provide a foundation for political and economic stabilization of Ukrainian democracy. To ensure that this can be implemented immediately after the end of the war, concepts, financing and details reconstruction should be developed early on.

Different players have their own ideas and interests as to what the reconstruction of Ukraine should look like after the end of the war.

For Europe and the European Union, it means greater security through having a democratic and economically stable neighboring country that provides Ukrainians with a livable homeland and, as an EU membership candidate, makes a valuable contribution to the Union.

Economic operators from the EU, the USA and other industrialized countries see Ukraine as a promising resource and sales market for their goods.

For the Ukrainian government, it is crucial to maintain its ability to act independently, despite reliance on external support.

Ukrainian civil society wants to help shape the future development of the Ukrainian state in accordance with the principles of participation, transparency and government accountability.

Reconstruction offers an opportunity to establish new structures instead of inefficient, outdated ones, to reform Ukraine according to EU standards and to shape the country as "Green Ukraine" with future-oriented, environmentally friendly and energy-saving projects.

17.2 Plans and assurances

The costs of rebuilding Ukraine are rising steadily due to the ongoing hostilities and Russia's deliberate destruction of Ukrainian infrastructure.

In June 2022, the first reconstruction conference for Ukraine took place in Lugano (Switzerland). At the conference, the European Union committed to rebuilding the country in close cooperation with the Ukrainian state and civil society and introduced a corresponding platform. A similar platform was also created by the G7 countries, and further conferences were held by other institutions.

> Ukraine can count on the EU's full support. We are ready to take responsibility at international level in rebuilding a democratic and prosperous Ukraine. This means that investments will go hand in hand with reforms that will pave Ukraine's European path.
> Ursula von der Leyen, President of the European Commission

17.3 Possible Sources of Funding

Several sources of financing for Ukraine's reconstruction are being considered:

- *Direct aid and loans* from states, communities of states and international organizations such as the EU, the G7, the World Bank, the European Investment Bank, etc., which have pledged or are already providing support. Such measures are usually linked to certain conditions and are regarded as "help for self-help". Historically, the best known of these is the US *Marshall Plan* for the reconstruction of Europe after the Second World War.

> **The Marshall Plan**
> The "Marshall Plan," officially the European Recovery Program (ERP), is a US economic development program for the reconstruction of Europe after the Second World War, which was initiated by US Secretary of State George C. Marshall. From 1948 to 1953, it provided 16 European countries (including defeated Germany and Austria) with loans, raw materials, food and industrial goods.
> The Federal Republic of Germany (FRG; "West Germany") mainly received food, fuel and medicine as part of the Marshall Plan. Germany had to later repay only a part of this aid. After 1990, the ERP assets were also used to rebuild the economy in the former GDR and are now used for economic development.

In February 2024, the EU heads of government agreed on a "Ukraine Facility." This program will provide Ukraine with up to €50 billion in the form of loans and non-repayable grants in several tranches from 2024 to 2027. The disbursement is conditional: Ukraine must demonstrate quarterly progress on reforms necessary for EU accession.

- *Russian assets* abroad. These include frozen funds of the Russian central bank held in European and international bank accounts, assets of sanctioned (government-affiliated) Russian companies, as well as the luxury assets and bank accounts of the sanctioned Russian oligarchs. Appropriate political and legal mechanisms are being developed to ensure that these assets can be used without the owners' consent.

In the European Union, €210 billion from the Russian central bank have been frozen. In 2023, the Brussels-based financial institution Euroclear earned approximately €4.4 billion in interest from these holdings. In 2024, the EU decided to allocate this interest revenue to Ukraine for defense and reconstruction. The EU und the G7 countries agreed in 2024 to grant Ukraine a loan of approximately €45 billion ($50 billion) as part of the *Extraordinary Revenue Acceleration (ERA)* loan initiative. The funds are to be disbursed to Ukraine by 2027 to finance urgent budgetary needs, military goods, and reconstruction. Repayments will be covered by interest income from frozen Russian assets. The first ERA tranches have already been transferred to Ukraine by mid-2025.

- *Reparation payments* by Russia. Reparation payments are usually determined either in a peace treaty after the end of hostilities or unilaterally by the victorious powers.
- *Private investments* with profit prospects. Due to the risk of destruction, such investments are usually only possible after the end of the war. However, smaller projects in the western regions of Ukraine, where there is no ground fighting, are already underway.

In November 2024, the international trade fair *ReBuild Ukraine* took place in Warsaw for the fourth time. As part of the event, the European Commission hosted its first EU-Ukraine investment conference to mobilize private investment. European companies were invited to submit their project proposals for investments in the Ukrainian economy, which are to receive EU support.

Further Reading

https://commission.europa.eu/topics/eu-solidarity-ukraine/eu-assistance-ukraine/recovery-and-reconstruction-ukraine_de; https://at.usembassy.gov/de/70-jahre-marshall-plan-in-oesterreich/

Plan for Russia 18

18.1 Colonial History

The Russian Federation, as Russia is officially called, is the largest country in the world in terms of territory. It comprises over 80 federal subjects (i.e., parts of the federation) and is a multi-ethnic state. This means that the state consists of different ethnic groups and nationalities, each with their own language, culture and religion. Over the centuries, Moskow has conquered these regions and continues to control them through authoritarian power and an intense policy of Russification. Liberation movements and the pursuit of self-determination by these oppressed groups and peoples have long been an inherent part of the political and social reality in Russia's multiethnic state.

After the First World War, the liberation movements of the colonized peoples led to the collapse of the Russian Tsarist Empire and the emergence of new states. The Russian Bolsheviks (Communists) under the leadership of Vladimir Lenin used overwhelming military force and many human sacrifices to bring former colonies back under Russian rule—as part of the newly founded Union of Soviet Socialist Republics, USSR or Soviet Union.

Under the pressure of independence efforts and disintegration processes, numerous countries of the Soviet Union declared their independence in 1990–1991 and held corresponding referendums. The USSR was finally dissolved at the end of 1991. The 15 Soviet republics were replaced by 14 new nation states and the Russian Federation, which itself comprised many peoples and nationalities.

18.2 Peoples of the Russian Federation

The disintegration process linked to the Soviet collapse also occurred within the Russian Federation itself. Chechnya and Tatarstan, previously autonomous Soviet republics within the Russian Soviet Federative Republic, declared their independence. After the referendum confirming their independence, they practically functioned as independent states for years. Other autonomous republics, e.g., Bashkortostan, Yakutia (Republic of Sakha), Karelia, Kalmykia, Chuvashia, Buryatia, Tuva, etc. declared their sovereignty or asserted the primacy of their own laws over those of the federation. Other regions (autonomous oblasts and districts) sought more self-determination and changed their legal status to a republic, such as the Republic of Dagestan and the Republic of Kabardino-Balkaria.

In the following years, the Kremlin re-established control over the emerging regions. Most of them signed the new federation treaty with Moscow as early as 1992, which restricted their rights. The Republic of Tatarstan, with its capital Kazan, did not sign the treaty, but gradually lost its independent status through special agreements and legal changes.

The Kremlin used excessive armed force to roll back the secession of the Chechen Republic of Ichkeria (as it identifies itself). The first Russian-Chechen war under President Yeltsin in 1994–1996 ended with a peace agreement. During the ceasefire, Russia prepared for a second offensive. There is strong suspicion that Russian secret services staged provocations or terrorist attacks, which Moscow used as a pretext for the second Russian-Chechen war in 1999–2000.

After the complete destruction of the Chechen capital Grozny, the flight of many locals and the occupation of Chechen territory by the Russian army in 1999–2000, Moscow integrated Ichkeria/Chechnya into the Russian state structure with the help of local warlords. The current Chechen ruler in the service of Moscow, Ramzan Kadyrov, is particularly known for his brutality. Armed resistance to Russian rule over Chechnya continued to varying degrees into the 2020s.

The political leadership of the Russian Federation under Vladimir Putin continues the imperialist government practices of the Tsarist Empire and the Soviet Union. These include in particular:

- Repression of dissenters. Local autonomy movements are violently suppressed and severely punished.
- Centralized decision-making. All important decisions are made centrally in Moscow, local authorities have few self-governing rights.
- Exploitation of natural resources (oil and gas, rare ores, diamonds, agricultural products), extraction of resources, economic exploitation, and indebtedness to

Moscow. The locals receive hardly any corresponding financial returns and live in poverty.
– Instrumentalization for the goals of the center. A disproportionate number of members of indigenous peoples such as Buryats or Chechens are being used for the war against Ukraine.

In its resolution in June 2024, the Council of Europe stated that in the war against Ukraine, conventional military attacks by the Russian Federation "go hand in hand with a systematic, state-directed policy of Russification of the occupied territories, imperialist and neo-colonial historical revisionism and the denial of a distinct Ukrainian cultural identity for people under occupation." The resolution also attested the Kremlin the same pattern of action within the Russian Federation:

> Furthermore, the Russian Federation is pursuing a Russification policy towards numerous indigenous peoples in the country, progressively erasing their cultural identities by restricting the use of their languages, especially in the education system, reducing the domains of their cultural expressions, distorting their history and depriving them of their historical memory, as well as by capturing and prosecuting ethnic minority activists.
> Point 3 of Resolution No. 2558 of the Parliamentary Assembly of the Council of Europe, June 26, 2024

18.3   Accompanying Democratization

History shows that large empires that are held together by force are not viable in the long term.

The future of the nationalities and peoples of the Russian Federation, including the ethnic Russian people, depends on whether they can achieve democracy and self-determination.

Since the beginning of the large-scale war of aggression against Ukraine in 2022, voices have increasingly been raised in favor of *democratization* (= building democracy), *decentralization* (= transferring decision-making power from the center to local political actors) and *demilitarization* (= eliminating offensive weapons and reducing the army) of the Russian Federation.

Some of the active decentralization and liberation movements in the Russian Federation are: the Chechen Republic of Ichkeria in Exile (Chechnya), the Committee of the Bashkir National Movement Abroad (Bashkortostan), the "Free Ingria" movement (St. Petersburg), Smolensk Republican Center (Smolensk), "Sakha Resistance" movement (Yakutia/Sakha), "Free Kalmykia" movement (Kalmykia) and others.

The Free Nations of Post-Russia

The Free Nations of Post-Russia Forum (FNPF) was established in 2022. The 14th conference of the forum took place in Vienna, Austria, in December 2024 (see Fig. 18.1), and the 16th conference took place in Washington, USA, in June 2025.

The declared goal of the forum is a change in Russia towards democracy, *"deputinization"* (= elimination of Putin's influence), *de-imperialization* and *decolonization* (= independence of the former colonies or subjects of the federation), demilitarization and renunciation of nuclear weapons as well as economic and ecological change.

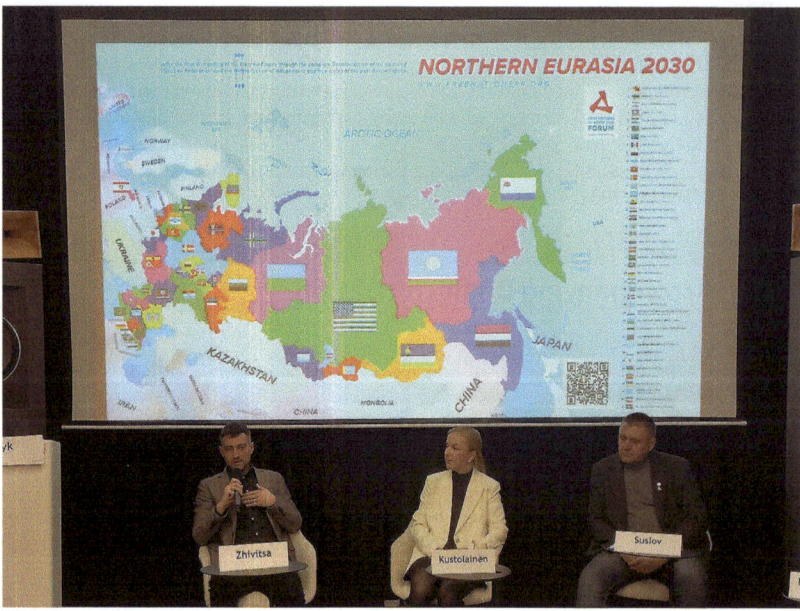

Fig. 18.1 Conference of the Free Nations Post-Russia Forum (FNPF) on December 13, 2024 in Vienna, Austria. (Photo: Oleg Magaletsky, www.freenationsrf.org)

The representatives of these and other initiatives describe their understanding of future development in the region in the following ways:

- The internal processes within the Russian Federation are largely taking place without attention or influence from abroad. Europe in particular would benefit from knowing this in order to prepare for possible scenarios.
- A potential peaceful dissolution of the federal state and an orderly disposal of nuclear weapons would require international support.
- Hostile attacks against the West, disinformation and destabilization of the democratic order in other countries as well as the war against Ukraine would come to an end.
- Newly emerging states would now have their own resources (oil, gas, other natural resources) and successfully enable the economy and prosperity of their citizens. Through treaties with the individual states, the European Union, for example, would not be dependent on a powerful authoritarian state.
- New states in the Far East could weaken the dominance of the People's Republic of China in the region and possibly contribute to democratization for the oppressed peoples of the Chinese regime (Manchuria, Uyghur East Turkestan, Tibet).

The idea of the Russian Federation dissolving is a familiar and feared scenario in the Kremlin. At the beginning of 2012, Vladimir Putin, then Prime Minister of the Russian Federation (having previously held the office of President in 2000–2008), published an article entitled "Russia: the national question." This article was part of his election program for the then upcoming presidential elections in March 2012, which Putin won. In the article, Vladimir Putin warned of ethnic conflicts of interest that could "tear Russia apart."

In February 2023, Putin spoke in an interview with the Russian TV channel "Rossiya 1" about the emergence of "Muscovites" and "Urals" in the event of the disintegration of the federation and that the West could only accept Russia "into the so-called family of civilized peoples in parts, each part separately."

Russia's war of aggression against Ukraine is inextricably linked to internal Russian processes. This complex interplay will have a lasting impact on the future of both countries, but also on the global security order and international relations. The world is witnessing a historic turning point, the consequences of which we will only fully understand in the coming years.

Further Reading

https://pace.coe.int/en/files/33685/html; https://www.freenationsrf.org; https://www.forbes.ru/society/485381-putin-predupredil-o-poavlenii-moskovitov-i-ural-cev-v-slucae-raspada-rossii; https://www.rbc.ru/politics/23/12/2021/61c4489e9a79475d87db1441

MIX
Papier aus verantwortungsvollen Quellen
Paper from responsible sources
FSC® C105338

If you have any concerns about our products,
you can contact us on
ProductSafety@springernature.com

In case Publisher is established outside the EU,
the EU authorized representative is:
**Springer Nature Customer Service Center GmbH
Europaplatz 3, 69115 Heidelberg, Germany**

Printed by Libri Plureos GmbH
in Hamburg, Germany